# MASTERING PEOPLE MANAGEMENT

**FINANCIAL TIMES**

# MASTERING PEOPLE MANAGEMENT

**Your Single-Source Guide to Becoming a Master of People Management**

Executive editor **James Pickford**

London   New York   San Francisco   Toronto   Sydney   Tokyo   Singapore
Hong Kong   Cape Town   Madrid   Paris   Milan   Munich   Amsterdam

PEARSON EDUCATION LIMITED

Head Office:
Edinburgh Gate
Harlow CM20 2JE
Tel: +44 (0)1279 623623
Fax: +44 (0)1279 431059

London Office:
128 Long Acre
London WC2E 9AN
Tel: +44 (0)20 7447 2000
Fax: +44 (0)20 7447 2170
Website: www.business-minds.com

First published in Great Britain in 2003

© Compilation: Pearson Education Limited 2003

Note: Licences have been granted by individual authors/organizations for articles
throughout this publication. Please refer to the respective articles for copyright notices.

ISBN: 0 273 66192 2

*British Library Cataloguing in Publication Data*
A CIP catalogue record for this book can be obtained from the British Library.

10 9 8 7 6 5 4 3 2 1

Typeset by Pantek Arts Ltd, Maidstone Kent
Printed and bound in Great Britain by Ashford Colour Press, Hampshire

*The Publishers' policy is to use paper manufactured from sustainable forests.*

# Contents

# Introduction

Companies traditionally find competitive advantages in access to greater financial resources or technological innovation. To sustain the success these advantages confer, however, managers now acknowledge a third requirement: the company's processes and structures must allow employees to realize their full potential. People must be satisfied in their work, and believe that executive rhetoric is reflected in reality. This is the concern of human resources management or people management, and the questions it raises affect not only HR managers but general managers of all kinds.

In October 2001 the *Financial Times* newspaper launched *Mastering People Management*, a series of eight weekly supplements examining the issues surrounding people in organizations and the practices devoted to managing them. This book contains the complete articles published in the series, as well as further essays from industry experts and noted academics.

*Mastering People Management* offers the general manager answers to the most important and topical questions in the field of HR. What organizational structures allow people to perform well in companies? How should business goals be reflected in individual and team objectives? What processes should govern recruitment and training? What are appropriate ways of appraising performance? How should employees be compensated? How should managers tackle failing morale in the workplace?

A persistent theme is the need to link the activities of the HR department with the overall strategic process and the question of HR's role at board level. Company reports may intone the relevant cliché – "people are our greatest asset" – but until managers show how selection, motivation and reward policies affect the bottom line, HR is likely to remain outside the centres of corporate power. It has clearly moved on from its original role of administering pay and provisions, but without broadly recognized standards of performance measurement, it will continue to face scepticism in its aspirations to a higher status. Several authors address this issue and describe how innovative companies are answering the critics by fashioning a new role for HR.

This book is published at a time of growing economic and ethical uncertainty in corporations around the world. Financial scandals at US corporations Enron and WorldCom have been exposed under the searchlight of accounting scrutiny; more may follow. How will this affect the role of HR more generally? In the short term, an ailing economy encourages cost cutting and restructuring, and often job losses; people managers must carry out these tasks with great skill if they are not to repeat the worst excesses of 1980s-style re-engineering.

In the longer term, it may provide an opportunity for HR managers to grasp a role as the ethical standard-bearers in organizations of the future. Their central role in reward programmes, employee discipline, recruitment and selection places them in a unique position to set the firm's standards for acceptable behaviour internally and in its relations with customers and shareholders. Companies that can demonstrate their integrity in their dealings with stakeholders stand a better chance of recruiting talented employees and improving performance from a committed workforce.

Many distinguished academics and industry experts have contributed to *Mastering People Management*. The Wharton School at the University of Pennsylvania and Insead in Fontainebleau, France, led the participating schools, alongside Michigan, Harvard, Rutgers and Henley, to name a few. Each author has striven to find an international perspective on the issues, linking general principles with best practice. Our thanks go to all of them in their efforts to create an invaluable guide for anyone with responsibility for managing others.

James Pickford, *Editor, FT Mastering*

# The role of
# **people**

1

# Contents

**M**astering People Management opens with a broad examination of the role of human resources (HR) in the organization and the ways in which people management has changed over the centuries. Dave Ulrich sets out the agenda of the HR manager, while Richard Donkin traces the historical landmarks of people management. Finally, Malcolm Higgs looks at where HR might be heading in the next decade.

# The evolution of a
# professional agenda

Dave Ulrich Is a professor
of business administration
at the University of
Michigan Business School.

Managing people is a role that all executives must master.
Here, **Dave Ulrich** outlines underlying principles and
practice, their development and how they are likely to shape
up in the future.

**M**anagers, in their weaker moments, may like to imagine that there is an ultimate aim or conclusion to their work. In reality, whether they manage organizations, resources or people, new problems appear as old ones re-emerge, and the work of transformation and competitiveness is never done. This is as true of managing people as anything else, but it is easy to lose track of the evolution of human resources, its concepts and relationships with the wider organization.

The appalling events of September 11, 2001 have put the skills of managing people – in particular the pastoral responsibilities that managers are rarely called upon to exercise – in a new light for many organizations. Another skill, that of handling redundancy or lay-offs, was in limited demand during the dotcom boom at the end of the 1990s. It is likely to be needed again.

So it is timely to review the development of human resources, as a profession and as part of every manager's role, and offer suggestions for the journey ahead.

The concepts behind HR have evolved over millennia, but they became more structured during the 1930s, when companies set up industrial relations departments. Before then, employees were often considered as assets to be bought. During the depression, companies responded to unions by forming industrial relations units to negotiate terms and keep records on working conditions.

In the 1940s, selection tools began to be more aggressively deployed. During the second world war, tests were devised to place soldiers in the "right" units. This trend evolved in the 1950s with a focus on personal change. It was the decade of training groups and development experiences, when intervention would make employees more productive.

The 1960s and 1970s shifted attention to legal issues. In addition, compensation systems began to emerge with pay for performance, flexible benefits and stock options. Personnel departments ensured that policies were lawful and efficiently administered. The 1980s moved the agenda further to thinking about systems rather than just people. Human resources systems were integrated and aligned with strategy. The HR focus began to treat people as strategic investments and a source of competitive advantage for the company.

The 1990s continued this focus, with an emphasis on the organization, not just people. By highlighting teamwork and organization, HR began to work with the management team to deliver strategy. A profession developed, with a body of knowledge, standards and expected outcomes.

This short history shows that HR matters. It aims to ensure that people and organizations perform at their best. HR professionals are included in forums where significant decisions are made. The strategies they develop are soon integrated into mainstream managerial practice. Rather than disparage this history, it is important to build on it for the future.

## The journey ahead

How can HR continue to add value? Value is defined by receivers more than givers. In the case of HR, receivers include employees (who become more committed and competent), customers (a greater market share is achieved through intimacy with customers), investors (adding to shareholder value through intangible assets) and organization (more capabilities to succeed). Four factors can be identified for HR providers in creating this value: contribution (how they work with others), content (what value they add when they contribute), channel (who does HR work) and competencies (what they need to know and do). Mastering each of these becomes a milestone for the journey ahead.

### Contribution

To add continued value, HR must be more than a partner – it must be a player. Players contribute. They are engaged and add value. They are in the game, not just at the game. They do things that make a difference by acting as coach, architect, designer, facilitator and leader.

> HR professionals can coach business leaders to raise employee and organizational productivity by setting standards, giving feedback and becoming personal leadership trainers.

Coaches inspire, teach and train. They enable people to learn from the past and adapt behaviours for the future. HR professionals can coach business leaders to raise employee and organizational productivity by setting standards, giving feedback and becoming personal leadership trainers.

Architects turn ideas into blueprints. They make sure that what is built fits with the environment and space available. HR players, similarly, draft plans for how organizations can and should be built. They lay out the choices for talent, structure, making decisions, information flow and other processes to ensure alignment of organization with strategy goals.

Designers and deliverers turn ideas into actions. HR managers need to ensure they create systems (for example, staffing, rewards, training, development and organization design) to meet business goals. Ensuring ideas are implemented is critical because many good ideas don't happen.

Facilitators pay attention to how work gets done. They focus on who is involved and how to improve work. HR players facilitate when they bring resources (talent, money and time) together to accomplish goals.

Leaders act as role models for what they preach. HR players lead when what they propose to others they first demonstrate in their own function. Too often HR hypocrisy exists where more is preached than practised.

### Content

Out of these roles, a question arises: "What are the issues that will occupy HR managers?" Without identifying the content, or issues, for HR, contribution has no direction.

HR adds value when it helps an organization develop capabilities to compete and win business;

these capabilities become intangible assets when they give investors confidence in a future stream of earnings. They include the following:

- *Attract, retain and motivate talent.* Talent combines competence and commitment. Competence requires specifying future skills; commitment implies writing contracts that engage employees intellectually, emotionally and behaviourally.

- *Act with speed.* Speed comes when leaders have the capacity to make decisions, to remove bureaucracy, to provide discipline in implementing projects and in removing cherished ways of doing things.

- *Instil learning.* If lessons have to be continually re-learned, they will not be maintained. Learning occurs when individuals, teams and organizations generate and generalize good ideas; when ideas from one setting or time are applied to another; or when theory becomes reality.

- *Craft a shared mindset.* Organizations have an identity, or image. This establishes a company's brand in the minds of customers and creates value. The identity also becomes the desired culture or values among employees. A mindset shared by customers and employees brings value to both. Customers pay a premium for the brand; employees feel loyalty to the values.

- *Innovate.* Organizations that can innovate have a stream of ideas that become commercially viable; they have an ability to turn individual creativity into collective innovation.

- *Assure accountability.* Aspirations should exceed resources. But aspirations without commitment to execution become dreams that add no value. Organizations with accountability have the ability to turn idea and ideals into behaviours and outcomes.

- *Invest in leadership.* Leaders embody the brand of the company in their behaviour and results. Building leadership means making sure leaders at all levels have the right attributes and create the right outcomes.

- *Assure strategic clarity.* Some companies know where they are heading and how they will get there; they have clear strategies, goals and objectives. Other organizations remain active but unfocused; they have strategies for the old, not new, world.

These capabilities may become the bedrock of an organization and intangible assets for investors. More directly, they may be the basis for the deliverables of HR. These capabilities are not exhaustive but they expand the traditional HR focus on talent alone. While innovation in recruitment, training and building commitment are valuable, HR will have to do more than attract and motivate talent.

## Channel

Who does the work of human resources management? This question has several answers. As the work expands, those tasked with doing it also evolve. Let me suggest seven constituents who do and will do HR work.

First, line managers are ultimately accountable and responsible for HR work. Line managers make the decisions governing how work gets done. They demonstrate their commitment to HR by being the visible, public champions for initiatives. Second, corporate HR professionals design policies and procedures, building enduring values and ideals that permeate the company. They are also responsible for nurturing employees, for shaping programmes to implement the chief executive's agenda and for ensuring that the company presents a united front to outsiders, such as investors and large customers. Corporate HR is likely to become more streamlined, focused on long term policies that shape values.

Third, HR managers work in business units. They work directly with line managers to clarify strategy, carry out audits and make investments in HR-related areas. In future, HR generalists within business units may become more business-focused and able to broker their services. Fourth, HR professionals work in centres of expertise where they come together to share knowledge. They deliver functional excellence by doing internal consulting with business units. They also share knowledge across business units through creating menus of choices. They form relationships with outside vendors who have deep knowledge and they bring that knowledge into the company.

Corporate HR is likely to become more streamlined, focused on long-term policies that shape values.

Fifth, HR managers work in telephone and online service centres, which grew up in the 1990s to handle administrative tasks. Call centres allowed employee questions to be answered in a more co-ordinated way. As one HR executive said, "If they move the HR work 400 yards, they might as well move it 3,000 miles." Much of this work may be outsourced. Sixth, HR work may be done using technology. Administration can be done by people for themselves. Self-reliance, self-sufficiency and self-service will become increasingly popular as HR departments enable employees to deal directly with the company.

Finally, HR work may be outsourced. Some of the outsourcing may be done with consultants who aim to transform external expertise into internal insight. Other outsourcing may occur through partnerships and alliances. Knowledge does not have to be owned to be accessed. Through some alliances, expertise may be shared across boundaries. Such alliances are likely to continue as different sources of expertise combine around common interests.

These skills will enable HR managers to contribute value. Are they there yet? No. But, with knowledge of the past and a vision of the future, HR will evolve – and relish the journey.

## Competencies

In research with about 18,000 respondents, Professor Wayne Brockbank and I have discovered five domains of competencies covering knowledge, skills and capabilities:

- *Knowledge of the business*: finance, marketing, strategy, globalization, technology and other business functions.
- *Delivery*: the latest research in functional HR.
- *Managing change*: the ability to make things happen quickly.
- *Culture management*: how companies create patterns of behaviour and mindsets among employees and customers.
- *Personal credibility*: how to build personal trust by living the values of the company and having an informed point of view.

These competencies are evolving to include:

- *measurement*: of the impact of HR;
- *technology*: used to deliver HR work; not seen as a threat;
- *intangible assets*: work with investors requires mastery of trends in finance and market valuation;
- *globalization*: exploiting knowledge, adapting to local conditions and instilling global thinking.

# More than just a job:
## a brief history of work

Richard Donkin is editor
of FTCareerPoint.com, the
*Financial Times'*s
recruitment website.

The concept of work is a slippery one, says **Richard Donkin**, who finds its future in the hands of technology.

Two and a half million years ago in the Olduvai Gorge, Tanzania, our ancestors were using roughly shaped rocks as tools. This is the first evidence we have of the human family engaged in the process we now know as work. Whether what they were doing at the time would have been viewed or described as work is debatable.

Work is a slippery concept, as much about mood and emotion as it is about product or outcome. We have the Bible to thank for perhaps its most popular definition today – as something we would rather not be doing. Adam was told to leave the garden of Eden "to till the ground from whence he was taken". The consequences of ignoring God's command were spelled out by St Paul in his letter to the Thessalonians: "If any would not work, neither should he eat."

The problem with these biblical interpretations of work as punishment is that work has chimeric qualities. It can be difficult yet satisfying, arduous yet enjoyable, well paid yet stressful. At its worst, it can be drudgery, at its best uplifting. It is an instrument of power and exploitation, a catalyst for change; it is a part of our identity and the only way we know of getting things done. This article traces the evolution of work and identifies moments in history when the relationship between employer and employee changed for ever.

## The emerging shape of work

For most of human existence, up to about 10,000 years ago, work manifested itself as hunter-gathering. But even in this period there was division of labour. The skills needed to fashion a hand-axe, throw a spear or butcher an animal had to be acquired and practised. The hunter-gatherers were nomads who needed everything they possessed.

But, looked at in another way, they had all they needed. This was, in the words of anthropologist Marshall Sahlins, "the original affluent society".

That said, archaeologists have identified 50,000-year-old grindstones. So at least one process more readily identified with modern definitions of drudgery has an ancient history. When people discovered edible grains growing in the fertile plains of the Levant, they began to settle and farm. Human society had crossed an important watershed. It was able to create a surplus, freeing some people from the need to undertake physical work and others to engage in the construction and expansion of towns and cities.

It was in this society – the longest period of recorded history – that types of work began to define social class and that skills developed into artisanship. The undertakers of ancient Egypt had refined their skills to a degree that would never be surpassed. The pyramid-builders displayed extraordinary expertise. But what came to be known as civilization had a price. Rome and Athens were societies in which most manual labour was undertaken by slaves, a working class of people who lived, Aristotle observed, "under the restraint of another".

In fact, what may be the first reference to something that would later be identified as human resources management concerns the welfare of slaves. The Roman agricultural writer, Columella, wrote in *De Re Rustica*, a work on farm management in the first century AD, that improving the living and working conditions of slaves and the payment of some reward would repay itself in a greater enthusiasm and willingness to work.

This "enlightened self-interest" would be a hallmark of the strides achieved in personnel management by Robert Owen, a 19th-century industrialist. His ideas in worker education, working hours and employee behaviour at his textile-mill complex in New Lanark, Scotland, paved the way for UK legislative reforms outlawing the employment of children in factories. By this time Britain was at the forefront of another great upheaval in the organization of work.

Well before this upheaval, the condition of slavery had passed almost seamlessly across Europe into that of serfdom within the feudal system. In turn, serfdom dissolved into sporadic working arrangements governing the lives of agricultural workers. The artisans, meanwhile, had organized themselves within guilds, the forerunners of trade unions, in the way they regulated pay rates, protected their members and organized apprenticeships. However, work for many people remained piecemeal up to the late 18th century. The idea of packaging work as a job, with defined hours for starting and ending the working day, was novel up to the years 1760–1830 – the period designated by the historian Arnold Toynbee as the time of the industrial revolution in England.

Before the spread of the factory system, many individuals could be relatively flexible in their working hours. This was not to say that agricultural labourers did not work long and hard or that coercion did not exist. However, the popularity of saints' days and local feasts, and the arbitrary choice of some people to prolong the weekend by the observance of "Saint Monday", preserved a spirit of independence across many trades and forms of working.

People's working and worshipping patterns, for that matter, were governed to some extent by the measurement of time. St Benedict had introduced the hourly bell to parcel the daily regime of prayer, psalm-singing, sleep and physical work of those who followed his "rule" and bell towers were adopted across Europe to designate hours of devotion, whether to God or to the employer.

## Factory production

It was not until employers began to concentrate production in mills that measuring working time became precious in the pursuit of productivity and profit. Textile manufacturing introduced its early entrepreneurs, men such as Thomas Lombe, Richard Arkwright and Jedediah Strutt,

It was not until employers began to concentrate production in mills that measuring working time became precious in the pursuit of productivity and profit.

to the possibilities of gathering workers under one roof to maintain and run the machinery.

There were several reasons for this concentration. Mill machinery usually required a central power source – river water in the case of Arkwright's first mill at Cromford in Derbyshire, then steam; the machines were often protected by flimsy patents and entrepreneurs were anxious to preserve their secrets behind closed doors; new materials such as wrought iron allowed simpler, cheaper production of larger working spaces; finally, teams of low-skilled workers were needed to run the machines. Typically, early mill workforces comprised the wives and children of independent weavers who were encouraged to live nearby in cottages built to house a handloom on one floor. The idea of exploiting the whole family as an economic unit was familiar enough to farm workers, but the factory provided the attractive dimension of regular paid work.

The factory system was perfectly placed to take advantage of a surplus of labour arising out of the escalating practice of land enclosure. Before enclosure, commons and open fields had sustained an elaborate collection of freeholders, leaseholders, cottagers and squatters who were able to subsist if not prosper in the strip-field system. Enclosure destroyed what the historian E.P. Thompson has called the "scratch-as-scratch-can subsistence economy of the poor" and with it their independence.

In Scotland, the Highland clearances had created even greater misery and for many there was a stark choice between factory working, emigration or the workhouse. When Robert Owen built a school within his mill complex in 1814 and declared that children up to the age of 10 would attend lessons rather than work, some of their parents lamented the loss of a worker. The exploitation of children was resisted only by the more liberal elements of society. Owen was a rare combination of entrepreneur and social reformer. Unusually as a mill owner, he also recognized a link between employee welfare and productivity.

The flux of ideas emanating from the Age of Enlightenment, revolution in France, the growth of international trade and the rise of trade unionism contributed to the need for better regulation and organization of labour. Adam Smith's description of the 18-stage division of labour in the manufacture of pins in his *Wealth of Nations*, coupled with the mid-19th-century expansion of the steel and rail industries, only strengthened the demand for improving and streamlining the productivity of workers.

## Analysis of work

In 1881, Frederick W. Taylor, a foreman at the Midvale steelworks on the outskirts of Philadelphia in the US, discovered the potential of an improved stopwatch that allowed the precise measurement of elapsed time, and began experiments that would transform the relationship between worker and supervisor. By breaking down work into its constituent parts, he standardized tasks that had hitherto comprised specific skills, jealously guarded by individual artisans. This enabled him to fix more accurate and usually more demanding times for "piece work" – the kind of work where a set rate was offered for a particular task.

The case for work study had been made by Baron Charles Dupin, the founder of mechanics' institutes that sprang up in France, Britain and the US in the 1820s. In the machinery of production, argued Dupin, the worker was in the first rank. A specific application of Taylor's ideas among a group of hand-picked labourers at Bethlehem Steel about 40 miles north of Philadelphia demonstrated how one worker, Henry Noll, was able to achieve prodigious work rates day after day, loading pig-iron on to railway trucks.

When Taylorism was further refined, absorbing the motion studies of Frank and Lillian Gilbreth, and described as an efficiency movement called Scientific Management, it began to attract worldwide attention. When work was condensed into a specific action, such as the turn of a screw, by engineers designing the moving assembly line to make Ford Model-T cars in 1913, the industrial age had finally succeeded in creating the human tool envisioned by Dupin. Some, like Aldous Huxley, author of *Brave New World*, viewed Ford's production line with alarm. Charlie Chaplin chose to lampoon the system in his film, *Modern Times*. Chaplin placed his faith in human nature and recognized that no system, other than slavery, could retain people indefinitely in jobs devoid of satisfaction, skill or intellectual input.

Workers placed their faith in the trade union movement and the industrial dispute became an ever-present feature of manufacturing throughout most of the 20th century. Some management teams were more confrontational than others. Companies such as Western Electric in the US and many of the big Quaker manufacturers pioneered styles of management that focused on human relations, temperance and community within the workforce.

The first world war witnessed the large-scale use of psychometric testing in the selection of recruits for the US Army. Industrial psychologists such as Hugo Munsterberg had outlined the case for studying human behaviours in the workplace. At the same time pioneer occupational psychologists such as Walter Dill Scott were telling large companies that they could improve the quality of their workforces through the use of psychological profiling.

## Shadows of the modern workplace

Division of labour, work study, industrial relations, increasingly sophisticated selection techniques and workforce administration created a strain of management devoted solely to the maintenance of a productive, efficient and competent workforce among large public and private sector employers. Max Weber, the 19th-century German sociologist, had outlined a bureaucratization of administration. Coupled with the disciplines and processes of scientific management, it helped to create a cadre of personnel managers whose role was identified and outlined in the 1920s by Thomas Gardner Spates, director of industrial relations, then vice-president of personnel administration at the General Food corporation in the US.

Personnel management, along with other disciplines such as finance, marketing and operations, was yet another diverging branch in the evolution of work. The increasingly structured class system in the workplace identified white-collar supervisory and administrative roles assisted by members of the professions – lawyers, accountants, actuaries – in controlling an army of manual workers.

External expertise such as management and recruitment consultancy was also developing in these inter-war years to feed and feed off the large corporation. At the same time, the artisan tradition was upheld at its highest level by industrial scientists, chemists, biologists, technicians, civil engineers and architects. Outside these spheres were other professions – teaching, medicine, journalism and those whose jobs were maintaining the fabric of society and public order, the police, the military, fire fighters and public administrators. When asked "What do you do?", anyone could give a clear answer.

In the 1950s, the middle-class, besuited executive became a recognizable type, identified in William H. Whyte's *The Organization Man*. Organization man was a lifelong employee following a career path leading, with promotions, to ever-increasing status until it would peak at a certain level or, in a few cases, the chief executive's office. The futurists Alvin and Heidi Toffler regarded 1956 as a landmark in the history of work since this expanding breed of white-collar worker outnumbered blue-collar workers in the US for the first time.

The ordered office, the typing pool and structured tiers of management in the large organization may well have reached their zenith about this time but the workplace was still characterized by an "us and them" distrust between managers and unionized workers. Work for most employees, however, was not ordered in a fundamentally different way than it had been since the industrial revolution. Most of the changes, such as paid holidays, collective bargaining and shorter working weeks, had been secured in hard-fought campaigns by trade unions. A job was still a job.

Union muscle in the UK and the US was diluted in the 1980s era of Reaganomics, when the western industrial base was eroded by recession, automation and competition. In particular, Japanese industry had pursued scientific management to new levels of refinement, focusing on process and quality.

Finally, in the late 1980s, the process approach was applied to the top-heavy tiers of management. The lifelong career cycle enjoyed by middle managers was shattered in a wave of redundancies.

If business process re-engineering broke the psychological contract that had promised loyalty in

## The lifelong career cycle enjoyed by middle managers was shattered in a wave of redundancies.

return for job security, rapid improvements in computer technology, including data-processing software, removed further administrative responsibilities. The costs associated with redundancies alongside the weakening of union power and membership led managers to begin experimenting with flexible working, using a proportion of temporary and agency workers for cyclical work and one-off projects. Employee hybrids began to emerge – interim managers who would work on a project or act as a stop gap, then leave; agency-employed information technology professionals to install computer networks or programs; and self-employed service sector workers for almost every function.

At the same time, social trends such as the widespread availability of the contraceptive pill, lengthening periods of education and cheaper air travel were influencing the profile of the labour market. More women were entering the workplace. They sought careers with which they could identify themselves, as men had done for centuries. Careers were becoming contracted into shorter spans as people entered paid work at a later stage and retired earlier. Employees were becoming increasingly mobile as professional qualifications became standardized.

Then came the internet and the mobile phone. These allowed many professionals greater choice over their hours and place of work, and opened up new possibilities for independent careers. More and more people, particularly in the rapidly expanding IT and communications sectors, were able to work at any time and in any place.

Throughout the late 1990s people across the generations, for a host of different reasons, were exploring the potential to work as free agents outside the confines of the organization. The focus seemed to be shifting from the job to work. Even full-time, "permanent" employees were being urged to update their skills in anticipation of change.

Has work reached yet another watershed as significant as those of the agrarian and industrial revolutions? It may be too early to answer this, but the combination of social trends, demographics and the rapid expansion of communications technology bears many similarities to the factors that created the manufacturing base some 200 years ago. Who knows what is waiting around the corner?

This article is based on the author's book, *Blood, Sweat and Tears: The evolution of work*, Texere, 2001.

## Further reading

Ashton, T.S. (1948) *The Industrial Revolution 1760–1830*, Oxford University Press.

Drucker, P. (1999) *The Practice of Management*, Butterworth Heinemann.

Owen, R. (1991) *A New View of Society and Other Writings*, edited by Gregory Claeys, Penguin.

Viteles, M.S. (1933) *Industrial Psychology*, London: Jonathan Cape.

Whyte, W.H. (2000) *The Essential William H. Whyte*, Fordham University Press, includes selections from *The Organization Man*, 1956.

Wild, R. (1972) *Mass-production Management*, Wiley.

Wrege, C.D. and Greenwood, R.G. (1991) *Frederick W. Taylor, the Father of Scientific Management*, Myth and Reality, Homewood, IL: Business One Irwin.

Wren, D.A. (1994) *The Evolution of Management Thought*, Wiley.

# Beyond operations
## to partnership

Malcolm Higgs is dean of Henley Management College and a professor of management studies.

Evidence is mounting of the effect people management can have on corporate performance. Now, argues **Malcolm Higgs**, HR managers must address their relationship with the top team.

Over the past decade, managers have begun to emphasize the importance of HR strategy and the need to align it with the overall strategy of the business. However, it is less clear whether this change has been driven by HR practitioners seeking a more significant role or whether it reflects a more profound shift in thinking about the significance of people management. This article explores the changing terrain of human resource management.

Although the phrase "our people are our most important asset" long ago became a cliché, few organizations appear to respect the principle in their day-to-day practice. Why should this be so? Perhaps because, until recently, there has not been much evidence that focusing on people management has any impact on the performance of an organization.

In addition, HR managers have too often relied on advocacy, without supporting their reasoning with business-based arguments. More recently, though, the case has been shaped in terms of sharper business imperatives. Organizations are becoming aware of the impact of skills shortages and the "war for talent". Leading and highly respected chief executives are publicly stating the importance of winning the "talent wars". During his time at GE, for example, Jack Welch pointed out that organizations which are successful in attracting and retaining more than their share of talent will have a sustainable competitive advantage.

Research is also beginning to show clear links between people management issues and business performance. Academic Dave Ulrich has shown that investors' valuation of businesses is significantly affected by intangible assets, which can account for anything up to 55 per cent of variation in market value. Such "intangibles" include:

- the ability to develop committed employees by aligning individual and organizational values;
- the quality of the leadership of the business (not just the chief executive, but the broader leadership team);

- the ability to work in a way which avoids "turf wars" between different functions or departments;
- the capability of employees to acquire skills and work in new ways;
- the ability of the organization to change and make changes stick.

Research in the UK by the Chartered Institute of Personnel and Development has also demonstrated links between good HR policies and practices and both productivity and product quality. Similar results have been found in European studies.

It seems evidence is accumulating of the increased importance of human resource management and its practices. Furthermore, it raises questions about more strategic aspects of HR:

- What are the implications in terms of the HR function?
- What are the competencies required by HR practitioners operating in such a role?
- Where are these "new" HR practitioners to be found?
- How will HR be seen in terms of its position in the career path of potential senior executives?

## The role of HR

The role of the HR function has moved from a welfare and administrative role ("pay and rations") to the provision of an increasingly professional range of policies, practices and services. Growth in employment legislation has fuelled many of these changes. Equally, line managers in many organizations have viewed this shift with suspicion, as HR has adopted more of a policing function.

A new view of the role of HR is clearly required. If people management is crucial to business success, then the HR function must undergo some substantial changes. First, HR managers should no longer assume full responsibility for, and control of, all people-related matters; instead they should become valued advisors to line managers in these areas. In many of today's most effective organizations, line managers fully accept their accountability for people management. The HR function in such organizations tends to be focused on building the

> It is essential that HR keeps in touch with business trends and issues and their effects on working practices.

capability of line managers to fulfil their people management responsibilities in a flexible and productive way. Second, the HR function must broaden its remit from purely operational matters towards a more strategic approach. HR managers must participate in strategic discussions within the business and, importantly, add value to these discussions as a business partner.

In moving towards a greater partnership with the business, HR must turn its attention outside the business, benchmarking against other organizations, and collecting and analyzing data on competitors. However, research has to go wider than analysis of people management practices. It is essential that HR keeps in touch with business trends and issues and their effects on working practices.

HR no longer primarily represents employee perspectives; today it is also a pillar of business and contributes alongside all other functions to building the commitment and loyalty of employees. So, it needs to be in a position to anticipate what changes are required, rather than responding to line managers' requests for change. This does not mean that their needs, views and opinions should be ignored; rather, these should be linked to an educated view of issues and developments and the effect these have on business plans, strategies and performance. HR practitioners need to be able to act as change managers by making a compelling business case for changes that are needed to support business strategy.

HR needs to move from being a specialist function that is ancillary to the core business to becoming an integral part of the company. Line managers as well as HR professionals must change their attitude towards HR if this is to happen. It not only entails a new relationship between HR and other functions but also requires line managers to accept their accountability for people management and devote more time and effort to fulfilling this role.

## The future model

A growing number of organizations have begun to work with HR in the ways outlined above. Their experiences, together with broader research, have led to a way of looking at HR that is based on the extent of focus on people and strategy. Figure 1 shows a model based on these dimensions.

The activities within each of the quadrants are significantly different. The potential roles in each quadrant have implications in terms of how the HR function is structured, resourced and developed.

- *Change capability builder.* In this role, HR managers help the organization lead and facilitate change. This encompasses not just HR-related changes, but all change and transformation processes. Why should this fall within the HR function? Because evidence shows that a major cause of failure in change initiatives is that managers do not take account of people-related issues. The role is often implemented through internal consultancy. Some global organizations have, within the last few years, moved all of their change and transformation teams into the HR function.

- *Provider of advice and service.* This role is concerned with delivery of HR services and advice, to both line managers and employees. Such services range from pay and benefits administration, to recruitment administration, training and employee legislation. For many, this is seen as "typical" HR work. Others have outsourced it, allowing the scope of the HR function to add value to the business. Large and diversified organizations which have not done so have taken the

opportunities for cost reduction offered by providing this function as a shared service.

- *Planning and metrics.* HR must develop ways of measuring the implementation of its policies. These monitor HR performance and provide important information for the business. Many organizations have tried to develop and use business metrics (such as the balanced scorecard) that go beyond financial measures and attempt to value intangible assets. In organizations using the scorecard approach, it is common to find that the HR function is accountable for its implementation and use.

- *Strategy and policy formulation.* HR managers must show a clear link between business strategy and HR strategy if a true business partnership is to develop. They must formulate people management policies that add value to the business. Sometimes this function is accountable for the direct care of the business's strategic people resources. For example, senior-level succession management and development may sit within this role.

Although few organizations think about HR in terms of strategy formulation, a significant number of global companies are moving in this direction. They have realized that the "new" HR roles require different capabilities and competencies from those traditionally associated with HR. This leads us to the second important question: "What will it take for HR managers to succeed in the new role?" Furthermore, should HR have board-level representation?

## Seeking success

Many researchers have explored the nature of the skills and competencies required by HR practitioners. The research of Ulrich and others into HR competencies has created a picture of those that add value to a business. Most important of these is "personal credibility" – meaning having a track record of success; instilling confidence; asking important questions; providing candid feedback; and providing alternative insights on business issues. In addition, HR requires the ability to manage change (and the ability to place the change in a business context) and to help others contribute effectively. Cultural sensitivity demands the ability to challenge the status quo

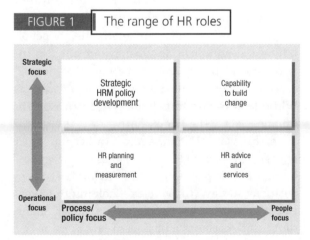

| FIGURE 1 | The range of HR roles |

BEYOND OPERATIONS TO PARTNERSHIP | 17

and establish clear links between the business and the organizational culture. Business acumen is critical, not only in its own right but also in terms of how it is used within the other aspects of the role.

Other competencies include:

- *Business knowledge and understanding.* This goes beyond knowledge of the business of the specific organization and its issues. It is increasingly important that those in leading HR roles have a breadth of business understanding. They need to know about the nature of business generally, strategic issues, market developments and what drives success in their organization.
- *Delivering relevant HR practices effectively.* The basic expertise, in terms of the range of HR topics, tends to be assumed as an entry-level requirement; the really valuable competence is the ability to apply this expertise in a way that adds value to the business.
- *Effective management of change processes.* Increasingly organizations are looking to senior HR managers to lead change, to have expertise in terms of change tools and technologies, and to make the case for change, facilitating, developing skills and coaching others.

An argument has been made that if HR is central to supporting business success, it needs to be a function that carries a board-level appointment. However, this argument, and the associated debate, misses the point. It is not a question of functional representation at board level that is important but rather the extent to which board members (and in particular the chief executive) have developed an attitude encompassing people issues in their planning and decision-making processes. A growing number of senior HR practitioners who believe in the strategic importance of people have nonetheless identified the core issue for effective change as the strength of their relationship with the top team – rather than whether they are personally on the board.

In practice, some feel that board membership may compromise the ability to facilitate change.

The key to the future role of HR is about how it becomes a business partner.

They believe they would see better business results from advising and coaching the top team rather than engaging in "functional warfare" as a member of the board. The key to the future role of HR is about how it becomes a business partner.

## Whence HR leaders?

Many of the above competencies could equally be applied to other functional areas within a business. The main differentiator is the delivery of HR advice services. Even here, the emphasis is on delivery in a way which adds value to a specific business and is aligned with business needs.

Perhaps, then, companies should consider bringing more broadly skilled business managers into senior positions within the new HR function. Many companies are pursuing this route already. If this becomes common practice, what is the potential role for those who have an HR background and have developed the other competencies that are required? One answer is to move them into line management roles, in the same way as line managers can move into HR roles. Such integration is already happening. For example, the European head of a major oil company was formerly head of its HR function. This sends a powerful signal to employees of the value of people management.

To date, little consideration has been given to how successful HR leaders work in practice. The most skilful HR leaders have developed their ability to coach and support the corporation's leaders. Perhaps the combination of the personal competencies and a deep understanding of people issues and organizational behaviour enables the seasoned HR practitioner to become the "people" coach and advisor for the top management team. While this is difficult, it may in future be the unique role for the HR executive.

In this way, HR managers can become more engaged in formulation of business strategy and be in a better position to link business strategy with day-to-day HR policies – helping to ensure that the mantra of "people are our most important asset" becomes a business reality.

## Conclusion

Given the view that people will play a significant role in the future success of businesses, perceptions of the role and contribution of HR functions need to be updated. This article outlines how thinking and practices have responded to significant changes in the business environment. If organizations commit to and execute these changes, there is a real possibility of their securing more viable and sustainable businesses in the long term. The effort and commitment to such change should not be underestimated. However, the business benefits can be considerable.

## Further reading

Guest, D., Michie, J., Sheehan, M., Conway, N. and Metochi, M. (2000) *Effective People Management*, Chartered Institute of Personnel and Development.

Richardson, R. and Thompson, M. (1999) *The Impact of People Management Practices on Business Performance: A literature review*, Chartered Institute of Personnel and Development.

Ulrich, D. (1997) *Human Resource Champions*, Boston, MA: Harvard Business School Press.

# Strategy and **performance**

**2**

# Contents

# Introduction to Part 2

**People management** is often considered a "soft" subject, reliant on the vagaries of human nature to achieve its results and with little in the way of quantifiable results. The authors in this part challenge this perception, describing how the activities of the HR department can and should be measured against expectations. Only then, they say, will the management of people be treated as central to company strategy and performance.

# Aligning HR with business goals

Justifying investment has become part of the human resources agenda as it takes on a strategic role. **George Dreher** presents a framework for assessment.

George F. Dreher is a professor of human resource management at Kelley School of Business at Indiana University.

The traditional way of thinking about gaining competitive advantage was to focus on a company's financial, strategic and technological capabilities. However, well over a decade ago management theorists and consultants began to reason that these must be supplemented with what they called "organizational capability".

Writers such as Dave Ulrich and Dale Lake argued that in addition to competing merely on price through financial capability, or product quality and innovation, high-performing companies engaged in an explicit competition for the most capable people. They argued that this competition went well beyond simply hiring the best people – to win, companies needed to attract, retain, motivate and develop talented people through effective human resource practices.

Accomplishing this, however, appears to require more than simply giving the traditional personnel or human resource management (HRM) function more power and influence. It requires a different way of thinking about people management. One goal of this article will be to introduce this way of thinking, commonly called strategic human resource management (SHRM). However, in the process, another objective may be served. This objective is directed at the general manager but also should be of interest to the HR professional because, if achieved, it will define what clients should reasonably expect from this class of service providers. Here the aim is to help the general manager become a better and more informed consumer of the services provided by in-house HR professionals and by a growing number of consultants. To this end, a framework is outlined that helps make judgements about the quality of these types of services. In particular, the types of issues that HR managers should be able to address will be presented and discussed.

Talent management practices and the essence of human resource management vary greatly across companies. In some companies HR specialists might be considered employee advocates, in others HR has become a set of highly developed administrative functions (with specialists devoted to staffing, pay, development, performance management and industrial relations) and in others they act as advisors to line managers.

By contrast, companies that have reached the SHRM stage of development treat HR staff as strategic business partners. But what is a strategic business partner? Edward Gubman, a former consultant with Hewitt Associates, suggests that the role aims to align business strategy and people to achieve extraordinary business results. This does not simply mean implementing business strategy through talent management practices – it means a more complex form of business practice integration. To introduce a little terminology, it is about creating both externally and internally congruent staffing, reward and development practices.

## Internal congruence

Something that distinguishes SHRM is a concern for the "internal congruence" of talent management practices. Three issues need to be addressed when considering this concept. First, managers must focus on the behaviours they want to promote. Many attitudes and practices are more difficult to change than one might think. Academic Barry Staw provided one of the earliest discussions of this. He found that only when several changes were enacted at once could entrenched behaviour be modified. An isolated change in staffing, reward or development activities is unlikely to do the job. Instead, managers must "throw the kitchen sink at the problem", to use Staw's phrase.

Next, managers must ensure that staffing, reward and development practices do not conflict. Consider a company that wants to influence the quality of its employees' teamwork. This company's practices might include:

- using a performance management system that focuses on the individual;
- providing team training in group interaction skills;
- having team members hire new members;
- having teams deal with grievances and discipline problems;
- giving bonuses to individual employees for meeting quality goals.

> Managers expect that providing high wages will lead to a large and highly qualified pool of applicants and that they will be able to hire the cream of the crop.

The first and last practices support behaviour that may conflict with the aim of improving teamwork. The promotion of individual task performance would tend to result in competitive behaviour within the team and discourages co-operation.

Finally, managers must ensure that inter-related practices support each other. Suppose an organization designs its salary hierarchy so as to make it a generous payer in its sector. Managers expect that providing high wages will lead to a large and highly qualified pool of applicants and that they will be able to hire the cream of the crop. But what if the organization does not also invest in a high-quality selection system? Without an effective selection system, the organization will never be able to take full advantage of its pay policy.

## External congruence

Examining the business environment and aligning HRM practices with key features of this environment creates another form of congruence – external congruence. This is at the heart of developing a contingency perspective – or the view that practices should be consistent with other aspects of the organization, especially business strategy. The development of this approach was pioneered by academics Randall Schuler and Susan Jackson. Their work revealed connections among competitive strategies (such as innovation, quality enhancement and cost reduction), desired role behaviours and a typology of HRM practices.

Ideas about aligning HRM practices with business strategy tend to begin with a framework for classifying companies. For example, in *The Talent Solution* Edward Gubman links three strategic business styles (operations, customers and products) and three distinct kinds of workforce strategy. Operations companies focus on deliver-

FIGURE 1    Role of human resources in strategy formulation

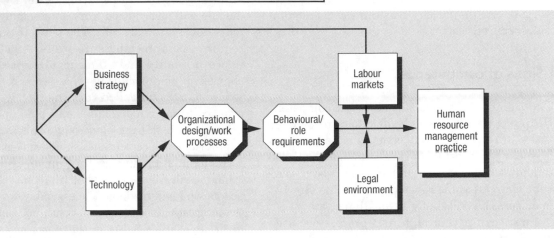

ing the best quality or value to customers. They tend to focus on improving work processes as a way to reduce costs and improve market quality. Gubman argues that with efficiency, order and process as their base, operations companies:

- compete by building teams to deliver high-value, low-cost processes;
- emphasize creating motivation and esprit de corps;
- measure process- and results-oriented outcomes and reward what is measured;
- build a culture of continuous improvement.

Companies that focus on product design and innovation or on customer-focused or customized solutions require different workforce strategies. For example, product-based companies need to foster innovation and risk-taking among certain employees. Staffing, reward and development practices to do this will differ from practices needed to support customer service or process improvement.

The link between business strategy and HRM system design is shown in Figure 1. It considers several contingencies (not just a company's business or tactical strategy) and works at the level of a targeted job class. It suggests a more decentralized approach than is taken by many companies. As the figure shows, the first step in the alignment process is to consider the business strategy and manufacturing- or service-oriented technologies that characterize a business environment. These attributes will dictate, in large part, how work needs to be organized and structured. How

work processes are ordered, in turn, will reveal which types of employee behaviour (and their associated competencies) are needed to accomplish specified objectives.

Decisions about HR practices come from an analysis of the behavioural requirements of the job, taking account of the labour market, and employment laws and regulations. While not explicitly shown in Figure 1, costs associated with implementing and maintaining the system must be compared with the likely returns. To be useful, the rate of return must meet or exceed the rate of return from other investment options.

Finally, Figure 1 reveals that HR specialists have a role in strategy formulation. That is, SHRM is not just about implementing a business strategy; it can inform decisions related to a variety of strategic issues. It is not so much knowledge of HRM practices that informs strategy formulation but knowledge of internal and external labour market conditions. For example, when German carmakers built assembly plants in the US, labour market analysis informed the decision about where to locate the sites. Labour market analysis can even influence the use of technology and facility design. An article in *The Wall Street Journal* reported that in 1997 General Motors planned assembly plants in Argentina, Poland, China and Thailand. Some plants are highly automated and expensive to build. However, when constructing the Argentine plant, the company took advantage of lower labour costs by depending much more on workers and using a lower automation ratio than normal. So, the factory was built at a substantially reduced cost.

## Signs of competence

The framework above suggests that competent HR professionals should be able to resolve linked issues in response to any changes in people management practices. It also suggests that they need to know about internal and external labour markets. Here are some concluding thoughts on what managers should look for in an HRM strategy.

First, can a thorough and process-oriented explanation be provided about why a prescribed HRM practice is properly aligned with business strategy? In addition to knowing about strategic models and how they relate to HRM practices, managers should have an understanding of the processes accounting for this relationship. That is, can the effect of a change in business strategy on HRM practices be traced through the model? Whereas general classification schemes may provide limited guidance when aligning a company's business and workforce strategy, the notion of a direct link masks a complex reality: role requirements can vary across organizational levels and occupational types, even within the same company. There is no substitute for the careful consideration of the behavioural and role requirements of a targeted class of jobs when addressing issues of HRM policy.

Next, have changes to HRM practices adequately considered the labour market? Managers must account for the skills, values and other competencies possessed by current and future employees when managing change. Assume that a company has adjusted its business strategy to stress product customization. This change will require greater manufacturing flexibility, so production will be switched from an assembly line to four-people assembly cells. The new processes will require team members to work together to improve quality and efficiency. Because of the changes in manufacturing processes, a consulting team has recommended that the pay system be changed from an individual bonus plan to a team-oriented gain-sharing plan. While this may seem appropriate, the consultants should not make this recommendation unless they have also determined, using labour market analysis, that the people who will be doing the assembly work have the interests (for example, in continuous improvement) and skills needed for this new role.

Third, have changes to practices addressed all the legal aspects? Employment and labour laws vary greatly across countries and cultures. Even something that may seem neutral, such as a downsizing initiative using job performance as the primary factor in making lay-off decisions, may create problems. In the US, if this procedure adversely affects members of classes protected by the employment sections of civil rights laws, the employer may need evidence that the performance management system is of high quality and "job-related".

Fourth, when changing a practice, have managers checked for conflicts with other practices? This, of course, is a question directed at the issue of internal congruence. The previously described change to a team-oriented pay plan will have implications for how the company trains employees and manages the staffing process. For example, team members may need to learn skills related to the quality improvement process.

Finally, have managers examined the costs and returns associated with a prescribed change? It is likely that most outcomes can be achieved if the employer is willing to spend enough money and devote the time and resources needed. However, the SHRM perspective demands that decision makers treat HR issues in much the same way that they treat other investment decisions. HR managers should stress the need to consider simultaneously the costs and financial returns associated with proposed changes in practices.

There is no substitute for the careful consideration of the behavioural and role requirements of a targeted class of jobs when addressing issues of HRM policy.

## Conclusion

Human resources executives and consultants often say their function needs to be aligned with business strategy and that they should be treated as partners at the strategic level. To do this, they need to show that their investment in recruits will generate reasonable rates of return. Further, their proposals must be compatible with other HRM practices and with technological and strategic changes. There is no simple template for formulating talent management practices, such as focusing on a company's strategic direction and core values. The connection between HR and business strategy can be made only by a rigorous analysis of internal and external factors.

## Further reading

Gubman, E.L. (1998) *The Talent Solution*, New York: McGraw-Hill.

Porter, M.E. (1980) *Competitive Strategy*, New York: Free Press.

Schuler, R.S. and Jackson, S.E. (1987) "Linking competitive strategies with human resource management practices", *Academy of Management Executive*, 3.

Staw, B.M. (1986) "Organisational psychology and the pursuit of the happy/productive worker", *California Management Review*, 28.

Ulrich, D. and Lake, D. (1990) *Organisational Capability*, New York: Wiley.

# The link between
## people and strategy

Brian E. Becker is a professor of human resources at the State University of New York at Buffalo.

Companies often treat workers as a cost, rather than as a source of competitive advantage. **Brian Becker**, **Mark Huselid** and **Dave Ulrich** suggest a way of valuing the most important intangible asset.

Mark A. Huselid is an associate professor of human resources strategy at Rutgers University.

Organizations increasingly rely on intangible assets for competitive advantage. Research, brands, customer relationships and capabilities such as organizational flexibility and culture are recognized as sources of value creation. Yet managing these intangibles as assets when conventional accounting often sees them as costs is a challenge.

Nowhere is this more obvious than when dealing with people. Even in tough economic times, managers recognize they are in a "war for talent" but often treat people as an overhead to be minimized. Instead, human resources should be managed as a strategic asset and HR performance measured in terms of its strategic effect. This requires a different perspective on what is meant by HR and a new understanding of how it creates value. Both line managers and HR managers need to think of HR not in terms of a function, or isolated practices, but rather as an "architecture" that must be structured and managed to create value.

## Architecture

Conventional thinking about HR reflects the paradox facing line managers. If people are the "most important asset", why is the HR function often thought of as an administrative overhead? In large part this perspective has been justified by the traditional emphasis on administrative efficiency and compliance. As innovation, speed, flexibility and intangible assets become more important, however, all managers need to break out of their functional perspective and consider the strategic value of HR.

Simply put, when senior line managers describe "people" as a strategic asset, they are describing the strategic aspects of employee behaviour; they are focusing on employee performance that implements company strategy. But just as organizational performance is a function of both people and systems, the appropriate HR system is required to

Dave Ulrich is a professor of business at the University of Michigan Business School.

select, develop and reward employees in ways that produce those strategic behaviours. This system is the set of policies and practices that describes the way people are selected, developed, appraised, rewarded and so on. (The HR function is the administrative home of the company's HR staff.) While line managers often play a central role in managing an HR system, HR staff must still have the competencies to drive this process.

## Strategic asset

It is easy to understand why organizations talk about people as an asset but manage them as a cost to be minimized. The costs are easy to see but the value creation is not. Because of the traditional perspective on HR, companies have no way to measure its strategic performance. Nevertheless, intangible assets are an increasingly important source of company value, of which human capital ought to be an important part.

Academic Baruch Lev and his colleagues have shown that an increasing share of a company's market value can be attributed to intangible assets. Lev identifies sources of intangible assets, including what he calls "sharp execution". For example, when chief financial officer James Chestnut transferred most of Coca-Cola's tangible assets to its bottlers, he observed that the company's $150bn market value derived largely from its brand and management systems. The implication is that intangible assets are increasingly important for value creation and that strategy implementation and management systems are an important part of this.

HR can become a strategic asset because the ability to execute strategy well is a source of competitive advantage and people are the lynchpin of strategy execution. Business commentators write

HR can become a strategic asset because the ability to execute strategy well is a source of competitive advantage and people are the lynchpin of strategy execution.

that the inability to execute strategy is the primary reason for the failure of a chief executive. Our research demonstrates the same point. As part of a survey of 400 US companies, respondents were asked to rate the suitability of their strategy and how well it had been executed. Analysis showed that the ability to execute well had an impact on financial performance that was 10 times greater than strategic choice. Companies do a reasonably good job of choosing the right strategy, to the point where this is no longer a differentiator. What does differentiate companies, however, is the ability to execute strategy.

Equally important, strategy implementation is driven by employee strategic focus – the extent to which people understand how their job contributes to company success. It is critical that the entire organization, not just senior managers, be strategically focused. What determines such focus? Perhaps unsurprisingly, our research showed that what gets measured is what gets managed. Organizations with more balanced performance measurement systems (in other words, balanced scorecards) rated the strategic focus of their employees significantly higher than organizations that relied simply on financial data as the measure. Also, focus was driven by the strategic alignment of the company's HR system – when the organization's rewards, development and appraisal systems encouraged the execution of company strategy, workers' strategic focus improved.

Organizational assets take on a strategic role when they create competitive advantage. Talent, commitment and flexibility are desirable characteristics but are not sufficient to turn people into a strategic asset. Strategic assets are the set of specialized resources and capabilities that bestow the company's competitive advantage. The ability to align management systems and employee behaviour in ways that support strategy becomes an "invisible asset" that is idiosyncratic to a company and not easily imitated by competitors.

Most senior managers intuitively understand that human capital has the potential to be strategically important. There is little beyond anecdotal evidence, however, to demonstrate its impact on financial performance, much less the contribution of HR. This article has described how HR could become a strategic asset, but is there any evidence that it really can have an impact? Based on our research involving nearly 3,000 companies over the past decade, the answer is very clearly yes.

Our results show a clear relationship between what we call a high-performance HR system and various measures of company financial performance (market value to book value and accounting profits). A high-performance HR system is one that emphasizes employee performance in every aspect of the system, is internally consistent and is aligned with the strategy of the organization. When a company's HR system is measured using an index that captures these features, a 35 per cent improvement in a company's HR system index results in a 10–15 per cent increase in market value/book value.

## Management

How can these ideas be put into practice? HR has always been challenged to make a persuasive business case for its strategic significance because the link between HR and financial performance is rarely direct. A solution to the missing link is the concept of the strategy map developed by academics Robert Kaplan and David Norton. To replace traditional accounting measures they have suggested performance measures – the "balanced scorecard" – that capture not only the financial results of managerial decisions but also the underlying causes. The formalized result of this analysis, what Kaplan and Norton call a strategy map, describes what has to be done to implement strategy. However, as they acknowledge in a 1996 article, organizations have made little progress in developing measures of how people (or HR) make a strategic contribution.

The absence of relevant measures of HR's strategic performance reflects the focus of HR in most organizations. Just as form follows function in architecture, the available measures for HR performance no doubt reflect its traditional emphasis on administrative efficiency and compliance. In short, senior line managers and HR departments have a common problem. The former, who recognize the importance of implementing strategy, need to find a way to manage and measure the strategic role of people. Conversely, the latter – responsible for making

people a strategic asset – lack a framework that allows them to bridge the gap between HR and company performance.

Linking the perspective of the HR architecture with the strategy map provides a solution. Line managers and HR staff have a common interest in value creation through HR's role in strategy implementation. The HR architecture now has several important features that differentiate it from the traditional HR focus. These include:

- The motivation, competencies and structure of the HR function are guided by a "top-down" analysis of its strategic contribution.
- The measure of HR's strategic value lies in its contribution to goals identified by line managers using a strategy map.
- HR and line managers will be able to measure HR's contribution to financial performance beyond simply its effect on cost control.

## The transition

Once an organization begins to manage HR as a strategic asset, however, the measures of HR's performance must reflect that transition. Unfortunately, organizations too often fail to make the systemic changes that link HR to strategy implementation and simply try to raise the profile of people performance measures. Figure 1 shows the transition in measurement systems required.

Level 1 measurement systems reflect the traditional HR focus on transactional and administrative efficiency. For these companies HR "performance" is often based on comparisons to external benchmarks. As more organizations have recognized the limits of these measures there has been an increasing effort to give people measures more strategic significance, as reflected in the second level in Figure 1. The problem with the Level 2 approach is that, at best, there is a tenuous relationship between these people measures and business success. Neither line managers nor HR staff can identify the direct relevance of these measures for business problems. As a result, managers give little more than lip service to people goals and the performance of HR people is still judged largely by efficiency

FIGURE 1 | Measuring HR's strategic performance

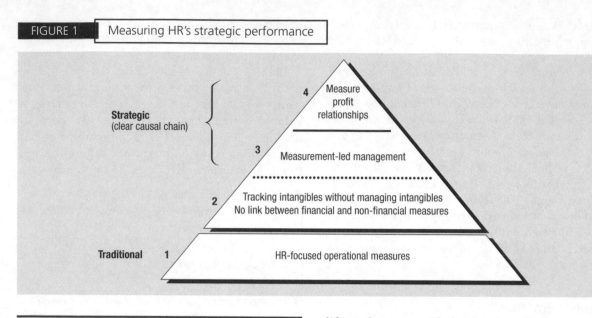

HR measures are tied directly to the development of a strategy map that outlines the causal logic of HR's impact on company performance.

measures. Operating at this level is frustrating for both line managers and HR people.

Level 3 measurement systems avoid these problems because the choice of measures is based on a systematic analysis of how intangibles, particularly HR, can influence strategy implementation. HR measures are tied directly to the development of a strategy map that outlines the causal logic of HR's impact on company performance. At this level, HR measures guide management decisions that drive strategy rather than simply reduce overheads.

Consider the example of a pipeline company that traditionally emphasized reactive maintenance policies for its workers. It became clear after developing a strategy map that pipeline reliability was an important indicator of customer satisfaction and, ultimately, financial performance. To improve pipeline reliability, the company put more effort into preventive maintenance. This in turn required employees to start diagnosing and predicting failures, analyzing

life-cycle costs and sharing knowledge. At this level there is a clear link between strategic behaviours and financial success.

Finally, Level 4 is the most sophisticated system because it measures both levels and relationships. This allows the organization to calculate the effect of HR in terms that are relevant to line managers. For several years, US retailer Sears Roebuck has been a leader in estimating the impact of intangible assets on financial performance. This allows managers' decisions to be guided by such specific relationships as "a 5-point improvement in employee attitudes will drive a 1.3-point improvement in customer satisfaction, which in turn will drive a 0.5 per cent improvement in revenue growth". More recently, Verizon Communications in the US has been measuring HR performance by its contribution to business and strategic goals (*see* Box 1), to the benefit of both HR managers and line managers.

## Conclusion

In practice, accepting that people are a company's most important asset means breaking with organizational systems that treat people as a cost to be minimized. Senior line managers understand that strategy is everybody's job; implementing it is the challenge.

Estimating causal linkages at Verizon Communications shows how a company can link HR practices and performance in a strategy map. Its network services unit (about 60,000 employees) proposed that market share was driven by customer valuation of service, which in turn was driven by customer service quality, brand advertising and inflation. HR managers created what they called the "employee engagement index". This was based on seven questions from an employee survey, giving a measure of strategic behaviour that was related to customer service.

The analysis supported their hypothesis and demonstrated the wisdom of their approach. For example, Verizon found that a 1 per cent increase in their index resulted in nearly a 0.5 per cent increase in customer service satisfaction. In other words, managers examined a section of their "strategy map" and tested the hypothesis that employee behaviour was an indirect leading indicator of an important strategic measure (market share). They measured the strategic impact of one element in the HR architecture.

Verizon managers were able to do this because they had a clear view of how employee behaviour affected strategy. Second, they recognized the need to collect and merge information from many sources. Third, the HR department had access to the necessary expertise in statistics.

A new perspective on HR is the foundation for meeting that challenge. It means that HR is more than a function and has the potential to be more than a cost. It requires changes in the relationship between line managers and HR managers, and a shared responsibility and accountability for strategic performance drivers. The potential benefits, however, are enormous. As a combination of organizational systems, routines and changes in the company's culture, the result is a source of competitive advantage that is not easily imitated.

## Further reading

Amit, R. and Shoemaker, P.J.H. (1993) "Strategic assets and organisational rents", *Strategic Management Journal*, 14.

Becker, B.E., Huselid, M.A. and Ulrich, D. (2001) *The HR Scorecard: Linking people, strategy and performance*, Boston: Harvard Business School Press.

Itami, H. (1987) *Mobilising Invisible Assets*, Boston: Harvard University Press.

Kaplan, R.S. and Norton, D.P. (2000) "Having trouble with your strategy? Then map it", *Harvard Business Review*, September.

Lev, B. (2001) *Intangibles: Management, measurement, and reporting*, Washington DC: Brookings Institution.

Stewart, T. (1998) "Real assets, unreal reporting", *Fortune*, July.

# Scoring goals for
## people and company

Linda Bilmes is a former assistant secretary of the US Department of Commerce. She teaches at Harvard University's John F. Kennedy School of Government.

Companies that invest in their employees perform better, says **Linda Bilmes**, who presents a measurement system and the evidence to support the claim.

While companies pay lip service to the importance of their people, in reality they invest in almost anything else – sales, marketing, brands, customers, distribution, IT, finance – to enhance performance. Yet the most obvious, and overlooked, source of strategic advantage is to use people better.

Companies have long used human resource policies to gain competitive advantage. In the 1880s, John D. Rockefeller linked managers' pay to company performance. Rockefeller gave shares to senior managers. "I would have every man a capitalist," he said. In 1914, Henry Ford doubled the average wages of his assembly-line workers. He claimed that better motivated workers made him more money and said the pay rise was "the finest cost-cutting move we ever made". From this view, the present economic downturn is an opportunity to spend time and effort in nurturing workers.

The viewpoint described in this article is based on a study by myself, Peter Strueven and Konrad Wetzker of the Boston Consulting Group, as well as my empirical observations while at the US Department of Commerce. To measure how well companies manage employees, we developed a "people scorecard" – a set of criteria that can be tracked and quantified. In the analysis, companies that scored highest earned higher shareholder returns than their competitors. Further, such companies enjoyed better employee satisfaction, greater employee loyalty and were able to weather downturns more easily. This article lays out the evidence and shows how to use it.

## The scorecard

Why are people neglected in companies? First, human resources is seldom at the centre of corporate power. Everybody knows HR is critical but, perhaps because it is often a female role, it continues to be treated as a support function. Moreover, HR itself has been too narrowly focused. In the scorecard, we judge companies on both "traditional" HR functions such as recruiting and performance evaluations, and on what we call intrapreneurship – creating an active, entrepreneurial culture in the company (*see* Box 1). Successful people-factor companies emphasize both.

Companies also neglect human capital because it is difficult to measure and the benefits of people strategy take time to emerge. However, there is growing evidence to link company performance and people management.

We used the scorecard as a tool to analyze more than 200 companies in the US and Germany. Data was gathered from published material and interviews with staff. The criteria in the scorecard are specific data such as days of training provided, type of training and choice of training subject. Each company was rated and compared with industry peers.

The results are striking. First, companies that scored highest had a higher total shareholder return than lower-scoring companies. In the US, top companies had an average annual return of 27 per cent over the period 1989–98, whereas the bottom ones earned 8 per cent. Companies with

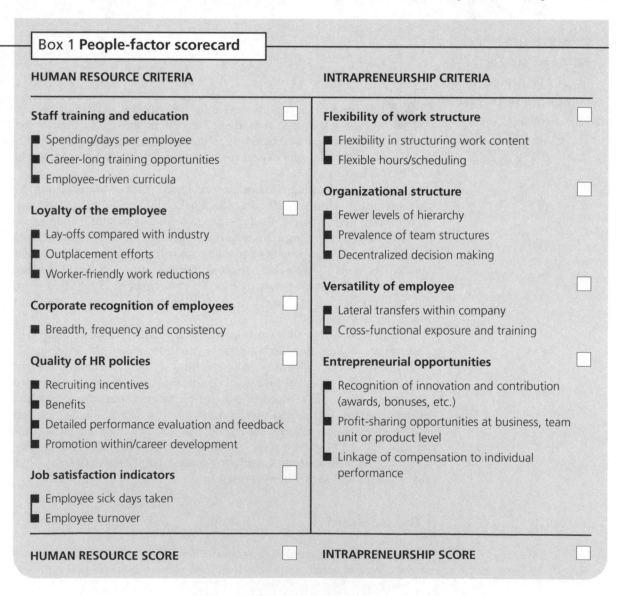

## Box 1 **People-factor scorecard**

### HUMAN RESOURCE CRITERIA

**Staff training and education** ☐

- Spending/days per employee
- Career-long training opportunities
- Employee-driven curricula

**Loyalty of the employee** ☐

- Lay-offs compared with industry
- Outplacement efforts
- Worker-friendly work reductions

**Corporate recognition of employees** ☐

- Breadth, frequency and consistency

**Quality of HR policies** ☐

- Recruiting incentives
- Benefits
- Detailed performance evaluation and feedback
- Promotion within/career development

**Job satisfaction indicators** ☐

- Employee sick days taken
- Employee turnover

### INTRAPRENEURSHIP CRITERIA

**Flexibility of work structure** ☐

- Flexibility in structuring work content
- Flexible hours/scheduling

**Organizational structure** ☐

- Fewer levels of hierarchy
- Prevalence of team structures
- Decentralized decision making

**Versatility of employee** ☐

- Lateral transfers within company
- Cross-functional exposure and training

**Entrepreneurial opportunities** ☐

- Recognition of innovation and contribution (awards, bonuses, etc.)
- Profit-sharing opportunities at business, team unit or product level
- Linkage of compensation to individual performance

**HUMAN RESOURCE SCORE** ☐  **INTRAPRENEURSHIP SCORE** ☐

middle scores had an average return of 21 per cent, which is close to the 19.2 per cent average annual growth in the Standard & Poor's 500 index. In Germany, companies with the highest score had a shareholder return nearly three times higher than companies with the lowest score and 35 per cent above the median. This contradicted the prevailing German view that companies pursue high returns at the expense of employees.

The second finding was that scores varied wildly. In each sector, we found a people-factor leader and a laggard. Pfizer, leader in the pharmaceutical sector, has been providing stock option benefits to nearly all employees since 1950. The least successful drug company offers such options to fewer than one in five employees and started to do so only in the early 1990s. Third, people-factor benefits take time to emerge. Over four years and longer, a pattern becomes clear, with those companies scoring highest on the scorecard enjoying strong performance versus their competitors. But people-factor companies sometimes forego short-term profits in pursuit of longer-term success.

In spite of its troubles, one of the best examples of this approach is US computer maker Hewlett-Packard. Over four decades, the company avoided lay-offs by using across-the-board pay cuts, sabbaticals, shorter hours and cancelled bonuses. It pioneered flexible hours, job shares, telecommuting, company-wide stock options and linking managers' pay to their rate of new product design. HP encouraged entrepreneurship, even investing in spin-offs launched by former employees and giving them "preferred-source" contracts.

Fourth, companies with high HR scores but low scores for intrapreneurship do not have superior stock performance. How can companies create entrepreneurial energy? Four Seasons Hotels is a good example. In the company that invented the mini-bar after a suggestion by an employee, ideas are welcomed and well rewarded. Four Seasons was also the first chain to introduce telephones and hairdryers in bathrooms, 24-hour services and free overnight shoeshine. Most of these innovations were suggested by employees.

So, HR should reinforce and foster entrepreneurial opportunity. Do good people policies create good companies, or vice versa? It is a fair assumption that better-managed companies are better at managing people. But beyond that, there is strong evidence that the best people-factor companies create an advantage in the market.

A company that does well on all parts of the scorecard seems to translate that into better performance through a more contented and loyal workforce. This was the conclusion of a survey of 2,000 US and German workers carried out for our research by polling organization Penn, Schoen and Berland Associates.

## Findings

The survey produced two main findings. First, investing in people-factor criteria strongly increased job satisfaction and loyalty. Overall, 34 per cent of US workers and 35 per cent of German workers described themselves as satisfied with their jobs. But among workers in companies that offered people-factor benefits, job satisfaction was much higher – 58 per cent of US and 63 per cent of German workers.

The features that most increased job satisfaction were allowing people to influence decisions that affect their work life, training and performance-linked pay. Similar factors increased employee loyalty. In the US, 46 per cent of workers said they were "very loyal" to their companies. But in companies that provided training, linked pay to performance and gave employees some autonomy, 58 per cent said they were "very loyal". In Germany, 86 per cent of workers in such companies were "very loyal", compared with 66 per cent in other companies.

The happiest and most loyal respondents were those who enjoyed both traditional HR benefits (especially training) and intrapreneurship. Employees who agreed with the statement "My company makes it easy for me to put my ideas into practice and to get credit for it" were twice

Companies with high HR scores but low scores for intrapreneurship do not have superior stock performance.

as satisfied, and twice as loyal to their companies, as those who disagreed.

The second finding was that a huge gap existed between what companies thought they provided and what workers believed they received. Most companies claimed to offer training, performance evaluation and employee involvement in decision making. Yet only a third of employees said they received such benefits. Moreover, the greatest gap was on attributes that people considered most important. For example, 71 per cent of respondents listed "I am able to influence decisions that affect me" as "very important", but only 34 per cent of employees agreed that they could do it.

The survey found little evidence of intrapreneurship. Top managers said pay was extremely important to them but only 41 per cent of such managers in the US (fewer in Germany) participated in a profit-sharing or stock option plan, and only 30 per cent said their pay was linked to their performance. Even in small companies, 60 per cent of employees said it was not easy to put their ideas into practice.

## Eight steps

Superior stock market performance and the powerful effect on employee morale together create a powerful case for the scorecard. Moreover, the fact that so many workers feel they do not receive people-factor benefits reveals the size of the opportunity. Companies can begin to create an emphasis on people by following eight basic steps.

- *Top-level commitment.* If a company is to transform itself into a people-focused organization, its leader must be dedicated to this aim. General Electric is a well-known example of a US company that has reaped the rewards of patient investment in its people. At GE it took a determined and focused leader (willing to write thousands of hand-written notes to employees) and several years. Jack Welch's vision, and his detailed attention to his workforce, allowed GE to focus on making every employee effective.

- *Workforce development planning.* A company must spend the time and effort to assess its workforce needs regularly. It should ask: "How will the market evolve?"; "How must the workforce change?";

## Employees value training and see it as a test of how much the company values them.

"How much outsourcing is desirable?" and benchmark workforce skills against current and projected needs. Such planning is necessary if the company is to provide meaningful and useful training, career development and performance evaluations for employees.

- *Develop versatility.* Skills development needs to be thought out and matched to the needs of the company and its employees. But companies should also use development to become more versatile. For example, the German construction company Bilfinger and Berger used the last recession to upgrade the skills of its workers and managers, so they learned new skills, such as languages and environmental engineering. While competitors shed workers, Bilfinger was able to take on more international jobs and different types of jobs. It gained market share and moved from seventh to third place in industry size rankings.

- *Training.* Employees value training and see it as a test of how much the company values them. Training boosted job satisfaction and loyalty for workers at all levels and companies of all sizes, in both the US and Germany. There is extensive literature on running effective training. The essential element of training for people-factor companies is that it must be linked to the personal and career development of the individual.

- *Retain good workers.* Staff turnover is inevitable and sometimes desirable. However, an essential ingredient of successful people-factor companies is that they are able to keep their top performers. The survey showed that the most direct influence on an employee's loyalty was linking compensation to performance. Such a link requires a fair and transparent way to measure performance. Leading people-factor companies such as HP and GE develop an annual individual performance plan for each employee, with feedback sessions every quarter.

- *Structure work.* Work needs to be structured so that people enjoy it. In addition, it should foster intrapreneurship. People-factor companies typically have flat hierarchies and decentralized decision making. In addition, some have come up with novel structures. US biomedical company Chiron allows its scientific staff to make "creative partnerships", which can be started up or ended easily, instead of going through a protracted legal process. Chiron's approach has yielded numerous innovations, including the discovery of the Hepatitis C virus.

- *Reward success*. People-factor companies reward success and mimic the reward structure of an entrepreneurial venture. To link performance and compensation, a company should design work plans for each employee that define goals, tasks and responsibilities, and specify how success will be measured. Further, attributes that support the people factor (such as creativity, teamwork and skills development) should be rewarded.

- *Communicate the people factor*. Chief executives who believe in the people-factor concept sound almost evangelical. William Steere, chairman and chief executive of Pfizer, says: "We get characterized for our balance sheet or our profit and loss but in the end [people] truly characterize a corporation."

## Conclusion

The people factor is a simple concept: investing in human creativity delivers high returns in terms of job satisfaction and shareholder returns. Implementing it takes sustained attention to a set of basic rules. In the current economic climate, managers preoccupied with short-term returns from cost-cutting often run against the grain of the people factor. Our evidence suggests that companies with the foresight to see beyond immediate difficulties will emerge from the downturn with renewed strength.

## Further reading

Wetzker, K., Strueven, P. and Bilmes, L. (1998) *Gebt uns das Risiko zuruck*, Munchen: Carl Hanser Verlag.

# Organization and change

# Contents

# Introduction to Part 3

**L**arge-scale change is hard for complex organizations to carry out. Aside from the strategic and logistical difficulties of a merger or restructuring, managers can face daunting problems relating to people management: resistance to change, culture clashes, morale problems and training gaps. As the authors in this part show, managers need to market change programmes to employees, not simply plan the physical or financial details.

# Seeking an
## edge in mergers

Randall S. Schuler is a professor of human resource strategy and founder of the Center of Strategic Human Resource Management at Rutgers University.

Susan E. Jackson is a professor of human resource management at Rutgers University.

Most mergers and acquisitions fail, say **Randall Schuler** and **Susan Jackson**, and neglecting human resources issues is often to blame.

Regardless of industry, it seems companies cannot compete without growing through mergers or acquisitions. Consider the size, variety and number of recent deals: Daimler-Chrysler, Chase-JP Morgan, UBS-Paine Webber, Glaxo-Smith-KlineBeecham, AOL-Time Warner, Pfizer-Warner Lambert, Nestle-Purina and Deutsche Telekom-Voice Stream. The factors driving this activity are likely to intensify: economies of scale, deregulation, globalization, expanding markets, risk spreading and rapid response in markets. Although the pace of activity has slowed, even in the tough environment of 2000 the value of global mergers and acquisitions (M&A) activity exceeded $3,500bn.

In a merger, two companies come together and create a new entity. In an acquisition, one company buys another one and manages its new asset according to its needs. There are mergers of equals, such as those between Citicorp and Travelers to form Citigroup, and between Ciba and Sandoz to form Novartis. There are also mergers between companies of different sizes such as that between Chase and J.P. Morgan to create JPMorganChase. Similarly, there are two major types of acquisitions: those involving integration, of a type typically made by Cisco Systems, and those involving separation, such as between Unilever and Bestfoods.

Each type of merger or acquisition creates different people management issues. For example, a merger of equals often compels the two companies to share staffing implications, whereas a merger of unequal companies results in these being shared unequally. An acquisition that involves integration has greater staffing implications than one involving separation. Other differences are highlighted later in this article.

There are many reasons for companies to merge or buy. Companies in horizontal markets may seek market dominance or economies of scale. Those in vertical mergers may want to control channels to market. Hybrid mergers can help companies spread risk, cut costs, exploit synergies or defend market share. Or companies may seek critical mass, speedy growth, cash, deferred taxes and excess debt capacity. Not least, companies may want to expand their core competencies with fresh talent, knowledge and technology. In addition, companies that are successful and inventive in combining not only create value but develop a core competence in combination management itself. This can give the company an edge.

## Track record

With the need for mergers and acquisitions growing, and the base of experience expanding, it may appear that success is more likely than failure. In fact, consultancy AT Kearney reports, three-quarters fail. Further, only 15 per cent of mergers and acquisitions in the US achieve their financial objectives, as measured by share value, return on investment and post-combination profitability.

> Companies that are successful and inventive in combining not only create value but develop a core competence in combination management itself.

Why do mergers fail? Clearly, many things can go wrong. Expectations may be unrealistic, strategy hastily constructed and poorly planned or executed. Talent may be lost or mismanaged. Success may require an impossible degree of synergy and transition costs may be underestimated. Culture clashes between the entities can go unchecked. The merger may distract the focus of executives from the core business at a crucial time. Of these, culture clashes, gaps, or incompatibility and losses of talent are cited most frequently as reasons for failure (*see* Box 1). Conversely, reasons for success include lead-

### Box 1 DaimlerChrysler

Many commentators believe that differences of culture at Daimler and Chrysler made its merger more difficult. DaimlerChrysler believed the two cultures could be combined relatively easily. Cultural issues seemed to be addressed only when executives made statements about differences in the companies. Either they did not realize the implications of cultural differences or they chose to focus on operational and business synergies, hoping that culture would sort itself out.

During the initial stages, Chrysler president Thomas Stallkamp indicated that Daimler intended to adopt Chrysler's product development methods, which emphasized teamwork. Chrysler in turn would adopt Daimler's rigid adherence to timetables and its methodological approach to solving problems. However, evidence of the lack of co-operation soon emerged – demonstrated by Daimler executives' refusal to use Chrysler parts in Mercedes vehicles.

In August 2000, Daimler's chief of passenger cars, Juergen Hubbert, was quoted in *The Economist*:

"We have a clear understanding: one company, one vision, one chairman, two cultures." While it is true that since the departure of Robert Eaton (Chrysler's former chairman) only one chairman (Juergen Schrempp in 2001) runs the company, Hubbert's other assertions are in question. Although DaimlerChrysler may be "one" company in name, separate operational headquarters were maintained. Business operations continued to be separate, as shown by "Daimler's" decision to allow "Chrysler" more leeway in design and production, which more closely emulated the practices of the "old Chrysler". Each had its own agenda on different aspects of the market, making it difficult to discern a unified vision for the company. Finally, with the acknowledged existence of two cultures, how could DaimlerChrysler truly become one company with one vision? Dieter Zetsche, a trusted Daimler executive with extensive US experience, is now running Chrysler. His background may give the best opportunity yet to meld the cultures.

ership, clear goals, due diligence on hard and soft issues, a well-managed M&A team, planning for combination steps completed early, retaining essential talent and extensive communications. Thus, while there are many reasons for success and failure, some of the most important are directly related to people management.

## Three-stage model

Experience suggests a model of M&A activity that has three stages: pre-combination, combination (integration of the partners) and solidification and assessment. While these stages involve most business functions, the issues highlighted here are those closely associated with human resources.

### Pre-combination

There are several human resource issues in the first stage of M&A activity (*see* Stage 1). Of the many possible reasons for an M&A, a substantial number are human-resource related, such as the acquisition of talent. At companies such as Cisco and General Electric, retention of employees is often the prime concern. Here, action is announced to obtain that talent in the first place.

An important issue is the choice of a dedicated senior executive, such as Michael Volpi at Cisco, and a team to head the M&A process. As suggested earlier, one reason for failure is the lack of a leader who can focus all aspects of the process, one of which is seeking out target companies. After identifying potential companies comes selection. Regardless of how well the other stages may be accomplished, selecting the wrong partner is likely to diminish the chances of success. Further, selecting the right partner without a well-developed plan for the rest of the process will also threaten the merger or acquisition. Companies that have a better understanding of the process are likely to be more successful in their M&A activities. This understanding, however, has to be shared and disseminated because M&A activity is likely to affect everyone, particularly if the combination results in extensive integration.

Conducting thorough due diligence also has critical HR implications. "Many CEOs gloss over softer HR issues, including potential cultural problems, only to realize later that they've made a huge mistake," says Mitchell Lee Marks, a management consultant who has worked on more than 60 mergers over 15 years.

Yet a Watson Wyatt survey concluded that the priority assigned to HR and communication in due diligence was comparatively low. While other functions may be the essence of the "hard" due diligence process, the human resource audit, the "soft" due diligence, is gaining more prominence. Important areas include day-to-day business costs and potential liabilities, especially related to retiree medical benefits, severance pay and employment contracts. Due diligence can identify people who are crucial to the transaction, allowing the acquiring company to give long-term contracts to vital executives, or lower the value of the deal based on the possibility that these individuals might leave.

Cultural assessments are also entering the due diligence process. These involve describing and evaluating the companies' philosophies and values regarding such issues as leadership styles, time horizons, relative value of stakeholders, risk tolerance and the value of teamwork versus individual performance and recognition. With DaimlerChrysler, cultural differences, initially played down, became the reason for allowing business units to function as they wished as long as they achieved their goals.

An important finding from the Watson Wyatt survey was that the above HR issues are best addressed through planning. Experience and learning from past M&A activity can help inform the planning, but this learning process must also be well managed. Learning, knowledge sharing and transfer are acknowledged as important not only in M&A activities but also in joint ventures. These can be systematically supported by human resources practices.

### Integrating the companies

Regardless of the area of breakdown or weakness, when poor integration occurs, productivity and job satisfaction drop and employees begin to feel that managers care more about financial statements than product quality or people. Johnson & Johnson found that a systematic, explicit integration

**HR issues**

- Identifying reasons for the M&A
- Forming M&A team; appointing leader
- Searching for potential partners
- Selecting a partner
- Planning for managing the process
- Planning to learn from the process

**HR implications and actions**

- Knowledge and understanding need to be disseminated
- Leadership needs to be in place
- Composition of team affects success
- Systematic and extensive pre-selection and selection
- Conducting thorough due diligence of all areas
- Cultural assessment
- Planning for combination minimizes problems later
- Creating practices for learning and knowledge transfer

process is at the heart of a successful acquisition. All acquisitions require some degree of integration in day-to-day systems and processes, and in achieving synergies (*see* Stage 2).

Perhaps the most critical HR issue for this stage is selecting an integration manager. Mergers and acquisitions that are guided by such a manager retain a higher percentage of the acquired companies' leaders and their employees, and achieve business goals earlier.

What should the integration manager do? The role includes serving as a project manager, communicator, relationship builder, team leader, referee and negotiator. He or she should focus exclusively on the acquisition or merger and should not be one of the people running the business. Usually it is someone on loan from the business who can focus solely on integration issues. Such managers provide continuity between the deal team and management of the new company, and will be part of a steering committee. This group is responsible for setting the role, process and objectives of the integration and overseeing the progress of integration teams.

A second issue is picking a leader to manage the combined business. If an acquired business has unclear or absent leadership, the result will be crippling uncertainty, stalled product development and postponed decisions. Restructuring should be done early, fast and once only. This minimizes

uncertainty. One problem has been a tendency to restructure slowly and to rely heavily on people rather than structures and processes. A lesson learned from GE Capital's experience is that decisions about structure, roles, reporting relationships, lay-offs, restructuring and other career-affecting aspects of the integration should be made, announced and implemented as soon as possible after the deal has been signed. Creeping changes, uncertainty and anxiety that last for months are debilitating and drain value.

Experiences at Johnson & Johnson affirm this. They also suggest managers should not dismantle something until its use is understood and there is something to replace it, and that restructuring should not be confused with integrating – it is part of a larger process. To facilitate this restructuring phase, the leader can manage the process of change itself. There is no doubting the pressure of work caused by the need to manage integration as well as "doing the day job". Add to that the tendency for people to resist change and the shortage of qualified managers, and you have a recipe for an over-stressed, under-performing work environment.

Managing this involves preparing staff for the change, making sure they understand it fully, creating a schedule for the changes making the changes and then putting in place structures, policies and practices to support the operation.

## Uncertainty caused by unclear strategy, no HR assessment and insufficient communication can drive away staff.

The Johnson & Johnson study found that many acquired businesses lose essential people. Yet retaining these people is crucial to achieving goals through the transition period and the long-term competitive advantage associated with specialized knowledge. Uncertainty caused by unclear strategy, no HR assessment and insufficient communication can drive away staff. Selection needs to be aligned closely with incentives for employees to stay.

Companies that are skilled at M&A adopt several techniques:

- *Negotiating financial deals with essential employees.* Senior employees may be covered by agreements that allow stock options to be exercised when there is a change in ownership. To keep these workers from taking the money and running, acquiring companies often offer packages that mature over time.

- *Giving retention bonuses.* Companies offer cash to workers who stay through a merger or until a specific project is completed. In the US, for example, Florida Power, gave retention bonuses to 200 employees during the merger of its parent and Carolina Power & Light. It also increased severance packages to discourage employees who were

worried about pending lay-offs from leaving prematurely.

- *Writing employment agreements.* Employees who get financial incentives may be asked to agree to stay on for a specified time. Agreements are usually signed before the deal closes.

Managing communication is another way to retain and motivate employees. This can take several forms. Acquiring companies use the web, company intranets and e-mail to dispel rumours and keep employees informed. Some senior managers talk directly with employees they are determined to keep. When his former company, Intervu, took over software developer Netpodium, chief executive Harry Gruber met every engineer personally.

A final HR issue is the need to create policies and practices for learning, and knowledge sharing and transfer. As Johnson & Johnson found, many of the same lessons were learned repeatedly across business units as well as from other companies. Sharing those lessons enhances integration and improves the likelihood of success.

### Solidification and assessment

As the combination takes shape, it faces issues of readjusting, solidifying and fine-tuning (*see* Stage 3). These issues take on varying degrees of intensity, depending on whether it is a merger of inclusion rather than one of separation, or an acquisition of relative equals versus unequals. DaimlerChrysler, an acquisition of relative equals,

---

### Stage 2 **Integration of the companies**

**HR issues**

- Selecting integration manager
- Designing/implementing teams
- Creating the structure/strategies/leadership
- Retaining employees
- Motivating employees
- Managing the change process
- Communicating to and involving stakeholders
- Deciding on the HR policies and practices

**HR implications and actions**

- Selecting the appropriate candidate
- Creating team design and selection are critical for transition and combination success
- Communicating is essential
- Deciding on who stays and goes
- Establishing culture, structure and HR policies and practices

## Stage 3 **Solidification and assessment**

**HR issues**

- Solidifying leadership and staffing
- Assessing strategies and structures
- Assessing culture
- Assessing HR policies and practices
- Assessing concerns of stakeholders
- Revising as needed
- Learning from the process

**HR implications and actions**

- Elective leadership and staffing
- Creating and evaluating structure
- Melding two cultures needs assessment revision
- Concerns of all stakeholders addressed and satisfied

provides an example. It went through this for more than two years after the formal combination was completed, during which time there were several leadership changes in the Chrysler Group.

## Conclusion

Companies are increasingly using mergers and acquisitions to maintain and strengthen their market position. They are seen by many as a relatively fast and efficient way to expand and incorporate technologies. Yet success is by no means assured. On the contrary, most fall short of stated goals and objectives.

While some failures can be explained by financial and market factors, many can be traced to personnel issues. Studies confirm the need for companies to address human resource issues and activities in their M&A activities. HR departments can make a genuine contribution to merger success in partnership with line managers and employees.

## Further reading

Charman, A. (1999) *Global Mergers and Acquisitions*, Alexandria, VA: Society for Human Resource Management.

*The Economist* (2000) "The DaimlerChrysler emulsion", July 29.

A.T. Kearney study reported in Haebeck, M.H., Kroger, F. and Trum, M.R. (2000) *After the Mergers*, New York: Prentice Hall.

Vlasic, B. and Stertz, B.A. (2000) *Taken for a Ride*, New York: HarperCollins.

Watson Wyatt (2000) European results of the global M&A survey (http://www.watsonwyatt.com/homepage/eu/res/surveys/mergersandacquisitions/0600/index.htm).

# Time to get
## back to the basics

J. Stewart Black is an adjunct professor of business administration at the University of Michigan Business School.

It sometimes seems that there is nothing more to say about change, so why are managers still so worried about it? **Stewart Black** has some suggestions.

What could there possibly be that is new to say about change? "Change is important" – it's been said. "The rate of change is accelerating" – we've heard it all before. "The only constant is change" – so often repeated that it is past being a cliché. Yet although it has all been said before, people have yet to master the art of leading change. Academics Hal Gregersen, Allen Morrison and I found that of 130 executives in 55 different companies around the world, 85 per cent thought change management was a critical leadership capability. More importantly, almost the same number of these senior executives said that the skills for managing change among their high-potential managers were unsatisfactory. Other studies have found that between 50 and 70 per cent of change initiatives fail to meet their objectives or fail to meet them on time.

So, if it has all been said before, why aren't people any better at leading change? Is it simply that they are not listening? In fact, most managers around the world think leading change is important and most want to know how to do it better. It may be that the problem lies in the message and its messengers, not the audience.

## Back to basics

When I was younger, I was a striker in a football team. Things would go well until I had to pass the ball to someone in the middle of the pitch using my left foot. The coach stopped me and said: "You will never master this unless you go back to the basics." My research and consulting experience suggests that the same is true for change – to improve their ability to lead change, people have to go back to first principles.

What are the basic lessons of change? One is this: people do not change very easily. For example, fewer than one in five people who set a goal of losing weight succeed. In addition, just one in three people who start an exercise programme follow it through beyond the first two weeks. Given that change of any sort is difficult for people, one way of leading it is to understand why change fails. Such understanding lies in answering three questions: Why do people fail to see the need for change? Why, even when they see the need, do people fail to act? Why, even when they act, do people so often fail to finish – either because they have not gone far enough or fast enough?

## Mental maps

So, why do people fail to see, act and finish? Just as people use maps to help navigate on journeys, they construct and use mental maps – ways of thinking and communicating – to guide behaviour. Further, just as people discard physical maps that do not guide them well and keep the ones that do, they keep mental maps for only one reason – they have proven successful. Consequently, the first point to recognize is that most change is preceded by success. Whatever personal or organizational change may be required, it is preceded by something that has worked.

This is why people are slow to see the need for change. They use mental maps that have proven successful. Consider the following examples – one from cartography and the other from business. In 1545, a map was drawn showing the state of California as an island. It was created by sailors who went north up the Gulf of Baja with the mainland of present-day Mexico on the east and present-day Baja in Mexico on the west. The sailors turned around before reaching the end of the Gulf of Baja (where Baja and Mexico come

> Just as people use maps to help navigate on journeys, they construct and use mental maps – ways of thinking and communicating – to guide behaviour.

together) and sailed back down the gulf, around its southern tip and up the west coast of present-day Baja and California. They sailed north until they reached a great inlet in northern California. The ship was low on supplies and the crew was sick. The sailors concluded that this inlet was the northern tip of the island and that water circled around and back south to where they had stopped on their first northward journey in the Gulf of Baja. Thus convinced, they drew a map with California as an island. Even though over time evidence from other explorers indicated that California was not an island, this map persisted for 200 years before King Ferdinand of Spain finally declared otherwise.

While some readers might question the relevance of this story of unsophisticated navigators to the modern age, there are many similar tales in more recent times. For example, Ikea, the world's largest furniture company, stuck to a flawed map for a long time. Ikea sells its products in more than 100 countries. When it set up and expanded operations in the US, it did well in all areas except beds and bedding. With poor initial results, executives increased the proportion of marketing and advertising spent on beds, yet sales did not improve. Unfortunately, these executives had a mental map of the world in which beds were measured using the metric system. While this worked for the rest of the world, in the US the sizes of king, queen and twin reign supreme. Ikea persisted in trying to sell beds and bedding measured in centimetres for nearly three years before finally relenting. Once the company altered its map and changed to the US sizing system, sales of beds and bedding improved significantly through the 1990s.

Change fails, partly because people fail to see the need for it. They are deluded by their existing mental maps and have these maps for only one reason – they have worked in the past.

## Failure to act

Even when people see the need for change, they often fail to act on it. Why is this? If people do something well, the knowledge that they are doing it well is often more important to them than the question of whether it is the right thing to do. For example, IBM executives decided that making computers – mainframe computers, servers, PCs and so on – was the right thing in the past but not for the future. They encouraged managers to change their perceptions of the business to one that provided "solutions" to customers. However, employees were skilled in the competencies of the old map. In spite of understanding that "solutions" not "boxes" were the future, employees believed that if they followed the new map they were going to go from being very competent at the wrong thing to being incompetent at the right thing. For many this was not an appealing proposition.

Senior executives at IBM complained: "If these managers see the need for change, why aren't they changing?" The problem with the change programme was not the destination but the path to it. Many managers saw that the change required capabilities such as teamwork, customer relationships and global integration, for which they lacked the capabilities. Without a clear indication of how they could move from doing the right thing poorly to doing it well, they unsurprisingly chose to stay put. In other words, simply providing a new mental map with a clear destination was not enough. These managers also needed a realizable process that they could believe would get them from here to there.

People often fail to act on the imperative of change, not because they do not recognize the goal but because they don't want to go from being competent at the wrong thing to being incompetent at the right one.

## Failure to finish

There is a third barrier to change. Even when people see the need to start the change process, they often fail to complete it because initial efforts deliver less than brilliant results. Consider the ticket agent of an airline whose executives decide on a new customer-centred strategy. The company does a great job of encouraging new attitudes among its agents. The ticket agent sees the need for the change and understands why the new strategy is the right one. The company even provides the tools and training to help the agent believe there is a path that will lead from doing the right thing poorly to doing it well. So, the agent begins to follow the path. However, as with any new activity, initial attempts at providing the service aren't that good. Customers yell at, complain to and never thank the agent. Having put great effort into following the customer-centred plan and getting negative results, the agent gets tired and stops trying so hard. The change programme fails.

People are like the ticket agent. Sixty years of research into human psychology has clearly established that positive results reinforce behaviour and negative results kill (psychologists say "extinguish") it. Change fails because people fail to complete it. People tire of their early efforts to follow the new map and yield unsatisfactory results. So they quit and go back to an old map and behaviour.

## Remapping change

How can this knowledge be used to increase the chance of change succeeding? Just as there were three forces that oppose change, there are three methods that can kick-start it: conceiving, believing and achieving.

### Conceiving

How can people be helped to see the need for change? Just as physical objects require contrasts in light to be clearly seen, so mental maps require contrasts to be clearly perceived. People see new mental maps when the contrast is made simple and clear and when they are confronted with it. For example, Samsung Electronics is the leading brand of consumer electronic equipment in Korea. It enjoys premium pricing and placement in stores. The head of the company had a problem, however. He could not get senior executives to see that the map that they followed in Korea did not apply in the US. There, brands such as Sony, not Samsung, lead the rankings of consumer electronics.

The chief executive helped his executives see the need for change through contrast and confrontation. To be precise, he put them on a plane to visit important retailers in the US. The contrast of Samsung's premium position in Korea

## Even if people do see, there is no guarantee they will act.

and its bargain basement image in the US was made abundantly clear as the group went from store to store and saw their products not front and centre but often placed in bargain bins. This experience changed their thinking.

### Believing

Even if people do see, there is no guarantee they will act. So how can they be encouraged to act? On this issue long-term academic research provides clear insights. Three things need to be in place.

First, people need a clear target. In constructing a mental map for employees, managers must make sure that the target – be it a customer-centred strategy, a transformation of the supply chain, a merger or any other kind of change – is clear. Second, people must believe that they have the tools, skills and knowledge necessary to hit the target. The target can be as clear as day but if people do not believe it can be attained, they will never act to make it happen. Third, people must believe that if they hit the target, outcomes they value will follow.

Of these, rewards are the ones on which managers typically focus – they worry about money as though it were the only motivating reward. While most people do value cash rewards, research has demonstrated that money is only one of several powerful incentives. Praise, growth opportunities, recognition, a sense of accomplishment and a feeling of belonging are all rewards of equal power and yet with substantially lower cost.

### Achieving

Even after people get moving, a change programme will succeed only if there is a commitment to complete it. This requires "change champions" – not in the executive suite but on the manufacturing floor or in the retail outlet, where new ways of behaving can make the difference in results for the organization.

In summary, because early attempts to follow a new map generally do not deliver the desired positive results immediately, people get tired of putting in extra effort and getting poor returns on that investment. Champions must be there on the front lines to shout encouragement and praise. Without this counterbalancing influence, the natural effect of initial poor results will simply cause people to quit short of the finish line.

Change is complicated and challenging. However, managers can prevail if they recognize that success is built on a small number of important and basic factors. If they ever hope to make progress with the most complicated and far-flung global change initiatives, they must ensure that they have mastered these basics.

This article is based on a book with Hal B. Gregersen: *Remapping Change* (Prentice Hall, 2002).

## | Further reading

Black, J.S., Morrison, A.J. and Gregersen, H.B. (1999) *Global Explorers: The next generation of leader*, Routledge.

Fullan, M. (2001) *Leading in a Culture of Change*, Wiley.

Kotter, J.P. (1996) *Leading Change*, Harvard Business School Press.

# How to avoid the
## seven deadly sins

Managers continue to make the same mistakes when trying to implement change in their companies. Yet this need not be so, says **Jean-François Manzoni**.

Jean-François Manzoni is an associate professor at Insead specializing in the management of change. He is also director of the Insead-PwC research initiative on high-performance organizations.

**C**hange management used to be taught separately from "regular management". Those were the days when you could look at organizations and distinguish between periods of relative calm and shorter bursts of rapid change. This is no longer true. It is now a cliché to say that the only constant is change itself.

This recognition has led leading companies such as General Electric to make middle managers attend programmes designed to help them become better at leading and managing change. At GE, the course is called the "change acceleration process". These companies do not assume that managers automatically become better with experience at leading change. Instead, they support and accelerate managers' learning.

Introducing change in complex organizations facing increasingly demanding performance requirements is bound to involve a degree of difficulty. Still, given the amount of training and information available, one would expect that senior managers would increasingly avoid well-known mistakes and maybe discover new ones. Yet this is not so. This article highlights seven common mistakes made by senior managers when trying to implement change.

## Addressing causes

Most organizational changes aim to modify employee behaviour. Managers may want employees to become more customer-oriented, performance-driven, entrepreneurial or focused on shareholder value, to collaborate more across departments or to be less risk-averse or less bureaucratic.

Too often, managers work hard at addressing the symptoms of a problem without addressing its causes. Most of the time, they assume that employees know how to behave in the way the company wants, could do so if they wanted, but don't want to. This leads the company to develop incentives to encourage employees to adopt new behaviour. The company might want employees to become more innovative and propose ideas, so it institutes a suggestion scheme with rewards for the best ideas. The board might want managers to think in the longer term, so it produces a long-term bonus plan. Employees might need to communicate and collaborate better across functions. Therefore they introduce a sophisticated system to work from the same database.

Pressed for results and short of time, too many senior management teams latch on to the first plausible solution that seems to address the problem. Yet what about the underlying causes of the behaviour? Rather than simply trying to make symptoms go away, companies need to understand and address the causes that create the symptoms they see. Causes include structure, process, technology, organizational culture, the skills of employees and the behaviour of senior managers.

## Persistence

One of the factors mentioned above is culture. The question senior managers ask in this respect is: beyond modifying temporarily employee behaviour, how can I change the culture of the organization and make this behaviour "natural" for people?

It clearly takes much longer to modify the culture of an organization than it does to observe changes in the behaviour of employees. For example, managers can speedily make employees more customer-sensitive by using a forceful combination of rewards and punishments. This will not work equally with all employees and will not be sufficient to obtain perfect customer satisfac-

It clearly takes much longer to modify the culture of an organization than it does to observe changes in the behaviour of employees.

tion, but a strong investment in measuring customer service quality, coupled with powerful rewards for good service and heavy penalties for bad service, will modify the behaviour of some employees to some extent.

To become part of the organization's culture, however, this attitude will need to be repeated often enough, by a large enough proportion of employees, over a long enough period of time, for it to become progressively part of "the way we do things". To be repeated by enough employees for a long time, the behaviour will also need to be reinforced by the organization. And even when, after 5 or 10 years, it seems to have become part of the organization's culture, the company will still have to reinforce the point occasionally. This is where companies often get it wrong.

Senior managers regularly say that they no longer need to reinforce quality or customer service because "it has become part of the DNA of the organization". This analogy is dangerous. DNA is a permanent feature of human physiology, but the behaviour of employees in organizations is not. Years of customer service heritage under Colin Marshall's leadership at British Airways were not sufficient to withstand the strategic changes under his successor. Robert Ayling never said to BA staff, "Stop caring about customers", but his emphasis on cost reduction made it increasingly difficult for staff to follow their customer service heritage.

It takes years to build an element into an organization's culture, but only a few months to destroy the effects of this painstaking, persistent work.

## Over-focusing on content

Successful change clearly requires detailed planning. Too often, however, companies develop great project content – the details of what the project is intended to achieve – and forget to invest in examining how they will go about implementing it. For example, in 2000 the executive board of a large German multinational instigated a big change programme. There was a glamorous launch event, a catchy slogan and all the documentation and supporting instruments you could wish for. When asked about the implementation programme, however, executives replied: "That's it, the programme is launched. Now it's up to each unit head to cascade it to his or her unit." Even in German companies, with a reputation for the discipline of their managers, things don't happen this simply.

Most managers operate at or above capacity. They work long hours, take work home, go on short holidays and remain in contact by e-mail and telephone. They no longer have slack time. This means a change programme must fight its way to the top of their agenda for it to have a chance of succeeding. Programmes don't fight their way, but a group of people – a guiding coalition for whom this is a question of life or death – can force it on to the priority list. Whatever the change, these people will have to make sure that the following five elements are widely understood and shared:

- *Point A – where we are now – is no longer good enough*. It may have been sufficient before but not any longer. We must change.
- *Where is point B?* What does it look like? What skills and behaviours are needed?
- *How does one get there?* What's the general path? Where can we stop and review progress on the way?
- *It can be done*. This will not go away. The company will make this change happen and people can be successful in the new environment.
- *It's worth it*. The benefits exceed the costs of change and the pain of getting there.

## Too little time

A client once counted that in addition to his supposedly full-time job, he was a member of 18 committees and task forces. "I feel like a salami," he said, "sliced to death." While 18 is an extreme number, organizations too often assign managers to projects for too small a proportion of their time. At the risk of sounding simplistic, no one should be assigned to any project for less than a quarter of their time.

Managers assigned to too many projects and committees never have a critical mass of time and energy to have an effect on any single project. This proliferation of projects also occurs at the organizational level. One executive recently cited 300 projects occurring at the same time in his company. Another company employs 10 staff to track projects. These are sure signs of an excess of projects.

## The resistance fallacy

Most managers expect some "resistance to change" when they try to implement change. When managers are asked why people resist change, their responses tend to be strikingly similar:

- Resisting change is "natural", it's "human", although some people do seem to display it more than others.
- People are afraid of losing power, influence, prestige, money, career prospects or their job.
- Resisters don't see the big picture; they are too narrow-minded.
- They do not want to abandon their "comfort zone".
- They suffer from the "not-invented-here" syndrome.

Yet when asked why they have ever resisted an initiative within their company, a typical answer is: "Because I thought about what they wanted to do and I disagreed with the change. I did not think this was the right thing to do or the right way to do it." The claim of careful consideration followed by rational, measured disagreement is conspicuously absent from the same managers' explanations for why other people resist change.

Too often, managers who expect strong emotional resistance trigger that very response. They behave in such a way (guarded, secretive, untrusting) that they tend to encourage the hostility they predicted. For example, managers who anticipate trouble may not explain a forthcoming change to employees but try instead to spring it on them, with predictable consequences. Or managers may expect employees to resist challenging targets, so they push for even more demanding targets with the expectation that they will "make a deal" and settle around their initial expectation. It can never be known whether employees would have resisted senior managers' initial goal, but managers should not be surprised that employees resisted senior managers' "opening bid".

## The "just do it" fallacy

When they are pressed for short-term results and are convinced that it will be impossible to get employees to co-operate, too many senior managers resort to implementing change through directives: "Henceforth, you shall do this." Sending an executive order may give executives a temporary illusion of control. In real life, however, many such directives are neither followed by staff nor enforced by managers. The only thing such directives achieve is to weaken the credibility of the senior managers who signed them.

There is no doubt that often directives can and do prove effective. Directives are more likely to work well, that is, they are more likely to be implemented intelligently, flexibly and durably by the staff, when:

- there is a shared sense of crisis or when people yearn for a decision. The latter occurs when consultation has been going on for too long and is not converging, or when opinions divide between options, leading to deadlock;
- the directive is sent by a trusted and respected leader (who does not do this too often);
- top management is willing and able to enforce the directive;
- the organization has a disciplined culture and people are used to following orders.

Note, however, how limiting these conditions are. A clearly shared sense of crisis and a strong, charismatic leader are not everyday occurrences. Senior managers' ability to enforce directives is often limited by the difficulty of identifying who has complied. Finally, disciplined cultures tend to develop in organizations where trusted leaders have enforced directives for a long time, so staff have internalized the benefits of implementing orders. These also tend not to be the most entrepreneurial and innovative companies.

Executives' answers show that, as subordinates, they are well aware of the limitations of directives. Yet when they act as bosses, they suspend disbelief and assume orders will be followed. Executives must rely less on orders and more on well-managed implementation processes.

## Why do this?

The "case for change" has become increasingly driven by the demands of shareholders. Twenty years ago, most change initiatives were caused by companies encountering a crisis and needing to survive. Today, change is increasingly explained by saying that "shareholders are getting an annual return of 12 per cent and they would like 15 per cent". Even when chief executives do not present it in this way, employees are not fooled. For example, an executive in a Singapore civil service department recently explained how she was puzzled over the limited enthusiasm shown for her "productivity drive". After some discussion, she realized the change was perceived as a way of increasing the effectiveness and intensity of work – to allow the department to reduce the number of employees.

On one hand, executives are to be complimented for addressing issues before they reach crisis proportions. It is easier and better to change when you have the time and resources rather than when the knife is pressing against your throat. On the other hand, employees tend to be more willing to make sacrifices to help their organization survive than they are to increase shareholder returns. This does not mean executives must give up their desire to make their organization as competitive as possible in an increasingly Darwinian race. It does mean, however, that executives must give more time and attention to marketing their change project to employees. Managers expend time and energy identifying the value of their products and services for customers. They must do the same for their employees.

Empirical observation suggests that people are much more likely to accept painful changes

Today, change is increasingly explained by saying that "shareholders are getting an annual return of 12 per cent and they would like 15 per cent".

when they see how today's pain is connected to future gains. People must have hope that their sacrifices will bear fruits for them. Similarly, corporate projects that explicitly address employees' needs and preoccupations are more likely to gain support than when customers and shareholders seem to be the only beneficiaries.

Executives trying to sell pain to employees need to look hard for some gain, somewhere. A good question to ask about "new corporate visions" and "strategies" is: what are senior managers selling? Is there something in the "new vision" that makes it worthwhile for people to make sacrifices? What is in it for them? If you cannot find any gain in the offering, you know it's going to be a tough sell.

Carlos Ghosn, who led the revival of Nissan Motors on behalf of French carmaker Renault, was clear in this respect when he joined Renault. For years Renault managers had been working increasingly hard to maintain market share and become ever more efficient. Meanwhile, Volkswagen doubled the number of cars it was making. Shortly after arriving, Ghosn asked managers what it would take for Renault to sell twice as many cars after 10 years. He also initiated demanding efficiency programmes, specifying that some of the money would go to shareholders, some would be reinvested in improving processes to make more cars and better cars, and some would go back to customers through reduced prices to stimulate demand. This clear and ambitious positioning had a major effect on managers' attitudes and motivation. They were invited to abandon their defensive position and instead contribute to creating a great car company. In other words, they were given a better reason to go to work.

## Conclusion

Seven classic mistakes made by senior managers when approaching change have been discussed. In part, these mistakes continue to crop up because managers lack formal training in change management. Companies can no longer rely on managers accumulating change experiences, they must speed up their managers' learning processes. The second major cause of unsuccessful implementation of change is insufficient time and energy given to managing the process and marketing the change to employees. Too many senior managers underestimate how hard they must work at change to make it happen. Some things can be delegated, but leading change requires sustained energy.

## Further reading

Argyris, C. (1993) *Knowledge for Action: A guide to overcoming barriers to organizational change*, San Francisco, CA: Jossey-Bass.

Dutta, S. and Manzoni, J. (1999) *Process Re-engineering, Organizational Change and Performance Improvement*, New York, NY: McGraw-Hill.

Kotter, J.P. (1996) *Leading Change*, Boston, MA: Harvard Business School Press.

Senge, P. *et al.* (1999) *The Dance of Change: The challenges of sustaining momentum in learning organizations*, London: Nicholas Brealey.

# When internal boundaries
## become network relationships

Structured companies are dissolving into fluid networks of alliances. **John Storey** contends that managers have much to learn about coping with these changes.

John Storey is professor of human resource management and director of research at the Open University Business School.

Even a casual observer of international business cannot help but notice that organizations seem forever in the process of reorganizing. Why should this be so? Does it reflect economic reality or a superficial rearranging of the corporate furniture? Might these reforms simply be part of a cyclical fluctuation between centralization and decentralization? Do new organizational forms require different HR capabilities?

Certainly, in many cases reform disguises routine behaviour: some changes may simply correct the deficiencies of the last attempt at restructuring. However, it would be cynical to dismiss all restructuring in this way. One explanation is that there is no "best" structure. Economic and industrial changes have produced patterns of organizational restructuring. For example, after the second world war, growth in international markets based on mass production was accompanied by an expansion in the number of multinationals and led to the near-ubiquitous multi-divisional form (the "M-Form"). This was associated with hierarchy, planned career structures and large, centralized personnel departments overseeing expatriates and home-based staff.

However, with fragmenting markets, shorter product life cycles and greater variability of demand, the unwieldy nature of the multinationals became apparent. Since the 1990s, other forms have been ascendant, characterized by smaller enterprises, outsourcing, joint ventures and alliances. These require new capabilities among managers, which in turn require changes in people management. Figure 1 indicates the relationship between drivers, forms, capabilities and HR management (HRM). As Figure 1 shows, while the drivers create "needs" for forms and capabilities, there is also an interactive relationship between these forms and capability requirements. New methods of working and organizing require new capabilities; likewise, the capabilities required by the external drivers constitute a pressure for experimenting with forms. It is worth reviewing the main elements in Figure 1.

FIGURE 1    Links between new company forms and HRM

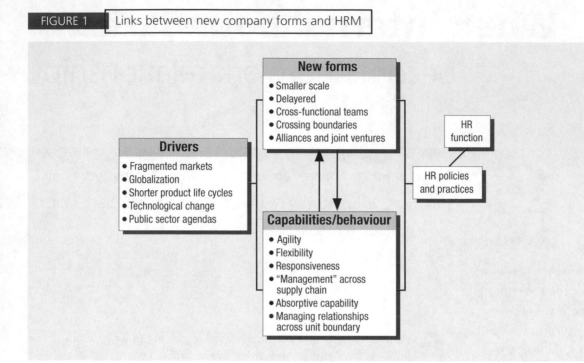

## Drivers

As mentioned, global markets have become more fragmented and turbulent. Product life cycles are shorter and customers require more options during the life cycle of a product. Meanwhile, technological change and the number of components in a product or service mean that few single businesses can fulfil customer demands on their own.

Similar challenges face the public sector: many governments have outsourced public services to the private sector and reformed organizations that remain. These reforms are explained as attempts to make bureaucracies more responsive to the public's needs. Nonetheless, they create pressure for new organizational forms and capabilities.

## Forms

Over the past 15 years, when measured by employee numbers, the size of companies and workplaces has decreased. Further, companies no longer rely on hierarchy and command as prime sources of direction and control. They have responded to turbulence and fluctuations in

demand by empowering employees, establishing cross-functional teams and taskforces, outsourcing non-core functions and focusing on processes rather than product lines.

In the 1980s and 1990s, the "strategic business unit" became the focus in divisionalized corporations. This period also saw dramatic growth in new enterprises funded by venture capital. These smaller, fragmented units, while more responsive, were severely limited in their access to resources and capabilities. The trend towards vertical integration, which characterized the corporations of the early to middle part of the 20th century, is being reversed. The value chain is becoming more clearly de-segregated as each component becomes the prime responsibility of a relatively independent unit or set of units.

> The trend towards vertical integration, which characterized the corporations of the early to middle part of the 20th century, is being reversed.

In consequence, new kinds of relationship between organizations are flourishing, including joint ventures and strategic alliances. The archetypal form is now the network organization or "N-Form", characterized by relationships that extend beyond market or contractual obligations. Companies in network relationships expect to share information, knowledge and learning. They expect to reduce risk by collaborating across the supply chain and thereby find mutually profitable solutions. Under these circumstances, competition is less between individual organizations and more between entire supply chains. But managing these new forms requires new capabilities.

## Capabilities

Companies need to be more agile and flexible under these conditions. Standard operating procedures and long reporting lines are no longer suitable. Rapid changes in customer demand require knowledge, or access to knowledge, to be distributed around the company. In addition, since managers increasingly work across boundaries, their ability to manage a complex supply chain is at a premium. Separate units need "absorptive capacity" – that is, the ability to make sense of, and internalize, information from partner organizations. They must be able to assimilate the knowledge they require and use it.

Where outsourcing has been established, employees must become skilled managers of contracts. Beyond formal contractual skills, they must be good at managing relationships across unit boundaries, which is where appropriate human resource management policies can help. Organizations may no longer need to own certain resources, but they do need to be able to access and use them effectively.

Examples of these trends can be found in many countries, though it is important not to assume that large organizations have abandoned traditional structural characteristics. Forms are still evolving. In a survey of 458 companies in Europe by academic Andrew Pettigrew and colleagues, 74 per cent reported an increase in horizontal linkages such as joint purchasing, sharing R&D across units and sharing marketing information. The survey also found extensive

evidence of increased outsourcing (65 per cent) and formation of strategic alliances (65 per cent rise). Reinforcing these findings, an Open University Business School survey of 2,700 companies in the UK revealed that 61 per cent were sharing knowledge with suppliers and 41 per cent were sharing it "with other organizations in the network". These developments were found to have implications for HR policies.

## HR policies

As companies become more dependent on each other, managing relationships becomes critical. Responsiveness and flexibility are required. Trust becomes important, along with the communication and sharing of knowledge. What are the people management implications? How, and by whom, is behaviour to be influenced?

Conducting relationships through the supply chain or through a network makes hierarchical control impractical. Equally, relationships are more complex than market transactions. Organizational structures are only one part of design. Other aspects include measurement, norms, expectations, culture and power – and these are often crucial in affecting behaviour. Some organizational reforms may present problems for HR. For example, the shift from a product-based mode to a process-based one can provoke anxiety and resistance. Employees may fear that re-engineering will result in job losses and extensive change. Maintaining commitment to the job and organization may be difficult during and after such reforms.

Narrow job descriptions usually have to be abandoned. For example, re-engineering consultants sometimes recommend that "workers" become "process performers". If managed skilfully, this offers opportunities as well as threats; roles may be enlarged as well as changed, and employees given more autonomy, responsibility and decision-making power. In the modern company, claims author Michael Hammer, there is no organization chart, no departmental manager and virtually no hierarchy. The new psychological contract offers initiative in exchange for opportunity. In the long run, he maintains, "the quality of an organization's coaching is a key determinant of whether it succeeds or fails. Process design alone is not enough. As more companies learn how to create the art of processes, the advantage will belong to those with an institutionalized capacity for staffing these processes with well-selected and well-trained people." In place of hierarchy, the process-focused organization will use cross-functional teams and taskforces. While some of Hammer's claims exaggerate actual practice, there is substantial evidence of extensive take-up of these forms.

Managers face important HR challenges as a result of these changes: how should they manage people who are not direct employees, and how can they maintain and develop relationships across traditional boundaries? Should outsourced workers on the premises be included in communications, invited to meetings and expected to be involved in commitment-building initiatives?

Where activities are outsourced, a critical issue is the potential loss of expertise. Once lost, certain activities and their associated capabilities may be difficult to recover. There is danger of "hollowing out" the organization. Innovation may be jeopardized if there is heavy reliance on strictly delineated services from external suppliers – even if service-level agreements are maintained and monitored. There is a major challenge for HR here if the organization becomes dependent on consultants and contractors.

The management writer Peter Drucker argues that companies will eventually outsource all functions that do not have a career ladder up to senior management. He contends that corporations once built like "pyramids" will become more like "tents" and managers will take responsibility for their own career development by exploring their competencies and making good deficiencies.

Outsourcing has other implications for HR. For staff transferred from the original employer to a service provider, different countries present different legal regulations. These typically require that prevailing terms and conditions of employment are preserved. In some cases, a task may be outsourced and the employees nominally transferred for day-to-day management purposes, while retaining their employment contract with the original employer.

Network organizations often grow out of the fact that resources and knowledge are difficult to locate within the boundaries of a single organization. These capabilities are more likely to be found distributed across a network of different businesses and contractors. If this is so, HR managers have a major task to identify, retain and develop such resources. Part of a company's know-how resides in being able to bring together relevant people and enable them to work together. In the boundaryless organization there are huge uncertainties surrounding who, if anyone, is managing these processes. In traditional organizations there were relatively clear boundaries between insiders and outsiders. Roles and lines of accountability were relatively clear. Under the network form, "contracts" (formal and tacit) are hybrid, that is to say, part market-based and part relational. In this environment, neither the traditional notion of win-lose competition nor hierarchical command is appropriate.

Instead of developing plans and strategies independently, planning in the network organization has to be co-ordinated and shared with other participants in the network. Information must be shared to allow managers to solve problems jointly. For example, GE Appliances collaborates with major suppliers. Together they plan for, and respond more quickly to, changes in demand and production schedules. Design, production, scheduling and sales data can be co-ordinated. Monthly sales data is shared with 25 suppliers.

Co-ordination of a value chain or network means employees need to be familiar with customer and supplier needs and preferences. One way in which this can be done is to invite suppliers and customers to meetings with employees, where outlines of goals, plans and problems can be explained and discussed. Workers can also be sent on customer and supplier field trips or seconded to these organizations. Further, companies may collaborate by giving taskforces specific aims across the value chain. A more ambitious step is to integrate information systems.

Co-ordination of a value chain or network means employees need to be familiar with customer and supplier needs and preferences.

## The HR function

To what extent do the new forms represent a threat or an opportunity for HR? In some respects these developments allow HR to adopt a more strategic role. Many failures in strategic alliances, mergers and joint ventures have been traced to a neglect of HR issues. This seems to present an opportunity. In addition, many of the challenges thrown up by the new forms put a premium on strategic thinking about human resources.

On the other hand, new forms – with an emphasis on devolved authority, flexibility and variability – may be inimical to HRM policies and procedures. In the past, personnel departments grew to a size where systems were uniformly applied across corporations. The classic age of the personnel department was that of the procedure manual. Contractual relationships are less conducive to investment in training, for example.

There is a paradoxical relationship between HRM as a relatively new movement and changing organizational forms. Old-fashioned personnel management flourished in bureaucratic structures with rigid job boundaries and detailed negotiations over minor contract variations; the HRM movement sought to overturn assumptions about its role in this environment. Yet large corporations favoured notions of "the human resource", career planning, commitment building and other tenets of HRM. A shift to small-scale enterprises interacting through short-term market transactions does not create a favourable climate for the exercise of HRM.

## Conclusions

New organizational forms require new ways of influencing behaviour. The traditional reliance on consistent procedures and rules seems misplaced when corpora-tions are increasingly fashioned around devolved, empowered and agile business units. Companies already face this dilemma. Following a period when many aspects of HR such as selection, development and career management have been devolved, down-sized HR departments are often uncertain about intervening in operational units. Some establish call centres to deal with enquiries; other routine processes are being handled via corporate intranets.

When activities such as recruitment, induction, relocation and payroll have been outsourced, what role will remain for the HR specialist? In a single organization, the question is difficult enough. When it comes to a supply chain or a network, it is evident that HR specialists have a great deal yet to learn.

## Further reading

Chandler, A.D. (1986) "The evolution of modern global competition", in Porter, M.E. (ed.) *Competition in Global Industries*, Boston, MA: Harvard Business School Press.

Child, J. and Faulkner, D. (1998) *Strategies of Co-operation: Managing alliances, networks and joint ventures*, Oxford University Press.

Drucker, P. (1993) *Post Capitalist Society*, New York: HarperCollins.

Hammer, M. (1996) *Beyond Re-engineering*, London: HarperCollins.

Pettigrew, A.M. and Ferlie, E.M. (2000) *The Innovating Organization*, London: Sage.

Storey, J. (ed.) (2001) *Human Resource Management: A critical text*, London: Thomson Learning.

Storey, J., Quintas, P., Taylor, P. and Fowle, W. (2002) "Flexible employment contracts and their implications for product and process innovation", *International Journal of Human Resource Management*, 13, 1.

# Facing up
## to uncertainty

Phil Hodgson is co-director of the Action Learning for Chief Executives Programme and co-director of the Executive Coaching Service at Ashridge Management College.

**Phil Hodgson** and **Dr Randal P. White** look at how managers can deal with unprecedented levels of ambiguity and uncertainty and still perform really well.

*If a man will begin with certainties, he shall end in doubts, but if he will be content to begin with doubts, he shall end in certainties.*
Francis Bacon, *The Advancement of Learning* (1605)

## Welcome to uncertainty

Dr Randal P. White is a principal in the Executive Development Group Inc, Greensboro, NC and an adjunct professor at the Fuqua School of Business, Duke University.

**W**hat shall I do about that new venture? Those sales predictions? That business lunch? How shall I handle that issue concerning my customer, my boss, or even my partner?

Chances are that while reading this you are putting off several decisions that you are facing. Let's ask a rather personal question. How confidently, really, are you facing up to these decisions and the actions that you will need to take? What's more, how certain do you feel about the outcomes? Do you have all the information that you need to make the decision? How many of these issues are surrounded by uncertainty?

Let us start in a very practical way. When everyone on the planet seems to be facing rising levels of uncertainty in their lives, how can we cope? If you ask people in sports and the performing arts what characterizes the very best performers, the ones who make the really hard seem easy, you will hear that the finest performers seem relaxed with their sport or their art. They have all the time in the world to strike the ball, play the note, hit the cue. On the other hand, the way to reduce performance is to add in too much stress and tension.

So if you are a manager who is facing unprecedented levels of ambiguity and uncertainty and you want to perform really well, then recognize that too much stress and tension is likely to get in the way. What is one of the prime causes of stress and tension? Ambiguity and uncertainty, of course.

## Start with the behaviour

We have spent the past 10 years looking at which behaviours help people cope most effectively with uncertainty. To be an effective leader you need to make decisions, often in the face of a lot of uncertainty. The more uncertainty surrounding a decision, the more the call for leadership. But people in leadership roles are frequently unprepared or unable to admit to the rest of the world the ambiguity they face and the feelings of uncertainty that result. Indeed, it was often believed that for a leader to admit to being uncertain was an outright failure of their leadership.

## The real work of leadership is embracing ambiguity

Leadership is what crosses the frontier between what we did yesterday and what we'll do tomorrow. We have argued elsewhere (*Relax, It's Only Uncertainty*) that the real mark of a leader is confidence with uncertainty – the ability to admit to it and deal with it. Just to be clear, we think ambiguity is how it is, and uncertainty is how you feel about it. So the effective leader is always coping with his or her feelings of uncertainty in the face of ambiguity.

Our research identified eight behaviours that seemed to be most effective in helping people cope with ambiguity. We called them "enablers" because although they are largely behavioural – i.e. you can learn to do them – some do require supporting attitudes as well. Arguably, the most significant of these is the first enabler, being a mystery-seeker.

*Once you eliminate the impossible, whatever remains, no matter how improbable, must be the truth.*

Sherlock Holmes

## Motivated by what?

Image that everything was attractive. Imagine that the more you didn't know, the more you wanted to know. Imagine that maybe wanting to know was too weak a description – there was a *need* to know that drove you from whatever else you were doing and pushed you to continually make further enquiries about the thing that you didn't know. Imagine insatiable curiosity. This is a mystery-seeker.

Mystery-seekers are curious about everything. They are attracted to areas that are unknown and to problems that appear to have no obvious solution. They question a lot; they want to know who and why and how. They seek to understand and at the same time use that understanding to explore further. Frequently, this exploration is of a playful nature. They experiment, they test things out – they put themselves in the role of both the experimenter and experimental subject. When they see a new building, they will stop and investigate it. They will take a new way home just to see if it is more interesting. They well explore a new road just to see where it goes. When you go for a walk with this person, they will continually be looking over fences, wondering what is over the next hill or around the next bend. They will want to change the walk based on what they've discovered and then to modify it further to go and investigate something. They won't stick to the plan if the plan prevents them from learning something or enquiring about something.

Mystery-seekers challenge others to be challenged by the unknown. This can make for discomforting company. You thought you were going to a business meeting to confirm the budget for a particular project, but instead you end up being drawn into a debate about how that product could be modified and used to create a new market somewhere. In times of pressure this can be seen as disconcertingly unfocused. And yet people who are highly motivated by mysteries can be extremely focused. They are almost obsessive in wanting to know more and finding out about the thing they don't yet know about. These people will also question things "for the hell of it" (and have been known to tear things

Mystery-seekers challenge others to be challenged by the unknown. This can make for discomforting company.

up and start all over again because they think it's the right thing to do).

Mystery-seekers actually seem to get energy from not knowing. Most people get some satisfaction when they discover the solution to a problem, but people who are motivated by mysteries seem to draw their energy when they *don't* have a solution. Yes, of course, they get satisfaction like everyone else when they have solved a particular problem. But the solving doesn't stop there. Once they have a solution, they will look for a second solution – a better one. And once they have a second solution, they will probably go on and look for a third and a fourth. For people who are strongly motivated by mysteries, it is the absence of the solution, the absence of knowing how something works, that is the really attractive part.

People who have been motivated by mysteries over the centuries have shown this insatiable curiosity and drive to continue to want to understand. And then having understood, they will want to go yet deeper. More than 400 years ago Galileo Galilei risked torture and imprisonment because the best solution he could find to explaining his astronomical observations was that the earth moved around the sun rather than, as the Bible implied, the other way round. His enormous curiosity kept him asking questions about sunspots, phases of the moon, the phases of Venus, the moons of Jupiter – he never stopped. Even when seriously ill and highly troubled by the pressure of the cardinal's inquisition, he continued to work on a theory about the trajectory of bodies fired from cannons.

Half a millennium later British inventor and entrepreneur James Dyson, in struggling to make a vacuum cleaner that did not require a paper or cloth bag, made more than 5,000 prototypes before he finally achieved the level of perfection he sought. Having made his first production model, he carried on developing, and that curiosity to improve on what was already improved upon and to enquire into yet further ways of developing new ideas could not be stopped. Just two years after its launch, Dyson's first product (an upright model) had become Britain's best-selling vacuum cleaner, overtaking sales of Electrolux, Hoover and Panasonic. A cylinder model launched two years later achieved similar success. Passionate about design and engineering innovation, Dyson says that success is made of 99 per cent failure. His persistent curiosity took his business to European brand leader in just five years against multinational competition.

But these people are not necessarily inventors in the normal sense. What is fundamental about them is that they are drawn instinctively to the edge of their knowledge rather than the centre of it. It is for this reason that we believe that being motivated by mysteries may well be one of the fundamental enablers underlying the ability to handle uncertainty. Mystery-seekers leave the comfortable and safe centre ground of accepted "truth" and move to the edge of their knowledge and their learning. They ask "why" and "what would happen if" and in general ask the difficult questions. Later we will return to this theme, as it seems to be a precursor to what we call "difficult learning".

## What happens if no one is very motivated by mysteries?

People who are not motivated by mysteries – who are not mystery-seekers – use patterns of behaviour in approaching the unknown that are narrow and unvarying. They aren't looking for variation in their life; in fact, they prefer things to be the same as they always were. They are not likely to go looking for new discoveries, new ideas or some other variants in their lives. Sometimes this is a survival mechanism. If you have been living in a state of civil war for the previous several years, for instance, the last thing you want is more change. What you want is to go back to things as they were – to the stability and the certainty that you used to enjoy. However, with traumatic situations put aside, the danger for an individual, an organization or a society that is not motivated by mysteries is that they will be unaware of or unprepared to take up new ideas and changes that occur.

Consider the management of *Encyclopedia Britannica*. Two hundred and seventy years of publishing tomes convinced the encyclopedia's leadership that there would always be a need for solid, leather-bound volumes that would be updated by an annual volume containing the highlights of knowledge and events of the previous year. Because of this view of the world, they rejected the fledgling Microsoft Corporation's overture to produce a version on CD-ROM. *Encarta*, a competing product, was born as a result of this rejection, but of course it didn't belong to Britannica. Britannica then faced chaos as it tried to retrench and catch up with the revolution that had taken place in the knowledge marketplace. What if a member of the senior team had been more motivated by mysteries – had been attracted to taking a new way home, for instance – wouldn't this crisis have been seen as an opportunity?

Motivated by mysteries is not a "mad scientist's syndrome" – it is a constant companion to everything else the individual surviving in uncertainty will do. But it should not be overplayed to such an extent that all other matters of everyday life and survival and planning ahead are diminished. It is said that Einstein, brilliant though he was, didn't always recall his own phone number or address. However, Einstein was clearly highly motivated by mysteries. He described himself and his approach in this way: "I have no special talents, I am only passionately curious" and "the important thing is not to stop questioning."

In everyday usage, being motivated by mysteries is about being attracted by the unknown aspects of new sources of data, new ideas, new opportunities. But it is also about integrating that curiosity into the rest of the skills and operations that we need to use. It's about being fluid: the great ideas of tomorrow are the questions of today.

## Difficult learning, or what did you learn today?

It has been our experience that those people and organizations that embrace uncertainty are often drawn to doing things, inventing things, providing services that others find more difficult to do, invent or provide. These individuals and organizations have *learned* to do the *difficult* and to some extent make it routine.

Being first is usually seen as having an advantage, although the so-called first-move advantage has been the downfall of an awful lot of dotcom start-ups. But the level of difficulty of something can be fleeting. On the one hand, the Fosbury Flop, a perfect score of 10 in compulsory figure skating, a triple Lutz, or 1,000 Mhz chip speed were once difficult but have become commonplace. So now, even an ordinary competitor is expected to do these things and an ordinary product is expected to have these features.

What is difficult to learn to do may be difficult for only the first learner or may be difficult for all who follow in his or her footsteps. Things that become easy to learn (or copy), those things that become commonplace, won't differentiate one actor from another, one organization from another. Those that remain elusive and hard to copy will be seen as special or differentiating.

For each of us, difficult learning is taking on something totally new. It is deliberately putting yourself on the steepest part of the learning curve. For both individuals and organizations, *true* difficult learning is doing what someone else has never done.

It is our belief that any organization that is trying to catch up with its competitors, particularly in the fastest moving sectors such as e-business, bio-tech or pharmaceuticals, will need to become good at difficult learning. In these fields, doing what your competitors did six months later than they did it is just not good enough. Your fastest moving competitors will already have moved on again.

## Overcome your fear of failure

How do you learn to handle difficult learning and how do you teach it to the rest of the organization? First, recognize that most of us were not trained to do it at school. Does that surprise you? Surely, you might argue, many of us worked hard at school and it certainly didn't seem easy at the time! This is where we come to the crux of difficult learning and why it is ... well, difficult. Difficult learning is difficult because it asks you to confront your fear of failure, of looking an idiot to yourself or others. Most of us have actually been trained by our school systems to avoid failure, which sounds reasonable enough until we realize that the fear of the failure is often what prevents us from learning what we need to learn.

Let's do some time travel. Take your mind back to when you were at school and the teacher asked the class: "What is the chemical formula for water?" You know what will happen next. You've seen this particular play many times. Those students who know the answer will call attention to themselves, while those who don't know will find something terribly interesting on the surface of the desk in front of them – and will do everything in their power to avoid attention. The practical learning is that when you are faced with something you don't know, you keep your head down and hope someone else deals with it.

Now fast forward to that same person at work and faced with a difficult situation in a public arena such as a senior management meeting. The chances are that they will take the same instinct they learned at school into their organization and when faced with something they don't know, their first reaction will be to keep their head down and hope that someone else will handle it. Is this what we want in our organizations? Of course not! But recognize that most of us – and our observations seem to apply around the world – have been through this major conditioning process at least 10,000 times as the result of our schooling.

It is at a fundamental level that we have to tackle fear of failure and the confidence to tackle more and more difficult learning. At schools we really want students who don't know something to jump up and shout: "I don't know, but I want to find out." Only if we fill the organizations of the future with people who are keen to explore their lack of knowledge will our organizations be competent at handling the things they don't know. Once organizations become competent at this, they can start making themselves competitive because they can vastly increase their rate of learning.

As one of our teachers of social psychology used to say: "We should hand you PhDs when we admit you. Then you have five years to convince us not

> It is at a fundamental level that we have to tackle fear of failure and the confidence to tackle more and more difficult learning.

to take them away from you." Translation: Show us you are willing to explore, make mistakes and engage in genuine learning, and then we will let you keep the degree as evidence that you are truly a learner.

## A final observation

Our expectation is that the trigger for developing your skills in these areas comes from being motivated by mysteries – by your curiosity and by your ability to take on a steeper learning curve – and to embrace difficult learning. The future organization will succeed because its employees will have no barriers to any area of learning and development and will be able to handle any situation and any learning opportunity. They will embrace the unknown in their search to provide goods and services that differentiate them from their competitors. And they will not fear the continual search for new and better products that will keep them ahead in their marketplace.

The leaders who emerge in these companies will embrace the unknown and they will relax in the certainty that there is *no* certainty.

## Further reading

Hodgson, P. and White, R.P. (2001) *Relax, It's Only Uncertainty*, FT Prentice Hall.

# Culture and the
# **workplace**

# Contents

# Introduction to Part 4

**C**ulture is the blend of beliefs, attitudes, ways of thinking and behaving that permeates an organization. It may not be consistent throughout a company, and because much of it amounts to subconscious habits in different groups of employees it is remarkably hard to influence, if at all. In this part writers describe how culture emerges, and how social and economic changes in the early 21st century are influencing corporate cultures throughout the developed world.

# A cultural evolution
## in business thinking

John Weeks is an assistant professor of organizational behaviour at Insead.

Culture is a well-established property of corporations, say **John Weeks** and **Charles Galunic**, yet managers still find it hard to influence. First, they need to understand exactly what it is and how it develops.

Charles Galunic is an associate professor of organizational behaviour at Insead.

**M**ost new ideas are bad. Managers are bombarded by buzzwords and fads fighting for attention. They protect themselves with good reason: most of these concepts promise more than they deliver. Some new ideas do get through the filters though, and become taken for granted as part of organizational reality. The question is: what happens next?

In 1982 *In Search of Excellence* by Tom Peters and Robert Waterman introduced the idea of organizational culture to managers. It transformed obscure ideas about the cultural aspects of organizations into a popular management fad. By the early 1990s, however, culture's star had been eclipsed by notions such as the learning organization and re-engineering, and Tom Peters had written *Liberation Management* to recant most of what he had said earlier about the beneficial effects of strong culture. Now, a decade later, the literature on organizational culture has still not fulfilled its promise of telling managers with any certainty how they can use culture to create organizations that are pleasant, passionate and profitable. Indeed, for the most part, it has stopped trying.

In fact, there is no straightforward link between organizational culture and performance. Instead, culture has come to be recognized as a fundamental aspect of business organizations. It cannot be seen independently of structure, incentives, technology and strategy, and must be managed in concert with them. Culture is so well established as a property of corporations that hardly a day goes by without reference in the business press to changing, clashing, merging or emerging corporate cultures. This is the legacy of the first generation of research about culture in organizations.

The problem is that the idea of organizational culture became taken for granted before there were compelling answers to basic questions. What is culture? How does it operate? Can it be managed? If so, how? When we are pressed for definitions, it turns out culture means different things to different people. No wonder, then, that leaders find organizational culture so difficult to manage and so often a wrecker of corporate marriages.

It is time to update our common-sense understanding of organizational culture to reflect research about the evolution of culture. This will mean discarding some cherished myths about organizational culture: truisms held over from its days as a management fad that have turned out to be false.

## Infectious ideas

It has become common to boil cultures down into one or two pithy adjectives. Yet when looking closely at well-known organizations, what do we find? Even in the most "entrepreneurial" companies, some parts are command and control. Cultures that look "cohesive" from one angle look insular from another. Such stereotypes, though not exactly wrong, are unhelpful oversimplifications that dissolve when it comes to managing the organizations they supposedly describe. Stereotypes would suffice if organizations were monolithic, but they aren't.

A better way to think of organizational culture is as a pattern of beliefs and behaviours, assumptions and routines – various elements of culture collectively called "memes" – distributed across the organization, usually in an uneven fashion. When new ideas arrive, they infect the minds of some people before others and of some people more than others. When a new routine proves successful in one part of the organization, it may or may not spread to other parts. Organizations are overflowing with initiatives, projects, programmes, best practices, ways of thinking and behaving, all competing for the scarcest resource of all: human attention.

Some ideas are explored, some practices are adopted. Others are ignored or abandoned. Some management fads find an audience, others are

quickly rejected. Some memes, in other words, spread from brain to brain in greater numbers than others. This is what is meant when people talk about organizational cultures evolving: it is the cumulative result of all of this competition among memes.

The tenets of evolutionary theory and the general idea of memes and cultural evolution are well described in books such as *Darwin's Dangerous Idea* by Daniel Dennett and *The Selfish Gene* by Richard Dawkins. In brief, whenever you have variation, selection and retention of a reproducer (be it an organism or an idea, belief or behaviour), evolution will occur. Selection assumes competition for a scarce resource, retention assumes the ability of the reproducer to copy itself accurately and variation assumes that this copying is not always perfect. Darwin's theory is that evolution occurred because nothing in life – in particular, no copying process – is faultless. There is something wonderful about that. More prosaically, anyone who has spent time in organizations can be sympathetic to the idea that they too reflect the idea that perfection is unattainable. But just how does cultural evolution in organizations work?

In organizations, culture evolves as a process of the selection, variation and retention of memes. Memes are competing for the chance of people in the organization noticing their public expression – in words, behaviour, cartoon form or whatever – internalizing them and then reproducing them. This raises the question: which ones will be selected for reproduction?

One reason for the selection of certain memes is that they contribute to the company's success. It makes sense for ideas and behaviours that help the organization do better to be selected more often than those that worsen its performance. You don't have to be a cynic, though, to see that exceptions to this rule may be more common. There are many reasons to expect cultures to evolve in ways that don't necessarily lead to better performance. In the first place, whether or not a particular meme contributes to success may not be as important as whether it is recognized as doing so. If managers misunderstand the source of organizational success or failure, they may reproduce the wrong memes. If they are ignorant of better practices elsewhere, they may think they are doing as

Cultures that look "cohesive" from one angle look insular from another.

well as can be expected and not recognize a need to change. Moreover, if managers are more interested in furthering their own career than in coming to the aid of their organization, they may be expected to reproduce those memes that they think further their self-interest. The culture of the organization, the distribution of its memes, will reflect this.

Managers shape culture in these two cases by using information technology and measurement systems to make the consequences of actions clearer and by using incentives to align individual and organizational interests. The meme's-eye view of culture suggests these efforts can be effective only if they are tightly integrated with business decisions that shape the day-to-day selection of which memes to reproduce.

Finally, it is important to realize that often people don't pay conscious attention to which memes they reproduce. Some they reproduce time and again simply out of habit. People tend to select a new meme on the basis of how well it fits with the memes they already have. And they reproduce others just because they are catchy. Academic studies by Bruce Kogut and Udo Zander have shown that whether an idea is imitated or not depends as much on how easy that idea is to imitate as on the content of the idea. In other words, some memes spread like viruses or like a tune that people can't stop humming.

Memes are selected not just because of their function or their fit but also because of their form. What this suggests for managers is that when it comes to new ideas, roles and structures, packaging matters. Even the best ideas will have no impact if they aren't sold to people in such a way as to get through their filters. Internal marketing matters.

## | Variation

Selection is only one part of the evolutionary algorithm, however. Selection's mill requires the grist of variation. There is an irony in managing memes. The very fact that most new ideas are bad means that people need more of them, not fewer, to survive in fast-paced environments.

This supply of diversity comes from three sources. First, memes may come from outside because people are brought into the company or because employees repeat ideas they pick up outside. Second, memes may be created serendipitously through mutation because mistakes are made in copying ideas and behaviours. Third, memes may combine, just as organisms are new combinations of the genes of their parents.

There is a big difference, though, between potential variation – which is huge – and realized variation. This is the difference between the memes that are available to the senses and those that are noticed. Only the latter have a chance of being selected. Now here is another irony. Research has shown that when the potential variation gets too large, the realized variation gets smaller. This is the result of information overload. People realize how little of the information available there is time to sort and select, so they may reject ideas just because they are new. The resulting anxiety can paralyse people into screening out anything but information close to what they already know. This can lead to the perverse result that the more diverse the workforce becomes, the less people learn from each other because they close their minds and seek out only those who are similar to themselves.

Just making information available and hiring more diversely, then, is not a solution. Managers can, however, increase the realized variation and so enhance the evolution of the organization's culture using several methods. The first is to allow more time and playfulness in the search for novelty. Keeping people focused on what they know well is a good way to reproduce ideas the organization already has, but a bad way to foster innovation.

The second method is to realize the costs as well as the benefits of socializing new employees so that although they look different, they act the same. Diversity in the workforce seems an irrelevance or a political correctness to many managers. When seen from an evolutionary point of view, though, diversity isn't just about the demographic characteristics of gender and ethnicity. It is about diversity of memes, of the ideas that people from different subcultures inside and outside the organization bring with them. Managing diversity means maximizing the possibility of those memes spreading. It means, in other words, learning from one another.

This requires the organization to have a strong set of core values that are widely shared and stable. The key, though, is that the core should be as small as possible while still creating this powerful identity. Everything else should be allowed to vary. Realizing the potential of this variation requires one more element: social networks. What is needed, in other words, are people who are networked into various subcultures and who can bring together ideas. This is how the recombination of memes takes place.

When it comes to networks, power is not just a result of having more contacts but of having more diverse contacts. Yet again, it is easy to see these networks as a luxury, not a necessity. Organizations with the latter view understand knowledge management not as a buzzword involving technology but as about their culture.

## Finding the balance

The flip side of variation is retention. Selection and variation are sexier subjects – literally, in the case of biological evolution – but without retention there is no evolution, just random change. People often talk about culture as if it had inertia. It seems to block change, or at least is often used as an excuse when changes fail. This is not automatically the case. Cultures change all the time: the distribution of memes is constantly shifting. It is not culture change that is hard, it is managing that change. Preserving a desirable culture can be as hard as changing one that is not liked.

Nonetheless, preservation seems to be something at which companies excel. Indeed, the economic historian Alfred Chandler suggests that the modern company replaced older structures of economic organization specifically because of its superior ability to retain increasingly complex knowledge accurately.

It is not culture change that is hard, it is managing that change. Preserving a desirable culture can be as hard as changing one that is not liked.

What may come as a surprise, however, is that people take this retention for granted at their peril. For example, quality in manufacturing is about increasing retention, making sure that production memes are reproduced in exactly the same way every time. The danger of focusing on variation and neglecting retention is that evolution requires a balance between the two. To see this, consider mutations – errors in the copying of memes. Perfect replication is difficult enough with memes expressed as words. People have a hard time repeating exactly what they have just have heard, and although they are better at imitating the gist of a message, misunderstanding is common. With memes that are expressed in behaviours, however, the problems are much worse.

Academics Christopher Bartlett and Sumantra Ghoshal give the example of the difficulty of accurately copying the "matrix form" of organizational structure. Many companies made the mistake of copying the easily observable characteristics of successful matrix structures, but failed to recognize and duplicate the subtle, underlying "memetic" expressions of compromise and consensus. So, these companies found their matrix structures worked worse than the models they were imitating.

The message of the evolutionary theory of culture, though, is that some of these errors will turn out to be innovations. Mutation is a failure of retention, but it is an important source of variation. As the science-fiction writer William Gibson says: "The future is here – it is just unevenly distributed." Selection, variation and retention work at cross purposes, acting as checks and balances on each other, and together they produce the splendours of evolution.

As this article has outlined, the meme's-eye view offers a powerful alternative to the old view that made organizational cultures seem so easy to describe and so hard to change. Part of the power, however, lies in the insight that there is much people can't control and shouldn't want to control if they want a well-adapted culture. This perspective suggests many ways in which culture can be shaped and points to the importance of day-to-day management over large-scale change programmes. It is a perspective, though, that urges our humility as much as it reveals our ability.

## Further reading

Blackmore, S. (1999) *The Meme Machine*, Oxford University Press.

Dawkins, R. (1976) *The Selfish Gene*, Oxford University Press.

Dennett, D. (1995) *Darwin's Dangerous Idea*, New York: Simon and Schuster.

Galunic, C. and Eisenhardt, K. (2001) "Architectural innovation and modular corporate forms", *Academy of Management Journal*, December (http://faculty.insead.fr/galunic).

Gladwell, M. (2000) *The Tipping Point: How little things can make a big difference*, New York: Little, Brown.

# All change in the
## customized workplace

Hamid Bouchikhi is a professor of strategy and management at ESSEC Business School, France.

John Kimberly is Henry Bower Professor at the Wharton School of the University of Pennsylvania and Novartis Professor in Healthcare Management at Insead.

As Copernicus discovered that the sun did not revolve around the earth, so managers must face up to employees who will not subordinate themselves to companies. **Hamid Bouchikhi** and **John Kimberly** examine the implications.

**F**ive centuries ago, the Polish astronomer Nicolaus Copernicus realized that the earth revolves around the sun, not the reverse. In management, we may be in the midst of a similar revolution, in which the relationship between the company and the employee is inverted and the "customized workplace" replaces the hierarchical, military-inspired model that has served so long.

Comparing the dominant managerial models of the past two centuries will help in understanding the concept of the customized workplace and how it differs from other management methods. This will also clarify the importance of flexibility – for the worker and for the company.

## Evolving models

More than tools and techniques, it is the company's flexibility and responsiveness to stakeholders that differentiates management models (*see* Figure 1). The 19th-century model, still alive in many industries and areas, does not respond to shareholders, customers and employees together. The company is often family-owned and managed as a closed system. Customers buy whatever is made available. Employees are hired and fired at will and have little voice or choice. For them, opportunity lies in finding a paternalistic capitalist who can make life less painful and the constraints of work more tolerable.

In the past 50 years, customers and shareholders have been more proactive and managers have needed to become more responsive to them. As a result, market-driven strategies and flexible organizations have developed. In contrast to the 19th-century model, 20th-century management is more open. The company actively listens to customers and shareholders and involves them in decision processes. In the 20th-

# The challenge for management in the 21st century will be to invent flexibility based on the employee.

century model, customers are the main drivers of the company's needs for flexibility and employees are required to adjust their work schedules, tasks, holidays, geographic assignments and jobs in light of these needs. Because they are at the receiving end, workers often complain about this kind of flexibility.

The challenge for management in the 21st century will be to invent flexibility based on the employee. To do this, managers will have to customize the workplace to suit both customers and workers. The company will have to apply the logic of marketing, developed for customers, to relationships with workers. Much as managers had no choice about dealing with shareholders and customers, they will also have to cope with the demands of autonomous and proactive individuals whose collaboration and commitment can no longer be taken for granted. Managers will have to adapt to the sociological context of this century.

## Sociological context

The challenges facing companies force us to move beyond the limits of conventional business thinking and consider the consequences of sociological trends. The foundations of management were established in the 19th century and built on a view of the worker as a reluctant individual whose efforts needed to be predefined, monitored and sanctioned. This still underpins much managerial action, but it is outdated.

According to British sociologist Anthony Giddens, post-traditional societies are marked by a declining role of tradition and hierarchy in governing people's attitudes and behaviour. Disenfranchised from tradition, the individual discovers a new form of autonomy and discretion in making life decisions. In this context, individuals draw on an extensive body of knowledge about social life and actively develop a sense of self-identity through strategic life planning. People are making choices in areas where before they did not or could not. For example, they are deciding about their physical appearance, sexual life and gender, parenting and eating habits. If the 19th century witnessed the advent of the

---

**FIGURE 1** | Management styles over three centuries

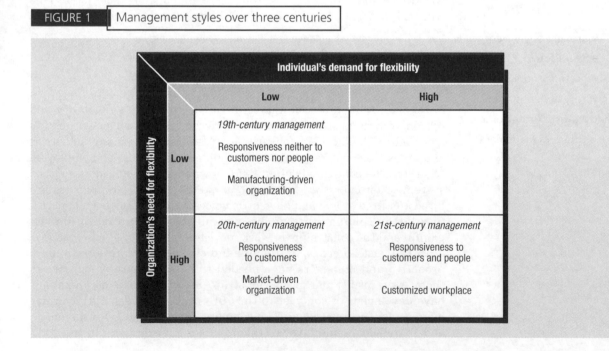

business entrepreneur, the late 20th century saw the birth of the life entrepreneur.

Caught between micro and macro social changes, the company faces challenges to its legitimacy. It is no longer perceived as favourably as it has been and is criticized on many fronts. The proportion of people for whom a traditional career is no longer the natural path is increasing and many of those who work for established companies are drawing less and less on the company for their sense of identity. Successive waves of restructuring and downsizing, and the development of a debate on employability, are inducing individuals to dissociate their fate from their company's.

The labour market in developed countries is already affected by these trends. Companies in traditional sectors, hampered by their unprogressive image, are finding it difficult to hire people. In other industries, companies are competing for a limited pool of talent. Younger people seem to be increasingly attracted to self-employment, entrepreneurial opportunities and the professions. And the business press regularly contains reports of high-flying executives who quit comfortable jobs to start a business, work as consultants, or simply to spend more time with their families.

These trends reflect a need for people to reclaim control over their lives. As the company listens to and involves people in these decisions, in the same manner that it has internalized the needs of customers, customization of the workplace will inevitably emerge.

## Collision coming

The Hawthorne experiments of the 1930s emphasized the importance of a motivated and involved workforce in achieving organizational goals. Techniques were designed to enhance motivation and involvement. However, in spite of such efforts, surveys continue to show low employee satisfaction and little trust in management. In a 1997 *Financial Times* article, Robert Taylor wrote: "At the other end of the satisfaction stakes, British workers were among the most discontented. 'Despite significant attempts at corporate restructuring and re-engineering,

employee attitudes towards the organization and the efficiency of their work are among the least favourable in Europe' says the [International Survey Research] report. 'Despite a strong commitment to total quality management in many companies, attitudes to the quality of work performance are more critical than in any other European country.'"

Unless we think, as some senior managers may, that people are never satisfied, this data may point to a more serious problem.

Managerial innovations had a limited impact because they were driven by the company's needs. People don't come first. The record of downsizings, restructurings and lay-offs is no doubt largely responsible for the distrust of management. Aaron Bernstein in a 1998 *Business Week* article reported the findings of another survey showing employees' trust in management had declined in the 1990s (less than 50 per cent in 1997). Even more telling, 70 per cent of senior managers thought that employees trusted management. The gap suggests that the reality of the workplace may not match the promise of management discourse.

After thriving on marketing and product customization, companies will have to transfer this mindset to their relationships with employees. Management will achieve the next Copernican revolution only when it acknowledges that its object – the individual – is no longer willing to sit passively on the receiving end of managerial policies and incentives. The life entrepreneur will no longer be the object but a subject of management. This evolution will require a genuine co-exercise of power instead of "empowerment", with its implication that power is "owned" by one party and delegated to the other.

## The new workplace

Because it represents a radical departure from accepted principles and techniques, the customized workplace cannot be conceived without a radical shift in thinking. The main differences between management models over three centuries are summarized in Table 1.

In contrast with traditional management, where structures and systems are derived from a

TABLE 1    Contrasting the paradigms

|  | 19th century | 20th century | 21st century |
|---|---|---|---|
| **Theory of personhood** | Interchangeable muscle and energy | A subordinate with a hierarchy of needs | Autonomous and reflexive individual |
| **Information and knowledge** | Province of management alone | Dominated by management and shared in a limited way | Widely diffused |
| **Purpose of work** | Survival | Accumulation of wealth and social status | Part of a life plan |
| **Identification** | With a company and/or the working class | Identify with a social group and/or company | The disenfranchised self |
| **Conflict** | Disruptive and to be avoided | Disruptive but tolerated. Settled through collective bargaining | A normal part of life |
| **Division of labour** | Managers decide Employees execute | Managers decide Employees execute thoughtfully | Employees and managers decide and execute |
| **Power** | Concentrated at the top | Limited, functional, sharing/empowerment | Diffused and shared |

pre-defined strategy, the design of the customized workplace will seek to balance what matters for the company (its strategy) and what matters for individuals (their life strategies). The above trends suggest that the individual will reclaim some control over fundamental aspects of work life: what to work for, content, when and where, how to accomplish the work, with whom and for whom to work, for how long to work, direction of career plan and skills needed to pursue the personal career plan.

People's needs and aspirations have historically been viewed as disturbances for management but they represent the starting point for the design of the customized workplace. Balancing companies' needs for predictability and effectiveness with diverse individual needs requires a new employment contract, one where managers and employees confront their strategic and life plans and seek common ground.

Although the customized workplace has yet to be invented, a few organizations display some of its characteristics. For example, at Semco, the Brazilian company discussed in Ricardo Semler's book *Maverick*, employees are involved in deciding about siting factories and buying machinery. Further, they have substantial freedom in setting their work schedule and control the investment of a portion of the profits.

At Metanoiques, a French medium-sized company specializing in collaborative software, there are no employees. Every member owns an equal share of the company and acts as an independent entrepreneur with profit and loss responsibility. The company does not operate from a head office and people are free to organize their own schedules. Internal collaboration is carried out through extensive use of information and communication technology.

The founder of Compagnie Française de Defense et de Protection sold this small French insurance company to employees and agents, and dismantled the head office. He hopes to create a "community of independent entrepreneurs" where associates are free to conduct their local business and use network-like mechanisms to co-ordinate with other members of the organization.

Therese Rieul, founder manager of KA-L'informatique douce, a medium-sized computer and software retailer, refuses to write formal job descriptions because she believes staff should design their own jobs. She believes managers should be concerned with outcomes and leave people free to work out the best way to do a task.

The customized workplace is primarily a philosophical attitude towards people manage-ment issues. It entails a replacement of the traditional hard-nosed, macho attitude with one that is more open to people's needs and more tol-erant of conflict and divergence. The customized workplace requires recognition of individuals as strategic life planners. In 20th-century manage-ment, even its most enlightened versions, the company is the only strategic planning agent. Managers form a strategy and then seek the opti-mal organizational and incentive structure to motivate people to implement it. In the cus-tomized workplace, people can influence strategy, in a sense more consistent with their own life strategies. This evolution will not come easily given the deep-seated belief that strategy belongs in top management's territory.

Sharing information and responsibility for the company's situation with employees is another ingredient of the customized workplace. Contrary to the idea that people never make decisions that can hurt them, sharing a problem with employees can be an effective turn-around strategy. Bertrand Martin, the former chief executive of Sulzer France, joined the company at the height of a crisis. Instead of devising a plan unilaterally, he told employees that the company's fate was in their hands and challenged them to find a solution with him.

Experience shows that people will commit a great deal of time, resources and self-identity in trustful relationships. After being pushed to the

background by "scientific management", the importance of trust in business life is being rediscovered. Trust must be put at the core of the employment relationship. Its importance is particularly evident in times of hardship. Only a trusting workforce can voluntarily make sacri-fices and explore with management every option to improve the organization's condition.

However, trust must be built before hard times, and for trust to grow, reciprocity is required. People will put part of their fate in managers' hands only if managers put some of their own fate in the hands of people. Reciprocity develops only when each partner in a relation-ship is potentially vulnerable to the decisions of the other. Managers who seek control can never establish trust.

In the customized workplace, individuals actively plan and negotiate their employment. Managers will find this transition difficult because they have used policies designed for aggregate groups, such as blue collar workers, hourly workers or part timers. In the customized workplace, people can no longer be managed in this way. They need to be treated as individuals. The challenge for managers will be to achieve sufficient predictability with individuals whose behaviour is less subject to control.

Achieving organizational predictability in the customized workplace requires mutual commit-ment and accountability. The customized workplace is not viable if it is made up of employ-ees who can change their behaviour or withdraw from the business at any time. The type of con-tract formerly reserved for senior executives will have to be more widely diffused. When people are bound to the company for a pre-determined time, they no longer fear being treated as dispos-able assets and the company can count on their full collaboration for the life of the contract.

Because it is based on participation, power sharing, trust, negotiation, reciprocity and com-mitment, the customized workplace will require adult, as opposed to charismatic, leadership. Because shareholders, customers and employees are equally important, the customized workplace will require a governance structure where the interests of stakeholders can confront and bal-ance each other.

In the customized workplace, people can influence strategy, in a sense more consistent with their own life strategies.

Are these ideas out of touch with the often harsh realities of the marketplace? Perhaps. But the kinds of changes described here have been developing over decades. Capitalism needed the better part of the 20th century to win the battle of the free enterprise. It will now have to win the heart and soul of the free person.

This article is adapted from a chapter by the authors in Chowdhury, S. (ed.) *Management 21C: New Visions for the New Millennium* (Financial Times Management, 2000).

## Further reading

Bernstein, A. (1998) "We want you to stay. Really", *Business Week*, June 22.

Giddens, A. (1991) *Modernity and Self-identity*, Stanford, CA: Stanford University Press.

Semler, R. (1993) *Maverick*, New York, NY: Warner.

Taylor, R. (1997) "Europe's unhappy world of work", *Financial Times*, May 14.

# Work as a
## life experience

John R. Kimberly is Henry
Bower Professor at the
Wharton School of the
University of Pennsylvania
and Novartis Professor in
Healthcare Management
at Insead.

Elizabeth F. Craig is a
doctoral candidate at the
Wharton School of the
University of Pennsylvania.

Trends towards workers rethinking the relationship between their working and private lives have been accelerated by recent terrorist attacks, say **John Kimberly** and **Elizabeth Craig**.

**M**ost people spend a large part of their lives in employment relationships. Do they do so simply to earn enough money to support a particular lifestyle? Is the exchange of time and talent for economic well being at the heart of the contract between employer and employee? Or is there a deeper explanation involving a sense of achievement and meaning?

In answering this, it should be remembered that today's employment environment is very different from that of a century ago. Then, common law covering "master" and "servant" governed relations between employers and employees. After a long period of labour unrest and market reform, such relations were embedded in a more bureaucratic, rule-bound system and were more equitable and less exploitative. Employees enjoyed greater job stability and security in exchange for loyal service.

A new employment era is beginning, one of flexible, non-bureaucratic organizations. People enjoy a growing power to choose among employment opportunities and to negotiate terms and conditions. What aspects of employment relationships are important to them as they make these choices?

Current rhetoric would have us believe that employability has replaced employment security as the basis for employment contracts and that people choose work primarily based on economic returns and professional aspirations. However, there are significant gaps between this rhetoric and the reality of employment.

## Employability

The employment security model is built on the exchange of time and loyalty for economic return and the possibility of more responsibility, status and reward. The terms of the contract, whether explicit or implicit, are clear: as long as the employee produces at levels acceptable to the employer, employment is assured. Because opportunities to advance are strongly tied to seniority, it makes sense to devote energy to the company. Loyalty was given in return for job security and individual careers tended to unfold within the company.

This model flourished after the second world war, a time of relative prosperity and steady economic growth. However, the 1970s and 1980s created a dilemma for companies. The loyalty they had engendered limited the flexibility they needed to meet the new challenges of global competition and technological innovation. Employees skilled in older technologies became a liability rather than an asset. Although workers could be retrained, many companies instead modified the terms of the contract with employees to emphasize "employability" over security. The new contract placed responsibility on the company to provide workers with the requisite job experiences and training opportunities to make them employable – whether with the company or elsewhere. Employees became responsible for seeking out opportunities and for managing their careers. Advancement and rewards were tied to achievement rather than to seniority.

The shift in the underlying contract coincided with other trends: part-time employment, increased use of contingent labour, outsourcing and project-based work. The result for the company was, in fact, increased flexibility. It could eliminate jobs and adjust staffing levels in response to competitive threats and the need for new skills and competencies.

The result for employees was less clear. If a company did provide the job experiences and

Company investments in employees' professional development were likely to engender loyalty even as they enhanced employees' opportunities in the labour market.

training opportunities central to the employability rhetoric, employees might be able to manage their careers successfully. The effect on employee loyalty and commitment, however, was ambiguous. Company investments in employees' professional development were likely to engender loyalty even as they enhanced employees' opportunities in the labour market.

Conventional wisdom holds that the shift from security to employability changed the way workers viewed the employment relationship. This "new deal" at work engendered a "free agent" mentality. When combined with robust economic conditions, the arrangement led many employees to strike deals of their own, changing employers often in response to sweetened offers and professional challenges. Employers found they were losing the people they wanted to keep as a "war" for talent intensified. And employees often found themselves paying as much attention to calls from headhunters and to job postings on the web as to their jobs.

## Transactions

The movement from security to employability represents a shift from relationship-based ties to transaction-based connections between employer and employee. In relationship-based ties, part of the "glue" binding employer and employee is social and psychological. Feelings of belonging and liking are promoted. One stays because one feels part of something "bigger" and one's personal identity becomes tied to the workplace. In a transaction-based model, by contrast, the decision about staying with an employer is a purely instrumental calculation. If an opportunity provides economic gain and professional challenge, there is reason to pursue it.

Has the shift transformed the average worker from a company loyalist to a free agent? Evidence is mixed. First, many companies have not in fact made this shift. There is a spectrum of commitment to employability, with high-tech and dotcom companies being more committed to the new model than others. Many adhere to the older model. However, while some companies claim to have made the shift, not all have implemented practices that actually enhance employability.

Finally, there is evidence of a backlash; people have found it hard to balance the demands of work with those of their personal lives.

People have discovered that market-based employment entraps at the same time as it empowers. In self-defined careers, there are no clear boundaries between the person and career. Because the limits on accumulation of skills and professional achievement are to a large extent self-imposed, and because performance pressures are unrelenting, one can for ever strive to become more employable. Eventually, lives become complicated, overloaded and stressful – and if satisfying, only in a narrow sense.

People are beginning to retreat from the employability model and to frame their sense of self and their lives in terms of balance and affiliation. The challenge is how to live satisfying lives in a world of employability. People may take into account how they wish to allocate their time across a spectrum of competing demands and opportunities, where they find a sense of community and how they derive a sense of meaning and purpose in what they do. The answer to the question of why people enter and stay in employment relationships goes beyond money and professional opportunity.

Psychologists, of course, have been saying this for years. However, it is a message that is easily overlooked by companies eager to restructure, downsize or reinvent themselves to address competition. And personal reappraisal of the employment relationship is a trend that was accelerated in the US by the events of September 11, 2001.

## September 11

People often reassess their lives and make purposeful life changes in the wake of tragedy. Understandably, the attacks in the US led people to question the priorities in life. Many commentators have discussed the impact of the terrorist attacks on people's views of life and work. Although some people returned to work with renewed dedication, many others questioned their choices and made changes.

Not surprisingly, some of the most immediate changes were seen among survivors of the attacks. Chuck Harcourt of Morgan Stanley's municipal bonds department told *The New York Times*: "Before all this, I'd be afraid to ask for a day off – or a morning off – to take my kid to the first day of school. It's true. We spent more time there than with most of our family members. Now it's just surreal to look at that skyline and to think we used to be in one of those buildings."

Even those who were not personally affected by the attacks examined their priorities: the place of work, family, friends and career success. There is anecdotal evidence that many people want to work less, spend more time with their families and friends and participate more in their communities. The press runs regular stories about people who are turning down job offers and promotions or quitting jobs that keep them far from families or that require too many hours at work or too much commuting.

It seems that in spite of the attention companies have paid to the work/life balance, they have not got it right and recent events have exacerbated the problems. Many companies have formal programmes aimed at enhancing employee retention and boosting morale. Some, for example, have attempted to become "family friendly", with flexible hours, on-site childcare and, in the extreme, concierge services. However, the problem of perceived imbalance remains.

The work/life balance campaign merely allowed employees to admit that they had lives outside work. Admitting that personal lives might sometimes take priority over their professional lives, however, was still taboo. In an environment focused on accumulation and achievement, the attention given to affiliation, community and meaning was squeezed out. A study in 2000 by academic Paula Rayman confirmed that people seek balanced lives, meaningful work and a sense of community from employment. Eighty-four per cent of people in their twenties and thirties cite a work schedule that allows enough time for family as the most important thing in a job. This is just as true for men as for women – both ranked family time as more important than money, power and prestige. In fact, 71 per cent of men would take a pay cut for more time with their families.

Market research by Yankelovich Partners into US values, lifestyles and motivations confirms an apparent shift in priorities. The firm's July 2001 survey found that 72 per cent of people in their twenties and thirties express a desire to do well at work, but also to have plenty of time left over for interests outside work. This figure is up from 56 per cent in 1999.

Marcy Scott Lynn, 29, who quit as a corporate communications manager for Levi Strauss after the terrorist attacks, told *Business Week*: "I don't want to die wishing I had done something that meant more." The magazine also described 34-year-old Nico Taborga's new-found need for community. A financial analyst for Cohen Financial, he lost all enthusiasm for his job after the attacks: "He felt more of a sense of community in the line to give blood than he did in his macho, me-first office."

These data indicate that people have been appraising how work fits into their lives and placing increasing importance on other parts of life for some time. Fifty-seven per cent of those in the Yankelovich survey said work was an important part of who they were. That figure, while significant, was down from 71 per cent just a year earlier. Significantly, nearly three-quarters of respondents said they were evaluating what things were working in their lives and what were not two months before the attacks.

As experience with the employability model has accumulated, assumptions about why people enter and stay in jobs have begun to show signs of wear. In the US and elsewhere, the events of September 11 both intensified feelings that had been emerging and effectively made it legitimate for people to give voice to their ambivalence about work and life choices. These events also prompted many to assert other priorities: a desire for affiliation and community, a search for greater meaning in life and choices about how to spend time.

## The future

Three themes emerge. People are seeking community. Whether community is found in church, synagogue, a volunteer service organization, social club or simply in friendship, it provides a sense of belonging and a sense of being part of something bigger than oneself. They are also seeking greater meaning in their lives. The brutal realization that life could be snuffed out

> Individuals, especially younger people who are just entering the workforce, do not bring with them any of the assumptions that underlie existing work practices.

without warning motivates a search for involvement in things that really matter and, in some cases, prompts a realization that life has become dominated by less consequential concerns. Finally, people are reviewing how they spend their time. They are open to new and different patterns of behaviour in balancing work and life.

Why are these themes significant? First, they help answer the fundamental question of why people enter and stay in employment relations. The emerging dissatisfaction with the employability model may be at least partly attributable to the emphasis it places on the transaction-based connection to the employer – and on monetary rewards and professional opportunity as the cornerstones of the employment contract.

Second, the themes provide clues for companies wishing to develop HR policies that encompass employees' changing priorities and beliefs. It may be that companies need to begin thinking about work more broadly as an experience in which relationships play a central role. Individuals, especially younger people who are just entering the workforce, do not bring with them any of the assumptions that underlie existing work practices.

This can be seen in the very different, casual, playful and diverse workplaces that have sprung up. By creating an employment "experience" that is more in tune with employees' needs and interests and more consistent with a younger generation's expectations, these companies have been able to attract talented, mobile, independent people. Although several such companies have fallen victim to the slowing economy, the new attitude is alive and well. Companies looking to become "employers of choice" would do well to determine how they might provide a similarly inspiring employment experience.

They might begin by designing an attractive employment experience much as web search company Google has done. Google attracts employees by selling the "experience" of working there. As well as offering employees a chance to be part of a community of people doing "meaningful" work, the company claims to treat family, leisure and personal well being as important parts of employees' lives. Employees can bring their children to work, enjoy a weekly game of roller hockey, park their scooters and pets in their cubicles, work out in the gym, then take a sauna or have a massage and sit down at a grand piano in the company's lobby when the musical urge hits.

Companies must recognize that work is only a part of employees' lives and must reconfigure their practices and expectations accordingly. Those that do so are likely to be able to attract and retain talented people, benefiting from their commitment whatever the duration of the relationship. Thinking of workers as consumers of employment experiences is the best place to start. Then creating employment experiences that engage the whole person is the next step.

## Further reading

Cappelli, P. (1999) *The New Deal at Work*, Boston: Harvard Business School Press.

Ciulla, J. (2000) *The Working Life: The promise and betrayal of modern work*, New York: Times.

Pink, D. (2001) *Free Agent Nation: How America's new independent workers are transforming the way we live*, New York: Warner.

Rayman, P. (2001) *Beyond the Bottom Line: The search for dignity at work*, New York: St. Martin's Press.

Rousseau, D. (1995) *Psychological Contracts in Organisations: Understanding written and unwritten agreements*, Thousand Oaks, CA: Sage.

Tulgan, B. (2001) *Winning the Talent Wars*, New York: Norton.

Yankelovich Partners (2001) "The Truth about Empowerment ... Getting it right in uncertain times", Monitor Report.

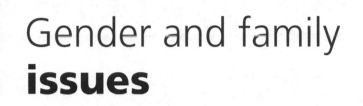

# Gender and family
**issues**

5

# Contents

# Introduction to Part 5

**A**ny company wishing to succeed in a competitive market needs to retain its talented employees. Managers are increasingly turning to the provision of more flexible, family-oriented benefits in the hope of attracting and keeping the best staff. As the authors in this part point out, though, any advances that companies have made in the good years are put under pressure in an economic downturn. And in the promotion and development of women managers, corporations still have much work to do.

# Lifting the corporate
## barriers to women

Herminia Ibarra is a
professor of business
administration at Harvard
Business School and a
visiting professor at
Insead.

Companies have started to do more to retain female employees, yet few are reaching senior levels. **Herminia Ibarra** investigates the forces that hamper women's career development.

No world-class company has solved the problem of retaining and promoting women. The "leaks in the pipeline" are obvious – women are hired at the entry levels in equal proportion to men. But that 50 per cent dwindles to less than 10 per cent at senior levels and further if one looks to the leadership of the company. Worse, for many companies these poor results persist in spite of efforts to address the causes of the exodus.

After a decade of experimenting with "women's initiatives", companies have learned about what works and what doesn't. Gone are the days when companies expected to improve recruitment, stand back and watch the intake grow. They now pay attention to career development and look for subtle barriers within their culture. Mentoring programmes and diversity workshops can help or hinder depending on their design and the extent to which employees support them. And work/family balance issues that are so easily attributed to women are among the central concerns of future leaders – male and female.

Companies are making progress, so why aren't they getting better results? It is primarily because they are not treating women's initiatives as change efforts: with a clear rationale, strong sponsorship and a realistic execution plan.

## Leading the change

Every change effort must start with a simple question: "Why are we doing this?" Without this, the plan will not get off the ground. For example, a senior manager of one UK company described a recruiting event in which a young woman asked what his company was doing about the "glass ceiling". He was not convinced about the company's initiatives but mentioned a recent programme. Later, the audience let

## If women do have higher rates of attrition, when do they leave and why?

him know he had seemed hypocritical in giving an answer devoid of conviction. The episode led him to create a group to build a business case for the programme.

### Build a business case

A business case serves two purposes. First, it tells people why they should support the proposal and shows it is not just rhetoric. Second, it tells external stakeholders what the company is trying to accomplish and why. As corporate scrutiny heightens, public opinion has become more important.

A business case is built on data. What is the gender composition of the entry-level pool? And of the places from which the company recruits? How do these figures compare with senior ranks? One transport company was sure it was building a good career path until managers looked at succession planning. It turned out that two and three tiers down from the top the figures were as bad as at the executive level. There was no career path.

Attrition levels are also important. Research by one investment bank found that women stayed with the company longer. The perception was that they were leaving in droves to stay with their children; in fact, men had shorter tenures because they were more likely to switch companies. If women do have higher rates of attrition, when do they leave and why? A Korn/Ferry study of women executives in the US who left for entrepreneurial opportunities showed that the main reasons cited for leaving were the opportunity to take risks, a seat at the decision-making table and generous pay for their performance.

A good business case also recognizes that figures tell only part of the story. It is easier to measure the opportunity cost of failing to attract or retain the best and brightest than to measure the long-term consequences of frustrating the contribution of those who stay.

### Have high-level champions

No change programme succeeds without leadership from the top. Women's initiatives flounder when backed only by the HR department. Sponsorship from the top means senior women and men in the company. For example, the division head of an investment bank started by sending the three most senior women on a leadership programme. He hoped they would learn what other companies were doing. More importantly, he wanted them to form a "guiding coalition" to help him lead the women's initiative.

Even if the chief executive is an ardent champion, without a united front, sceptics and detractors will highlight potential difficulties. This can greatly slow change.

### Invest in a diagnosis

To treat a problem, one has to find its root causes. Most people in companies think they know where the problems lie. However, competing explanations, interpretations and perceptions can be as numerous as they are varied. A good diagnosis, based on a broad cross-section of the company and reliable data, is a prerequisite.

Getting input from all groups that make up the organization is an important early step. The UK law firm Clifford Chance, for example, decided to involve women lawyers at all levels in a series of workshops designed to uncover why so few women were progressing to partnership. Including junior people is critical not only because they form the recruits for senior levels but also because generational differences often shape experience and opinion.

Diversity practices do not always travel well across national borders. US practices are often seen elsewhere as flawed by excessive political correctness. In some European countries, women still feel that women's initiatives amount to granting special, undeserved rights. And every organization has its local cultures. One group may be persuaded that the company is a meritocracy, while another may be convinced it is far from it. Managers must gauge these different viewpoints before selecting the right course of action.

The data on which such a decision is based must be accurate and unbiased. Exit interviews provide a harsh lesson. Psychological research has shown that once people have left a company, they explain why they left in ways that bear only a weak correlation with earlier reasons for leaving. Women, for example, may say they are leaving the company to stay at home with the children, when their true motives are more complex. Surveys of people who leave also uncover dissatisfaction that may just as well apply to those who stay. If you want to understand who goes and who stays, or who moves up and who derails, you cannot just study people who leave or the success cases because you will not know whether the others are any different.

## Benchmark

Any company can draw from a wealth of experience when planning women's initiatives. Different divisions – or competing organizations within the same industry – may have adopted easy, low-cost approaches. A common approach, for example, is for managers to participate in industry working groups that share best practices.

Once it is known what a reference group is doing, it is important to tailor the practice to suit both specific needs and local cultures. IBM Europe, for example, formed a multinational task-force to explore best practice on staff flexibility. In the US, it had good results with telecommuting. However, a survey pinpointed potential problems with attitudes towards working from home in other countries.

Mentoring programmes are another good example. Many organizations have jumped on the mentoring bandwagon without giving much thought to their own needs. One company, for example, launched a programme in which very senior people were assigned to mentor high-potential women. Later they discovered that what the group most needed was the detailed coaching that only someone closer to their level could provide.

## Manage expectations

Organizations worry about raising expectations with women's initiatives, fearing that everyone will expect results right away. It is certainly true that when a change programme is launched, expectations can run high. But that is exactly what managers want, otherwise nothing happens.

The trick is being able to raise urgency while setting realistic expectations. Interim objectives help and having the right comparison group is critical. When sceptics say, "There is not much we can do – our business is a 24/7 business and women just don't want to work like that", it helps to know how your company compares with others in the same industry. An interim goal might be an incremental move up in the rankings, relative to similar companies.

Accountability practices also help. Schlumberger, a Franco-American oil services company, for instance, has incentives for managers based on their ability to recruit women.

## Hard and soft levers

It is tempting to try to find the one programme or practice that will make all the difference and even more tempting to pick something tangible such as a daycare centre or a recruiting programme. But basing an initiative on one issue, or on issues that can be dealt with exclusively as a matter of policy, is a mistake. Managers increase their chances of success by intervening on many fronts and by using "hard" and "soft" levers. Hard levers are matters of policy that are identifiable, such as flexible work guidelines, recruiting practices and accountability targets. Soft levers involve culture and values and so are harder to identify and implement. They are concerned with the way people are developed and include mentoring and leadership training.

The challenge is how to design "hard" and "soft" levers that work together. Journalist Rochelle Sharpe found that US companies with excellent family-oriented benefits were among the worst in promoting women to senior levels. Flexibility practices are important but are no substitute for training and succession planning.

Managers increase their chances of success by intervening on many fronts and by using "hard" and "soft" levers.

# Career development

Career success requires three ingredients: the right assignments, mentors and a good network, and a credible image. An initiative that takes all three into account has a better chance of success.

## Access to important positions

The job histories of "star" senior managers invariably show that they have passed through certain posts. Historically, women have been less likely than men to get these jobs. A 1994 Center for Creative Leadership study, for example, found that women were less likely than men to be given start-up and turnaround assignments, precisely those that grow the competencies needed in a senior executive.

Deloitte Touche started its women's initiative by analyzing what assignments in each practice area provided better opportunities for advancement. Top-rated women were reviewed to ensure that they were assigned to high-visibility clients and strategic initiatives. This yielded good results in terms of new women partners. However, the results were disappointing for women moving from junior partner to company-wide leadership roles. To improve the proportions at the highest level, the company created an executive course that brought together top women partners to develop intangible skills such as leadership and negotiation.

## Mentoring and networking

Few make it to the top without strong mentors and networks. That is why mentoring programmes that link women at all levels with more experienced guides are now common. Yet no matter how good the connection, a single mentor is not enough. In a 1997 study of managers in four large corporations, I found that having a mentor matters less for moving up than having a broad mix of professional contacts that includes men and women.

That is why many organizations now supplement mentoring programmes with women's networks, conferences and off-site meetings. IBM, for example, started bringing together executive and high-potential women in 1997 to discuss barriers and possible remedies. From the start they discovered an unexpected pay-off – attendees found peers, mentors and role models they would never otherwise have met.

Events that bring together women from a variety of organizations are increasingly popular. "Women on Wall Street", an annual conference organized by Deutsche Bank employees, has grown from an internal company event to an institution that draws together thousands of women. Through such events companies can enlarge the pool of role models until the numbers at the top catch up.

## A matter of style

Women may drop out of the contest for top jobs because of subtle nuances of image and style. In professional services firms, for example, I found that women were much more likely than men to be described as "not aggressive enough" or "lacking in presence" in appraisals. These image problems were barriers to reaching partner status.

Acting on this finding can be tricky as organizations select their leaders on the basis of intangible but critical qualities, such as their ability to inspire others. Revamping performance appraisal forms to make such criteria more explicit is a starting point, but it will not be enough. Research suggests that part of the answer lies in helping women find role models from whom they can learn both substance and style. That is why networking events are so important. Many organizations also offer more intensive coaching and targeted executive development aimed at developing the more intangible skills of a senior executive. Until recently these were discounted as "remedial programmes". Today, with the increasing popularity of personal coaches, they are in high demand.

## Conclusion

When women make choices about whether to stay or go, whether to invest a lot or a little, much goes into the calculation. One side of the equation includes measurable variables: am I given important assignments? What kind of training is available? Can I balance work and home life? The other side weighs "soft" factors about meaning and membership: do I feel valued in this company? Are there role models for me here? Do I belong? To win the war for talent for women, companies will have to take account of both sides of the equation.

## Further reading

Ibarra, H. (2000) "Making partner", *Harvard Business Review*, 78, 2.

Kanter, R.M. (1993) *Men and Women of the Corporation*, New York: Basic Books.

Korn/Ferry International, Columbia Business School and The Duran Group (2001) "What women want in business: a survey of executives and entrepreneurs" (http://www.kornferry.com/focus/pubs_womens_study.asp).

Kotter, J. (1995) "Why transformation efforts fail", *Harvard Business Review*, 73, 2.

McCracken, D.M. (2000) "Winning the talent war for women", *Harvard Business Review*, November.

Sharpe, R. (1994) "The waiting game", *The Wall Street Journal*, March 29.

# Corporate help is at
## hand for working parents

Stewart D. Friedman is practice professor at the Wharton School of the University of Pennsylvania and director of the Wharton Work/Life Integration Project.

Ellen Galinsky is president of the Families and Work Institute.

As demand for childcare from working parents grows, companies have to be more creative in their provision. **Stewart Friedman** and **Ellen Galinsky** outline the latest developments.

Families with a working single parent or with both parents in full-time jobs have become the norm in the developed world and even among the growing middle class in some developing countries. As this trend continues, the need for novel and effective arrangements for the care of young children continues to grow. Although government policies in support of these efforts are evolving, the burden has been largely borne by private businesses in a number of countries. While companies have made considerable progress, the growth of their initiatives faces substantial obstacles, particularly as the economy weakens.

Since the 1990s, companies have tried to address the personal and family needs of their employees. Our September 2000 survey shows that leading US companies have moved from single-issue programmes and policies to meet the needs of employees with young children towards a more strategic, comprehensive approach. Many approaches are based on giving autonomy to employees about where, when and how they work.

In addition, the number of creative public-private partnerships has grown. In the process, some companies have taken an interest in the care of all children, not just those of their own employees. These companies are redefining their relationship with the community. Yet in a competitive world, businesses and community organizations face considerable challenges in advancing such programmes.

## Accomplishments

Two major trends are evident in the US. First, family-friendly policies have grown from a piecemeal collection of human resources benefits into a social movement characterized by a strategic, integrated approach. Unlike a decade ago, when the emphasis was on dependent care, many companies now offer comprehensive services that support the co-ordination of work and personal life. Second, and perhaps more importantly, workplace innovations increasingly depend on external stakeholders, such as communities, schools and government.

Companies give several reasons for supporting workers in their family or personal roles. Foremost is increasing competition in the so-called "war for talent" – the desire to recruit and retain the best employees – and the sense that helping staff to integrate work and personal life increases their desire to go the extra mile for the company. As employees have become more diverse, with a variety of lifestyles and family structures, companies have set up taskforces and committees to help resolve work–life issues using a range of programmes. Training is needed to ensure that employees are aware of how to make these programmes useful and that supervisors support their implementation.

Multinational companies such as Merrill Lynch and Glaxo offer programmes including childcare centres, summer camps, flexible work arrangements, help with dependents, resource and referral for childcare, tuition, adoption reimbursement and parenting education. They also offer back-up childcare, family childcare homes, before- and after-school programmes, family leave, flexible work arrangements, wellness programmes and campaigns for women's achievement.

Rather than imposing a standardized programme, some US companies such as Verizon Communications, Allstate and Prudential have designed flexible programmes to meet employees' needs. These programmes (in addition to those described above) include family illness days, college scholarships and preparation, summer camp, dependent care grants, lactation facilities, parenting seminars and materials, adoption assistance, employee recreation events and discounts, resource and referral.

Applying a comprehensive approach to work–life initiatives is not limited to large companies. Even small start-ups with limited resources realize the importance of a comprehensive work–life programme. For example, ECS, an environmental risk management specialist in the US, offers flexible hours, reimbursement of tuition fees, resource and referral services, extended parental leave, health programmes, adoption leave with subsidies and on-site childcare.

## Companies must continue to educate managers on the value of workplace flexibility and its compatibility with superior business results.

Federal agencies are also adopting a comprehensive approach. The US Department of Justice, for instance, has created a comprehensive work–life programme. Such programmes would have been unthinkable 10 years ago. Similar approaches are also evident in academia, for example at New York University. A decade ago the university had no maternity leave other than the statuary minimum of six weeks of disability. Now faculty members get a year off for the birth or adoption of a baby. This helps to level the playing field for female academics and encourages men to become more involved in family life.

Implementing such flexibility is never easy. Companies must continue to educate managers on the value of workplace flexibility and its compatibility with superior business results. At the heart of these approaches is a respect for employees' choices.

## Partnerships

Companies no longer assume they can address employees' work–life issues alone. They are increasingly becoming involved in some sort of public-private partnership to address childcare or education needs. In the US, such partnerships are developing at local, state and national levels. Some are aimed at improving the quality of, and access to, childcare and school-age care programmes; increasing the number of accredited programmes; and improving training and pay for providers. According to a survey by the Families and Work Institute, 11 per cent of companies with 100 or more employees are involved in partnerships between the public and private sectors.

For example, the American Business Collaboration for Quality Dependent Care (ABC) is a group of companies that aims to improve care for children and the elderly. Between 1995 and 2000, 18 lead companies and 50 local partners invested $100m to ensure high-quality dependent care services in communities for ABC employees. The group invests in communities that have large employee populations, as well as communities with critical business or employee needs. The needs of collaborating companies and employees shape the community strategy. Detailed assessments begin the process by determining workers' needs and care availability. The results are used to develop projects that aim to address specific issues. Participating companies make the final decision on whether to fund these projects.

Some companies have their own funds to foster private-public collaboration. These include major companies such as IBM, AT&T, Lucent Technologies, Johnson & Johnson and Merrill Lynch, which together have allocated over $100m to programmes. Such programmes have forged partnerships with local and state governments, universities and other social organizations. Companies have come to believe that it is partly their responsibility to address childcare and education, not only for their employees but for all children. Collaboration and public-private partnerships are seen as the best way forward. These companies believe that services for their employees cannot be improved without significant improvements in early childhood care. A number take the view that public private partnerships can be more effective in bringing about change than federal and state governments have been. In fact, Marriott has helped establish a group to address public policy, called Corporate Voices for Working Families. However, some business leaders remain wary of partnerships because they worry about becoming bogged down in bureaucracy.

These activities demonstrate that companies are expanding their definition of community as they enlarge their sense of responsibility – to the communities where their employees live and even nationally (a trend that has become even more pronounced since September 11).

## Doing business

Communications technologies have led to changes in traditional business models. Boundaries between work and other domains are becoming more permeable, and the speed with which we can move across these domains is increasing. Time at work can be used more intelligently, with a greater share of it dedicated to customers and other external stakeholders, including home and community, and less to low-value activities. At the same time, staying connected with people at work, at home and in the community is getting easier.

Yet these changes bring potential conflicts as well. The number of hours worked (often on site) is still used as a primary measure of an individual's productivity and commitment, even when a straightforward connection between time at work and results no longer holds. More creativity will be needed when measuring people's contributions.

Towards this end, Ford has launched a leadership development initiative for high-potential middle managers. Participants are required to experiment and demonstrate how they can improve results by integrating work, home and community lives. They receive feedback from participants and have to show that they can accomplish things without the constraints of place and fixed schedules. This experiment is expected to yield lessons on how to use communications technology and leadership methods, carrying a message of cultural transformation based on real-life examples.

Although respect for the employee and empowerment are at the core of the progress companies have made in the past decade, other forces are at play. Employees are expressing a greater need for control of their destinies. They are bringing a new set of values to their careers, with a greater emphasis on being able to make meaningful contributions to work and to society. Because the nature of organizations is shifting from hierarchical to horizontal and the need for teams is growing, it is only natural that employees exert more control; not just at work but in their whole lives, of which work is one part. Yet empowerment can challenge a workplace that is used to command and control. So, companies have to work out partnerships that combine autonomy with accountability. The key to successful change is to focus on results.

Another challenge is that boundaries between work and family life are blurring. For example, a May 2001 study called "Feeling Overworked" by the Families and Work Institute found that 41 per cent of employees are using technology to do their jobs during non-work hours and non-work days. This can result in the "every time, every place" work environment or, on the other hand, it can lead to a better integration of work with personal life. The former extends the burdens and stress of work beyond the work place, while the latter seeks to allow greater personal freedom and choices for employees.

Job design must allow for the full range of employees' needs rather than allowing flexibility only when the job structure permits it. Many more decision makers will be in dual-career families themselves and will be younger.

Changes in how business gets done could make it easier for working parents to be more available to their children, both physically and psychologically; with greater flexibility and control, parents are better able to focus on their children's needs. Yet the need for childcare by other adults will continue to remain strong – indeed to grow – and this need is most pronounced at the lower end of the socio-economic ladder.

## Support

The issue of childcare is especially problematic for low-wage earners. For far too many parents, the availability of adequate childcare can mean the difference between working and not working. Leading companies are coming up with novel ways to provide services for low-wage earners, but there is a long way to go before we see universal access to early childhood education and care in advanced economies.

One group of employees that typically have little access to work–life assistance is the childcare workforce. Bright Horizons Family Solutions, a childcare provider, offers childcare to its teachers at half-price and recently began offering a back-up childcare option to employees. This company is the only childcare organization ever to be named to the Fortune 100 Best Companies list.

The growing acceptance of family diversity has led to an increased awareness that the needs of low-income and hourly employees have not been met adequately. This is an area in which private-public partnerships could make a real difference and to which resources must be applied. The obstacles are substantial. Some employers whose workforce is dominated by low-wage employees,

## The growing acceptance of family diversity has led to an increased awareness that the needs of low-income and hourly employees have not been met adequately.

for example, have studied on-site childcare many times, but have never built a centre because there is not enough interest. Lower-paid employees may not use licensed care facilities because of cost constraints and instead use a neighbour, friend or family member or split shifts with their spouse.

## What next?

Companies have moved from single-issue programmes and policies to meet the needs of employees with young children to a more strategic, comprehensive approach. This approach is based on granting more respect and autonomy to employees about where, when and how they work, and developing the tools to make their decision making more effective.

Companies are engaging in more public-private partnerships and these experiences have led some corporate leaders to tackle the childcare needs of all children, not just those of their own employees. These companies are redefining the connection between company and community.

These changes could be either positive or negative for working families and their children. However, if employed parents, their employers and their social institutions develop programmes that invest in the whole lives of employees, the result will be a more productive workplace and a healthier and safer community – where children can continue to develop, learn and thrive as they seek their place in society.

## Further reading

Brownfield, E. (2001) *The Time Crunch: Work redesign and management in a 24-7 economy*, New York: Families and Work Institute.

Friedman, S.D. and Greenhaus, J.H. (2000) *Work and Family – Allies or Enemies?*, Oxford University Press.

Galinsky, E. (2000) *Ask the Children: The breakthrough study that reveals how to succeed at work and at parenting*, New York: Quill.

Galinsky, E., Skim, S.S. and Bond, J.T. (2001) *Feeling Overworked: When work becomes too much*, New York: Families and Work Institute.

http://www.familiesandwork.org and http://worklife.wharton.upenn.edu contain summaries of studies by the authors.

# Managing
# **conflict**

6

# Contents

# Introduction to Part 6

**Internal wrangling** between employees or departments can harm the implementation of company strategy and cost the company money, especially if parties turn to the courts for redress. Executives are now seeking ways of managing conflict before it comes to litigation, by putting in systems and policies to defuse disagreements at an early stage and identify the root causes of conflict. Writers in this part look at the concept of fair process in the corporate environment, and the kinds of conflict that can arise from having two different generations working side by side.

# Turning disputes
## to corporate advantage

Michael Alan Sacks is an assistant professor at Goizueta Business School, Emory University.

Arguments between staff can result in costly litigation. However, **Michael Sacks** and **Andy Lewis** believe a resolution system can turn conflict into a potentially creative force.

Andy Lewis is deputy director at the Georgia Office of Dispute Resolution and a director of Neutral Resources.

Companies are realizing that workplace conflict can be expensive and time-consuming. Resolutionworks, a US conflict management training company, recently reported that Fortune 500 executives spend about a fifth of their time on litigation-related matters. Companies usually pay thousands of dollars in lawyers' fees even when they win, let alone lose.

However, some companies have been able to cut significant costs when handling conflict. For example, Motorola reported a 75 per cent reduction in costs associated with litigation; NCR halved its legal costs and reduced the number of lawsuits brought against it from 263 in 1984 to 28 in 1993. In a survey of 652 companies, all saved more than $300,000 each and some saved millions of dollars.

How were these companies able to save so much? The answer lies in their use of integrated conflict management systems. This article shows how companies can design, implement and evaluate such systems. The approach goes beyond simply training employees in effective conflict management skills or setting up procedures to resolve specific kinds of dispute.

## Beyond skills

In recent years, companies seeking to cut the costs of conflict have turned to training seminars, where employees learn communication and conflict management techniques. A common theme of these workshops is to focus on interests rather than positions. For example, if an employee claims that a manager unacceptably interfered with a project, while the manager says plans were not communicated properly, they are likely to remain at a stalemate. However, underlying these positions are interests, and in separating the two, companies can often resolve the conflict. In this example, the employee's interest may have been to work with a level of autonomy, while the manager may have wanted a clear plan for the project.

By focusing on such interests rather than defending positions, the employee may agree to provide a plan for the project (meeting the manager's main interest) and the manager will trust the employee to handle the details (meeting the employee's main interest), producing a mutually agreeable outcome.

Another important topic in workshops is the notion that conflict is not inherently bad; rather, conflict is inevitable whenever many people with different opinions, interests, perspectives and cultures work interdependently towards common goals. For example, in any given company, there are many, often competing, ideas for how the company should proceed strategically, but all strive for the same goal of organizational success. Unfortunately, the company typically has to choose just one idea, causing managers to fight over whose idea will "win" and whose will "lose". The struggle for competitive advantage turns into destructive competition, fostering conflicts that can cause significant problems.

Conflict is productive only if it is primarily collaborative rather than adversarial. In the above example, a collaborative approach allows managers to offer opinions, discuss the merits of each and choose the strategy that most benefits the company – rather than individuals within it. This process focuses on what is best for the company and uses workplace conflict as a way of making that goal happen.

## Hierarchies

While skills-based workshops cover many important themes and are useful in addressing workplace conflict, ultimately the results are often disappointing. The problem is that conflicts are embedded in organizational systems that limit the effectiveness of these skills. In other words, people cannot use effective conflict management skills if there is no integrated system in place to support such efforts. In the first example, the employee and manager were negotiating as if they were equals. In real life, the manager

A well-planned and integrated conflict resolution system can overcome the challenges that hierarchy creates for workplace conflict resolution.

has power, which may make the employee reluctant to raise concerns. The same reluctance might exist among workers, who may be unlikely to deal with conflict for fear of being perceived as troublemakers. In the second example, managers have individual incentives to press for the adoption of their strategic ideas, even if these ideas are not best for the whole organization.

The situation worsens when a company places dispute resolution within the corporate hierarchy, because hierarchy often discourages individuals from discussing conflict. For example, a school implemented a dispute resolution process in which the head teacher was the formal arbiter of conflicts. However, the head teacher was also responsible for performance evaluations, promotions and discipline. Accordingly, teachers were reluctant to seek arbitration for fear that it would damage their job aspirations.

A well-planned and integrated conflict resolution system can overcome the challenges that hierarchy creates for workplace conflict resolution. Yet what should a conflict management system look like? How can managers assess whether their conflict management system is producing results for the company?

## Integrated system

Businesses have long recognized the value of arbitration for disputes at work and with trading partners. However, only in the past decade have some integrated skills training, arbitration, mediation and other tools to create systems for managing conflict. No two systems are alike – components differ, management responsibilities vary and policies are distinct. A common feature of successful systems is that the resources, goals and needs of a company are assessed, producing a tailored and informed system.

Planning is very important because a well-designed system does more than control conflict – it uncovers resources and creates value. It can turn a culture of competing individuals into one of collaborative team-mates working towards a common corporate goal.

Why do companies decide to manage their conflicts more carefully? Often it is prompted by a crisis, either within the company, industry or economy. It might be a messy class action lawsuit, a union-related dispute, or an economic downturn that requires cost-cutting measures. Changes in the law also might cause a company to examine its treatment of conflict. For example, in 2001, the US Supreme Court ruled in Adams v. Circuit City that virtually all agreements by employees to submit grievances to binding arbitration are enforceable, thereby precluding employees from suing their employers in court. This case, combined with the economic slowdown and several high-profile class action lawsuits, has spurred many companies to build conflict management systems.

A hastily designed system may offer immediate benefits. After the court verdict, many companies began requiring their employees to commit to binding arbitration for disputes. Such a policy may protect the company from a class action because it prevents classes from forming. However, companies that take a long-term approach tend to produce much higher returns in terms of system effectiveness and savings. In assessing workplace conflict before formulating policy, these companies often arrive at a more enlightened view on handling conflict. If managed poorly or avoided altogether, conflict can sink an organization; managed well, it can be a great resource for employee and company alike.

## Three stages

To produce an integrated conflict management system, companies must go through three phases: organizational assessment, system design and evaluation. Of these, the first is the most important, as it encourages organizational support, dictates design, informs implementation and gives a structure for evaluation. Unfortunately, most companies, in their haste, pay insufficient attention to assessment, or neglect it entirely.

## Assessment

The assessment phase considers affected constituencies, trends and costs of conflict, existing resources and goals of the system. Data should be gathered, analyzed and tested before crafting an integrated system.

First, managers must identify affected constituencies so they know where to look for trends of conflict and associated costs. A first group of such constituencies are those who are in direct conflict – for example, line workers who disagree over company policy, or women who feel discriminated against because of their gender – but may include shareholders, trading partners and unions. A second group consists of those whose jobs are indirectly affected by the conflict, such as HR managers, in-house and external lawyers, and employee and shareholder relations personnel.

Trends and costs can be identified from various sources. HR departments can provide internal data and industry trends. Lawyers can give information on lawsuits and changes in the law. However, there is a problem in that most workplace conflicts never come to the formal attention of the company. This is because employees rarely turn to formal dispute resolution for help – most conflicts are either handled without the knowledge of the company or are avoided altogether. Such information must be gathered from surveys and interviews with staff and other stakeholders. Only in this way can a company's situation and needs be assessed; it also helps in getting comments and support from those who will use the system.

The third step – analyzing resources – enables managers to see what is available and whether resources are co-ordinated. These may include human resources, employee assistance plans, a hierarchical system of complaint and appeal, and hotlines. The system should incorporate these and co-ordinate the services offered by each. Employees should have access to such resources and the freedom to choose between them.

The fourth component of assessment, the goals of the system, dictates the design and implementation of the system. In the assessment phase, many organizations begin to see that the value to be derived from a system is not just in preventing lawsuits and associated costs but in creating value

> Many companies hope their conflict management system will encourage collaboration, increased efficiency, greater tolerance for diversity and better working conditions.

by confronting conflict and addressing it early. For example, instead of allowing racial discrimination to fester over several years into a class action lawsuit, a well-designed system can uncover the needs and interests of a diverse workforce and help reap the full value of that workforce.

Most businesses aim to reduce the number of legal actions they face, the costs of legal services and the frequency and size of awards and judgements to complainants. These goals can be measured. The assessment phase measures the level of legal activity and costs in the company. By quantifying costs and measuring them over time, companies can assess the effectiveness of a system.

Other goals are more difficult to measure but are just as valuable. Many companies hope their conflict management system will encourage collaboration, increased efficiency, greater tolerance for diversity and better working conditions. Companies tend to track these by employee surveys that ask generally about the company's approach to conflict, or rate the workplace environment. A less common approach, though one growing in popularity, is to identify components within the broader goals of "increased diversity" or "better working environments". Companies can identify business-related goals that either comprise such goals or serve as a proxy for them. These subgoals might include a reduction in staff turnover or in sick leave. They can be measured in the assessment phase, traced and evaluated to assess the broader goals of the system.

### System design

The design phase addresses what goes in the system and how it is put together. The core components might be hierarchical appeal procedures, negotiation, coaching, facilitation, mediation, arbitration, an ombudsman, and skills training in communication and conflict resolution.

Managers should use their earlier assessment of how conflicts arise to select components.

Importantly, the system should be easy to use and fair. Those in dispute should be able to choose the components they wish to use. It should be easier to use the system than to avoid conflict and allow it to escalate further. Companies will place different emphasis on certain components. In Shell, most disputes are settled in the ombudsman's office, whereas in the US Air Force the ombudsman's office is contacted in only a few cases.

When designing a system, a company must allow input from all major constituencies. This helps it gather important data from those who will be affected by the system and to secure commitment from those who will use and support it. For example, when one company was designing its system, the head of human resources was replaced. His successor was unfamiliar with conflict management systems and opposed the idea. However, once the executive had the chance to learn about the system and influence its design, it went ahead. Support from important constituencies is essential.

### Evaluation

When companies perform the first two phases, evaluation becomes relatively easy. Assessment sets a baseline to be used for future measurement. Evaluation should then consist of periodic assessments, bringing in factors that might have changed, such as shifts in the economy, technology, or changes in the legal environment. Each can be identified directly or by benchmarking against other companies. Quantitative analysis allows the effects of these shifts to be separated from the effects of the conflict management system, producing a clear picture of the system's effectiveness.

### Conclusion

Many companies are realizing that investment in conflict management systems outweighs the return on investment in other areas. Cutting the cost of conflict is a challenge but has financial and organizational rewards. A rigorous process of assessment, design and continual evaluation will allow companies to achieve it.

## Further reading

Blake, R.R. and Mouton, J.S. (1985) *Solving Costly Organizational Conflicts: Achieving intergroup trust, cooperation, and teamwork*, San Francisco, CA: Jossey-Bass.

Costantino, C. and Merchant, C.S. (1996) *Designing Conflict Management Systems: A guide to creating productive and healthy organizations*, San Francisco, CA: Jossey Bass.

Rowe, M. (1993) "The post-Tailhook navy designs an integrated dispute resolution system", *Negotiation Journal*, 9, 3.

Sacks, M.A., Reichart, K. and Proffitt, T. (1999) "Broadening the evaluation of dispute resolution: context and relationships over time", *Negotiation Journal*, 15, 4.

# How to earn
## commitment

Chan Kim is the Boston Consulting Group Bruce D. Henderson Chaired Professor of International Management at Insead.

**The best-laid plans of managers will come to nothing if employees are not behind them. Chan Kim and Renée Mauborgne find fairness is the key.**

Renée Mauborgne is the Insead Distinguished Fellow and an affiliate professor of strategy and management at Insead.

Twenty years after its creation, British Airways had transformed itself from "Bloody Awful" to the self-styled "world's favourite airline". By 1997, employee morale and customer service had earned industry-wide acclaim. However, the strategy pursued by Robert Ayling, who had become chief executive in 1996, sapped employee morale, triggered unrest and jeopardized service. In the peak summer months of 1997, cabin crew walked out, causing hundreds of BA flights to be cancelled. Labour woes cost BA about £130m. What went wrong?

The airline's managers violated fair process – fairness in making and executing decisions. At a time when planes were full and profits were high, managers took employees by surprise when they announced a major cost-cutting programme. They did not discuss with employees why this was necessary, nor did they engage employees in the plan. Employees were not given clear messages of what they could expect. In the absence of engagement, explanation and clarity – the bedrocks of fair process – employees felt cheated, disrespected and vulnerable. They revolted.

We have spent the past 10 years studying the link between fair process and companies' abilities to make the wrenching changes needed to transform themselves. In this time, we have seen one common thread. With fair process, even the most painful and difficult goals can be accomplished while gaining employees' trust and co-operation. However, without fair process, even outcomes that employees might favour can be difficult to achieve.

## Communication

Consider Burmah Castrol, the UK lubricants company. Burmah Castrol devised an innovative system for water coolants used in metalworking industries. Traditionally, customers had to choose from several hundred types of complex coolants. Because of the delicacy of selecting the right coolant, products had to be tested on production machines before a purchase was made – a challenge that involved considerable expertise, costs and logistical difficulties for customers and salespeople alike.

An expert computer system promised to eliminate all that. Using artificial intelligence, it synthesized the knowledge of the company's experts in selecting and testing coolants. Customers got a leap in value – the failure rate under the expert system fell to 10 per cent from a 50 per cent industry average, machine downtime was reduced, coolant management was easier and costs declined. Moreover, the company came out a winner too – the sales process was dramatically simplified, giving time for sales staff to attract new customers while reducing the cost per sale.

Yet the expert system was doomed. All the wonderful benefits it offered sales reps – having a way to avoid the hassling part of their job and pull in more and bigger sales by standing out head and shoulders in the industry – went unappreciated. Not because the expert system wasn't great, but because Burmah Castrol's own sales reps worked to undermine its credibility with customers.

Why? In creating the artificial intelligence system, managers thought they were doing everyone a favour so they didn't bother to engage sales reps in the process, explain the rationale behind the system or clarify what would be expected of them. There was no fair process – fairness in making and executing decisions. Burmah Castrol's sales reps felt suspicious of managers' intentions and saw the expert system in a light managers had never dreamed possible. It was a direct threat to what sales reps viewed as their most valuable contribution – tinkering in the trial process. Feeling threatened, they worked against the system and sales did not take off. Great ideas matter, but as companies such as Burmah Castrol have discovered, so does fair process.

Fair process responds to a basic human need. Everyone, whatever their role in a company, wants to be valued as a human being and not as "personnel" or "human resources". People want respect. They want their ideas to be taken seriously and to understand the rationale behind decisions. In theoretical terms, they want intellectual and emotional recognition. Fair process has a

> Everyone, whatever their role in a company, wants to be valued as a human being and not as "personnel" or "human resources".

direct link to this recognition. The practice of fair process proves through action that there is an eagerness to trust and cherish the individual as well as deep-seated confidence in the individual's knowledge, talents and expertise. When people feel recognized for their intellectual and emotional worth, they demonstrate a willingness to co-operate and give their all. They are inspired to volunteer and share knowledge actively – essential processes in achieving high performance. However, when fair process is violated, companies induce the hoarding of ideas, foot-dragging and other counter-efforts, including sabotage.

These counter-effects are known as retributive justice. When people feel their intellectual and emotional recognition has been violated through a lack of fair process, they seek to redress the situation not only by demanding a return to fairness but also by imposing a penalty for their unfair treatment. Figure 1 traces the relationships found in our research. This explains why, without fair process, even great ideas can fail, as seen at Burmah Castrol. However, with fair process, even the most difficult goals can be achieved.

## Self-help

Take the example of Siemens-Nixdorf Informationssysteme (SNI). It was the largest European supplier of information technology when it was created in the early 1990s after Siemens acquired the Nixdorf Computer Company. However, by the mid-1990s, SNI had cut head count from 52,000 to 35,000. Anxiety and fear pervaded the company.

Yet Gerhard Schulmeyer, newly appointed chief executive in 1994, earned the trust and co-operation of employees at this tumultuous time. He did this neither by making large promises that satisfied employees nor by putting off the emotionally

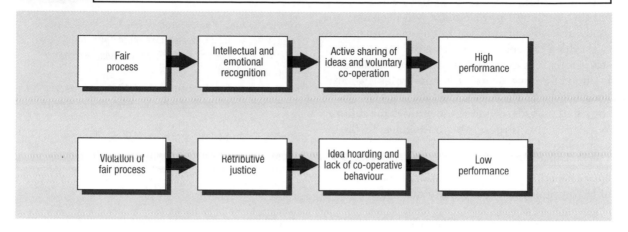

hard issues of restructuring. From his appointment, Schulmeyer went out to talk to as many employees as he could. In meetings with more than 11,000 people, Schulmeyer shared his mission of engaging everyone in turning the company around. He painted a bleakly honest picture of SNI's situation: the company was losing money in spite of efforts to slash costs. Deeper cuts were needed and every business would have to demonstrate its viability or be eliminated. Schulmeyer set clear but tough rules about how decisions would be made. People did not like what they heard, but they understood. He then asked for volunteers to come up with ideas.

Within three months the initial group of 30 volunteers had grown by an additional 75 SNI executives and 300 employees. The total grew from 405 into 1,000, then 3,000, then 9,000 as others were recruited to help save the company. Throughout, ideas were solicited from managers and employees alike concerning decisions that affected them, and they all understood how decisions would be made. Ideas were auctioned off to executives willing to champion and finance them. If executives did not think a proposal had merit, it would not be pursued. Although 20 to 30 per cent of proposals were rejected, employees thought the process was fair.

People pitched in voluntarily – mostly after business hours, often until midnight. In spite of accumulated losses of DM2bn, SNI was operating in the black and employee satisfaction almost doubled in just over two years, notwithstanding the

> Few companies have been able to muster such strong employee morale and co-operation during such a stressful corporate restructuring.

radical and difficult changes. However, intense competition finally led Siemens to sell the personal computer unit in 1998 to Acer, the low cost Taiwanese computer maker, and merge the other parts of SNI into Siemens. Yet few companies have been able to muster such strong employee morale and co-operation during such a stressful corporate restructuring. With many companies needing to restructure and change gears to become more competitive, they could learn important lessons from the way Schulmeyer exercised fair process at SNI.

Without fair process, managers will either find themselves facing a long, uphill battle to institutionalize much-needed changes or will have to back off as employees seek public support for managers' failure to pay intellectual and emotional respect to them.

## Key questions

To put fair process to work in your company, begin by asking: do we engage people in decisions that affect them by not only asking for input but allowing them to refute the merit of one another's ideas? Do we explain why decisions are made and why people's opinions may have been overridden? People can accept pain if they understand why it is necessary. Finally, once a decision is made, do we state the new rules clearly? Employees should be told the standards by which they will be judged and the penalties for failure. What are the targets and milestones? Who is responsible for what?

To transform themselves, companies need to earn the intellectual and emotional commitment of their employees. Fair process does that.

## Further reading

Kim, W.C. and Mauborgne, R. (1998) "Procedural justice, strategic decision making, and the knowledge economy", *Strategic Management Journal*, April.

Kim, W.C. and Mauborgne, R. (1997) "Fair process: managing in the knowledge economy", *Harvard Business Review*, July.

Kim, W.C. and Mauborgne, R. (1996) "Procedural justice and managers' in-role and extra-role behaviour", *Management Science*, April.

# Algebra lessons
## for older workers

Dr Karen L. Cates is an assistant professor of management and organizations at the Kellogg School of Management at Northwestern University.

Kimia A. Rahimi is a recent graduate of the Kellogg School of Management at Northwestern University.

Baby-boomers, who are used to paying their dues, may resent the forthright attitudes of younger employees. **Karen Cates** and **Kimia Rahimi** urge managers to learn what makes Generations X and Y tick.

Generation Y, made up of people born between 1978 and 1994, is entering the workforce. It shares the workplace with baby-boomers (1945 to 1961) and Generation X (1962 to 1977). These terms are often associated with the US, but young people everywhere emerge with their own voice, powered by affluence and characterized by a desire for change. Their arrival has sparked a good deal of debate, especially among older workers, as this new breed makes its professional needs and beliefs known.

## Who are they?

Generation Y has grown up in an era of technological advance and economic prosperity. More obsessed-over than any generation before, they have a confidence and optimism that comes from knowing that they are wanted. Their parents, who don't want to repeat the abandonment of the previous generation, shower their children with gifts, attention and esteem-building activities. Generation X is now a stable force at work. Rebellious, resentful and realistic in the wake of their parents' experiences of redundancies, as they move into management these former latch-key children have a no-nonsense approach, sometimes shocking older workers with their cut-and-dried decision-making styles. Older generations scrutinized Generation X when it entered the workforce. Generation Y now enjoys the spotlight – a source of bewilderment, frustration and relief all at the same time.

The plus side of working with late Generation X members and Generation Y results from their early childhood. They are used to being on the move and constantly stimulated by activities. They do their homework in the car between school and the soccer pitch. Their parents fill their days with activities. According to a 1999 study conducted by

> Coddled from an early age, Generation Y seems baffled when given a project to do. Initiative was not encouraged by parents who relied on acquiescence to get through their busy days.

the University of Michigan's Institute for Social Research, parents programme 75 per cent of their children's weekday time compared with 60 per cent in 1981 (leaving 6 hours a week of unstructured time versus 9.5 hours nearly 20 years ago). As a result, Generation Y grew up multi-tasking and knows how to make the most of every minute.

The downside of such a privileged, programmed childhood emerges at work in several ways. Generation Y doesn't want to perform the menial tasks of entry-level jobs and feels comfortable voicing its dissatisfaction. They are used to getting what they want. Coddled from an early age, Generation Y seems baffled when given a project to do. Initiative was not encouraged by parents who relied on acquiescence to get through their busy days. Further, expectations of wealth and opportunity born of the boom economy of the 1990s have left Generation Y seeking ambitious salaries very early. Their confident and capable demeanour with elders and their willingness to make demands belies their inexperience and need for guidance. Impatient with over-direction, they don't always know what to do with the reins when they get them. These bright new workers demonstrate the promise and frustrations their baby-boomer bosses experience at home with their own children. Only at work, the bratty behaviour doesn't seem so cute.

The oldest members of Generation Y are entering the workforce just as the baby-boom generation is poised to retire. Boomers outnumber Generation X employees by as much as 30 per cent, creating a labour shortage that employers will have to address, partly with Generation Y workers.

Not only will older workers need to manage the youthfulness of these workers, they will also need to manage rivalry between Generations X and Y: both will be vying for the baby-boomers' vacant positions. Generation X, the resentful, achievement-oriented entrepreneurs bred by downsizing of the 1980s, will not appreciate being leap-frogged as Generation Y earns fast promotions.

Younger workers bring opportunities and pitfalls. In spite of the recent downturn in the economy, competition for talent continues. Companies that understand the characteristics and motivations of Generation Y, and can manage the tensions in multi-generational organizations, will have a competitive advantage in attracting and retaining these employees.

## Implications

Managers at all levels must understand the expectations of the generations and use their strengths. Whereas Generations X and Y seek immediate recognition for successes, Boomers embrace the notion of "paying one's dues". Generations X and Y may appear ungrateful for opportunities, yet they cannot understand an organization's dedication to its "dead wood" (overpaid executives who seem unable to get things done). Boomers may view younger generations as slackers, always looking for free time. Younger generations are indignant when asked to do excessive overtime. Older generations might regard it as reasonable to entertain clients at home. The young have no such expectations – for them, work ends at the allotted hour.

There are benefits to the views of all generations, something that is not always easy to acknowledge. A company should identify how it can benefit from the expectations and values of each generation, and sell those benefits to others. To maintain the peace, however, assumptions about the organization and how it is understood by employees need to be modified and communicated. Everything, from the organization's vision to its human resources practices, needs to be evaluated for its message to the generations. Much of the "old way of doing things" is to be preserved, but much can benefit from a facelift.

### Vision

Vision statements may need more depth to motivate younger workers. Generations X and Y want to feel they are making a difference in people's lives or working for the good of society. Vision statements should include a value-driven component. For example, Ford updated its vision statement, which had been: "To become the world's leading consumer company that provides automotive products and services." It added: "In the process of meeting this vision, the company will focus on its customers, deliver superior shareholder returns and improve the quality of people's lives worldwide." This signals to younger workers that, at Ford, they are not just doing a job but also making a difference.

## Strategy

The vision for DuPont is to "dedicate ourselves daily to the work of improving life on our planet". To achieve this vision, the company has added "corporate citizenship" to its core competencies of "superior research and development" and "the ability to adapt".

Developing a competency in corporate citizenship means ensuring manufacturing policies include protection for the environment. Recruitment would focus on people whose values match those of the company. Performance appraisals would evaluate how well managers support environmental initiatives. Developing value-aligned strategies will demonstrate to younger workers that the organization follows through on these aspects of its vision.

## Communication

Younger workers communicate directly. They expect to be involved in decisions that affect them (much like they contributed to family decisions at the kitchen table). They seek direct access to leadership. Some organizations have responded by encouraging e-mail correspondence with top managers or scheduling online "chats" with the chief executive. Opportunities for direct upward communication are valued by these workers. Top-down communication processes are scrutinized by younger workers. They shun bureaucracy and politics and so do not enjoy power games. More concerned with doing their work so they can focus on other aspects of their lives, young workers want clear goals, adequate resources to do their job and for managers to let

them get the work done. For older workers used to politics and trading favours, this approach can appear naive. Younger workers wonder why companies let older workers waste so much time.

## Culture

In general, Generation Y is attracted to team-oriented cultures. Unlike members of Generation X, who are individualists and achievement-oriented, members of Generation Y prefer working with others and have a strong need for affiliation. Therefore, organizations should consider ways of encouraging team-oriented behaviour. These include designing offices to accommodate the sharing of ideas (placing desks in groups); assigning projects to groups of people who are evaluated on reaching the same goal; and ensuring that appraisals assess the team as well as the individual.

## Senior management

Younger workers admire honesty, integrity and ethical behaviour. They expect leaders to practise what they preach and see no distinction between levels within the organization when it comes to what is considered fair.

Companies that share the burden of salary cuts and redundancies across all levels are seen as more fair than those that target lower levels. The US government's agreement to bale out the country's airlines prohibits the use of the money for salary increases to executives earning $300,000 or more. Public response to this weak caveat was less than enthusiastic given the tens of thousands of employees expecting redundancy. The chairman and chief executive of American Airlines, perhaps sensing this, suspended his salary until the end of 2001.

Such gestures are not lost on young workers. Generation Y in particular is seeking a more

---

Generation Y in particular is seeking a more committed employment relationship and is looking for clues that everyone in the organization is in it together – for better or worse.

committed employment relationship and is looking for clues that everyone in the organization is in it together – for better or worse. If they are asked to follow rules that managers ignore, they will value the employment relationship less.

## HR systems

Managers should pay attention to the messages they convey when recruiting: the fairness of the appraisal system; the fairness of salaries and other rewards; and the apparent value placed on the individual when designing jobs and training systems.

### Hiring strategies

Young employees evaluate every step of the recruiting process, so organizations need to put their best foot forward at all times. Online advertising and targeted messages will be read by Generation X and Generation Y. Organizations may also want to send recruiting messages to their parents. A 2000 survey by the National Association of Colleges and Employers in the US found that 45 per cent of students say their parents' opinion of a potential employer is important. For a recent student recruiting effort, KPMG used posters featuring a picture of a middle-aged couple smiling into the camera. The text read: "Now that you've made your parents proud, join KPMG and give them something to really smile about."

Generation Y is used to older adults who spend time on nurturing them. Make them feel sought-after by having upper-level managers meet prospective candidates. Top managers who make time in their schedules demonstrate commitment to the candidate.

### Job design

When designing jobs, treat young workers as individuals who have specific goals. Managers should find out what is important to them. Based on these interests, employees should be given information on customizing their careers to give them control over their destiny and an understanding of opportunities. By giving them the tools to manage their own careers, managers will increase employees' commitment to the organization.

Baby-boomers often balk at asking what younger workers want. If open-ended questions are too threatening, give them choices. If the organization has selected them well, young workers' expectations should not be surprising or difficult to manage.

Defined goals and monitoring ensure inexperienced workers have early successes. Too much handholding can foster resentment, however. Give responsibility for manageable tasks to reduce errors and increase confidence. A focus on outcomes rather than processes will challenge and develop young employees.

### Training

Training should focus on specific skills needed to do the job as well as more general skills that can be used for developmental goals. Interactive training programmes that operate online can be customized, so allowing employees to learn at their own pace. Team-based training sessions allow employees to interact with their peers, a plus for Generation Y. Finally, mentoring programmes transfer institutional knowledge and reduce tension between generations by building understanding among workers.

### Performance appraisals

For young workers, the process of performance appraisal is as important as the outcome. Organizations should consider using a 360-degree appraisal process in which feedback is gathered from managers, peers, subordinates, customers and the individual. These assessments tend to feel fairer because they mitigate individual biases. Emphasis should be on employee development, especially the transferable skills that are a priority for young workers. They seek constant affirmation and feedback, suggesting annual reviews be supplemented with more frequent feedback. Informal talks, at least quarterly, help keep this group on track.

Generation Y is used to being applauded by adults and feels a pressure to excel. They may feel that any criticism is a sign of failure. Therefore, negative feedback should focus on behaviour that is under the employee's control and should describe how things can be improved. Boomers may feel this is taking too much time to stroke employees. However, frequent two-way communication is an oft-cited desire of all workers.

## Compensation and rewards

The carrot, not the stick, drives young workers to succeed. Traditional pay packages can be fraught with inconsistencies and unclear formulas. Further, in a survey conducted by Northwestern Mutual Life/Louis Harris, only a third of Generation Y respondents said salary was most important and many would not trade free time for higher pay and gruelling hours. Motivating young employees takes creativity and an appeal to their value systems.

To accommodate their varying interests, organizations can create flexible plans that allow employees to select benefits that are most important to them. Some benefits appeal directly to young workers: paid time off for voluntary work, days off to spend with family and friends, and tuition reimbursement. Non-monetary rewards carry weight as well. Consider memos of commendation that are copied to senior managers. Awards and gift vouchers show recognition without being costly. Young people need frequent feedback, but it need not blow the departmental budget.

## Start anywhere

A sixty-something graduate recently reflected: "We wanted what they want. We just felt we couldn't ask." Herein lies the truth: what young workers want isn't so different from what everyone else wants. However, young workers are asking for it. Granted, young workers can come to the workplace full of themselves and their ideas. And granted, they may not have the experience to manage or complete all of the ideas they bring. Having various generations working side by side can lead to stress and conflict. But it can also lead to creativity and opportunity.

The first step to making sure that generational differences work in favour of an organization is to acknowledge the differences. Then reassess the organization and the message it delivers to all of its employees through systems, policies and processes. Some of the changes that younger workers seek will be good for the organization as a whole.

## Further reading

Brooks, D. (2000) "The organisation kid", *The Atlantic Monthly*, April.

Coupland, D. (1996) *Generation X*, Abacus.

Howe, N. and Strauss, W. (2000) *Millennials Rising*, Vintage.

O'Reilly, B. (2000) "Today's kids", *Fortune*, July 24.

Zamke, R., Raines, C. and Filipczak, R. (2000) *Generations at Work*, Amacom.

# Law and **regulation**

# Contents

# Introduction to Part 7

**T**he story of employment law is one in which employees have, over the course of decades, won a succession of rights in the workplace. Any company wishing to carry out common tasks in HR – disciplining employees, adjudicating cases of discrimination, hiring staff or making them redundant – had better be well aware of the detail of laws that apply in all its territories, or face potentially protracted defeat in court. Globalization may be a powerful economic force, but it has yet to smooth out important distinctions in the world's legal systems.

# Employee rights and
## management wrongs

Dr Murray Fairclough is director of legal services at Abbey Legal Protection, a specialist provider of insured legal services.

Claire Birkinshaw is an employment solicitor and legal information manager at Abbey Legal Protection.

Employees enjoy more legal rights now than ever before. This makes it even more important for managers to know the law, say **Murray Fairclough** and **Claire Birkinshaw**.

The annual report of the Employment Tribunals Service shows that more than 130,000 claims were lodged by employees in the UK during 2000–01 – three times the number 10 years ago (*see* Table 1). The increase is due to new employment protection legislation and to a growing "compensation culture". Such trends are common to many countries and certain personnel issues are universally topical. These include disciplinary practice, discrimination and harassment, changing terms and conditions of employment, and redundancy. This article aims to encourage managers to familiarize themselves with the law and to take control of personnel matters. Failure to do so can prove costly.

| TABLE 1 | Employment tribunal applications |
| --- | --- |

| Year | Applications registered |
| --- | --- |
| 1990/91 | 43,243 |
| 1991/92 | 67,448 |
| 1992/93 | 71,821 |
| 1993/94 | 71,661 |
| 1994/95 | 80,061 |
| 1995/96 | 108,827 |
| 1996/97 | 88,910 |
| 1997/98 | 80,435 |
| 1998/99 | 91,913 |
| 1999/00 | 103,935 |
| 2000/01 | 130,408 |

Source: Employment Tribunals Service

# It is important to recognize that there is no global standard for employment contracts.

## The perils

Even the most reliable employees can cause problems and when they do, doing nothing is not an option. Ask the London Fire and Civil Defence Authority. It was recently ordered to pay £245,000 in damages to an employee for unlawful race discrimination. In the US, awards can be significantly greater. In August 2001, a New Jersey court affirmed a $1.6m jury verdict in favour of a male prison guard in a sexual harassment claim. In addition, in June a federal judge approved a $192m settlement of a class action on race discrimination brought by 2,000 African-American employees of Coca-Cola. These figures are not unusual. Ignorance is no defence, so managers must make sure they know employment law.

It is important to recognize that there is no global standard for employment contracts. Some jurisdictions, such as France, offer substantial protection for employees. Others, such as the US, offer considerably less in some areas of employment (for example, there are no statutory laws governing unfair dismissal) but significantly more in other areas (for example, US anti-discrimination laws are very broad).

Consider these scenarios:

- An employee with three years' service has a poor timekeeping record. His timekeeping has deteriorated over the past six months and he is now, on average, 20 minutes late each day. Informal counselling has failed to deliver any improvement.
- An employee has alleged that she is being sexually harassed by a fellow worker. The harassment is not blatant but it is unwanted.
- To keep up with competitors, staff hours need to change so that a call centre can be staffed round the clock rather than just during normal business hours.
- As a result of economic downturn, a business in the food production industry needs to shed more than 100 staff out of a workforce of 1,000.

Would your HR department know what to do in each of these cases?

Employment laws generally require both a just cause for termination and due process (for example, consultation and pre-dismissal meetings). In the UK, this is known as substantive and procedural fairness. In France, an employee can be dismissed only for a "real and serious" cause. In Sweden, dismissal requires "just cause" and in Germany, for businesses with more than five employees, dismissals of workers with more than six months of service must be "socially justified".

However, in the US, the practice of "at-will employment" covers about 80 per cent of employees. This means they can be fired at any time, for any or no reason. Other US employees have what are effectively fixed-term contracts, promising either employment for a specified period or to discharge the employee only for specific reasons. Whatever the contract, the employment relationship is seen as a private arrangement.

Bearing that in mind, consider again the four scenarios above.

## Disciplinary practice

All employers have problem staff. Some employees are a perennial problem, others may occasionally allow personal problems to affect their work, conduct or performance. It is clear these employees cannot be left to "get on with it" in the hope that their conduct or performance will get better. More likely, their behaviour will start to harm the business.

The solution lies in improvement, by effective disciplinary procedures. Disciplining an employee is an uncomfortable exercise. Procedures should not be viewed as a way of imposing sanctions. Rather, they should be seen as helping people whose conduct or performance is unsatisfactory to improve. Some businesses will have a separate procedure for performance issues, others will deal with all issues of conduct and performance through a single disciplinary procedure. Either way, it is important that the procedure is fair and is followed in a consistent, professional manner.

In the UK, employers with 20 or more staff have to specify disciplinary rules to go with the statutory written terms of employment. The Advisory

Conciliation and Arbitration Service (Acas) has produced a code of practice that sets out what a fair disciplinary procedure should include. In short, Acas recommends that allegations should be thoroughly investigated. The employee should receive details of the allegations in advance of any hearing and be given an opportunity to explain what happened and any mitigating factors. Recent UK legislation also allows the employee to bring either a trade union official or a fellow employee to the hearing. Finally, other than in cases of potential gross misconduct, a fair warnings procedure should be followed, comprising a verbal warning, a written warning, a final written warning and dismissal. Failure to follow a fair procedure may result in an otherwise fair dismissal being declared unfair by a tribunal. In the UK, the general rule is that employees with one or more years of continuous service with their employer can claim for unfair dismissal.

In Italy, disciplinary and grievance rules are statutory, requiring a disciplinary code to be displayed. The employee must be notified in writing about problems and be given five days to produce justifications. Sanctions vary from a verbal warning to dismissal, according to the nature of the breach and the employee's record.

In the US, there is no legal requirement to have a disciplinary procedure and to do so may be unduly burdensome on the "at will" relationship. That said, most employers will still wish to treat staff fairly and consistently by adopting non-contractual disciplinary procedures. In this respect, the UK provides a useful model.

Finally, documentation is the key to defending an employment claim, so managers should ensure the employee's personnel file is in order and contains the paperwork relating to appraisals, meetings, counselling sessions and disciplinary hearings.

And the "golden rule" is this: never try to counsel or discipline an employee when you are angry or upset.

## Discrimination

Much of the discrimination law in the European Union is derived from directives and the Treaty of Rome. The EU has become much more interven-

tionist in the area of equal treatment and directives have been approved that will soon be making their way into the national laws of member states. In the US, federal laws cover discrimination in areas such as gender, disability and age.

In particular, sexual harassment claims are on the increase. These are often expensive to resolve and they damage morale. Therefore managers should take measures to ensure harassment does not happen. The first step is to understand what sexual harassment is. Harassment is unwelcome physical contact or sexual advances. It usually creates a hostile environment. Examples include sexual innuendo, uninvited touching, comments of a sexual nature, requests for sexual favours and sexual jokes or pictures.

In the UK and the US, employees can claim harassment even if they have never complained to a manager. Employers can be liable even though they did not know harassment was taking place. Finally, there is no requirement for the employee to suffer tangible job detriment, such as loss of promotion or dismissal.

So, managers must have an effective anti-harassment policy and a complaints procedure with clear directions for reporting workplace conduct. The policy should not just be distributed or pinned on notice boards; staff should be given regular training on behaviour. The policy should inform staff that workplace harassment based on sex or some other protected classification will result in disciplinary action. Having such a policy will create a more business-like environment and reduce the likelihood of an employee succeeding in a claim. When complaints are made, employers must respond promptly, treat them seriously, investigate and take action.

Dealing with such claims is time-consuming, costly if lawyers are involved and can result in large damages against employers. While

While implementing policies takes time and effort, the litigation and liability costs of successful harassment claims mean that prevention is better than cure.

implementing policies takes time and effort, the litigation and liability costs of successful harassment claims mean that prevention is better than cure. In the UK, the burden of proof has recently been reversed for sex discrimination claims, so that once an employee proves facts giving rise to a prima facie case of discrimination, the burden of proof then shifts to the employer. In effect, the company must prove its innocence.

By comparison, in the US, employers can be held liable for same-sex harassment and harassment based on race, age, religion, national origin and disability. In the UK, there is no protection against discrimination on grounds of age, sexual orientation and religion (except Northern Ireland, which has laws on religious discrimination) but this is set to change as a result of the EU's Equal Treatment Directive.

## Changing terms

While the contract of employment will set out the terms of the relationship between employer and employee, it must comply with the law. For example, as a result of the Working Time Directive, employees within the EU must be given at least four weeks of paid annual leave. In the US, federal and state wage laws set overtime and minimum wage provisions. If workers are paid hourly, they are entitled to overtime pay of one and a half times their hourly rate for weekly work in excess of 40 hours.

In most countries, an employment contract is legally binding. This means any changes should either be in accordance with the contract or be agreed by the employee. In the UK, employees with one year's service can claim constructive dismissal if an employer changes a fundamental term of the contract and the employee resigns as a result. It follows that contracts should expressly provide that the employer is free to change the terms at any time. However, UK courts do not like such a broad approach and will interpret flexibility clauses restrictively. This is because there is an implied obligation not to act in a way that destroys trust. As a result, clauses permitting changes must be specific and reasonable.

In many jurisdictions, employers must consult works councils before changing terms or making redundancies. In Germany, these play a significant role in dismissals.

## Redundancies

Redundancy law has rarely been more topical. Following the terrorist attacks in the US in September 2001, Sabena failed and Swissair was on the verge of bankruptcy. KLM axed 2,500 jobs and British Airways 7,200 jobs. The US government gave the airline industry more than £10bn to see it through the crisis. Only time will tell whether the airlines will recover.

Employee termination – even in times of economic difficulty – always presents a risk of legal action. In the US, actions frequently take the form of discrimination claims (for example, an employee has been selected over another because of a protected characteristic), claims for failure to keep promises on compensation, claims for back wages and accrued holidays, and claims for failure to provide notice. In most cases, decisions that give rise to employment litigation are not ill-intended, rather they usually lie in simple ignorance of the law. Even the largest employers can fail to effect redundancies properly. In 2001, employees from Marks and Spencer's European outlets protested against plans to close its 38 European stores. A challenge in French courts was successful because M&S had failed to consult employees. Closure of the French stores had to be suspended for consultation. Under French law, injunctions in these circumstances are available. In the UK, they are not.

Reductions in the number of staff should be carefully planned and decisions communicated in a sensitive way. All issues relating to selection should be documented and employers must be consistent in their selection policies and in the procedure they use for carrying out redundancies. In the UK, there are three elements to redundancy: consultation, fair selection and consideration of suitable alternative employment. Ignoring any of these can result in an unfair dismissal claim. In Germany, employers must observe "social considerations". This means they must examine whether the selected person deserves less social protection than comparable employees. Social selection is related to length of service, age and the duty of the employee to support a family. Any employee who is unfairly selected and dismissed is entitled to bring proceedings, with reinstatement as the likely remedy. In Sweden, provisions are similar and redundant employees have priority rights to re-employment.

Of course, employers can "buy out" potential claims with termination payments. Such agreements must comply with the legal formalities and be carefully drafted. They may be invalid unless, for example, the employee has had independent legal advice.

## Conclusion

Companies that fail to comply with employment laws take serious legal risks. If the potential liability for compensation or damages were not enough, time spent in defending a claim distracts managers and legal fees pose a significant cost. Yet in spite of the costs, companies continue to break the law. Given that workers are becoming more familiar with the law and less tolerant of corporate misdemeanours, it seems safe to say that the number of claims will continue to rise. It may be a daunting task but managers need to ensure they keep abreast of the relevant laws and that they comply with them.

## Further reading

Acas (2000) Code of Practice on Disciplinary and Grievance Procedures (http://www.acas.org.uk/publications/pub_cop.html)

Blanplain, R. (2000) European Labour Law, The Hague: Kluwer Law.

Employment Tribunals Service (2001) Annual Report 2000-01, Stationery Office (http://www.clicktso.com).

Mayne, S. and Malyon, S. (eds) (2000) Employment Law in Europe, Oxford: Butterworths.

# HR practice:
## vive la différence

Mark Fenton-O'Creevy is a senior lecturer in organizational behaviour at the Open University Business School.

Various forms of capitalism across Europe influence the way relations between workers and employers are managed. **Mark Fenton-O'Creevy** sees little likelihood of a common approach in the near future.

Since the collapse of the Soviet Union, it has become common for commentators to declare "victory" for the capitalist system of economic and political organization. However, there is no universal form of capitalism. Even within Europe, one can find strikingly different forms. These differences influence the way human resource management is practised. This article reviews some distinctive forms and their consequences for HR.

In the UK, economic development has been marked (as in the US) by early industrialization and a long period of market development and capital accumulation. Hence the UK economy is characterized by the operation of markets. Relatively unconstrained labour markets have meant companies adjusting to demand by hiring and dismissing workers. This has relied to an extent on narrow job definitions and relatively generic skill sets, so that workers might be seen as a substitutable resource. Efficient capital markets have encouraged an arm's-length relationship between owners and managers. The UK labour market features job mobility, little legally mandated job security and, to some extent, low skill levels. There has been an emphasis on managerial autonomy and little employee representation by law.

In contrast, the Rhineland model seeks to balance the interests of company owners with those of other stakeholders. The exemplar is Germany, although it also applies, in a form, to the Netherlands and Belgium. In Germany, there is political commitment to a social market economy and social partnership. In practice, this means highly influential and centralized employers' organizations and unions, both of which influence HR policies.

The German economy developed later than that of the UK and has therefore had less advanced capital markets. Banks have been more important in supplying capital and have tended to develop long-term relationships with companies. Such relationships have led to a longer-term view of financial objectives. Another feature of the German economy is the set of employee relations institutions that developed out of the need for industrial peace during post-war reconstruction. Perhaps the most important element is the system of "peak bargaining", whereby wages and conditions for each sector are negotiated by employers' associations and trade unions. Wage bargaining is taken out of the workplace, so reducing tension. Employee representatives sit on the supervisory board of companies and *betriebsräte* (works councils) have the right to information, consultation or joint decision making on many HR issues.

Scandinavian countries also have less managerial autonomy in respect of HR issues, largely by virtue of strong labour unions. Changes in employment practices are subject to bipartite agreements, with the state acting both as a mediator and a guarantor. A legal framework ensures that conflicts are resolved at the company level. Labour unions are legally entitled to be consulted on issues such as mergers, downsizing and outsourcing. The Scandinavian model preserves the rights of labour unions to withdraw co-operation in the case of a dispute with management. However, the security granted by the national framework of government-backed agreements makes it possible for unions to get involved in developing collaborative agreements to improve the company's effectiveness.

The French model is different again. Although unions have significant power – often disproportionate to their membership – the scope of their powers is restricted. There is a tradition of managerial autonomy and even autocracy, based around an elite of managers educated in the *grandes écoles*. However, government legislation restricts managerial autonomy in many areas of HR practice (such as training and the use of temporary workers). Personnel departments must

> There is a tradition of managerial autonomy and even autocracy, based around an elite of managers educated in the *grandes écoles*.

maintain good relations with the Inspection du Travail, a public body that enforces employment legislation, particularly with regard to temporary labour. Unionization is only slightly higher than 10 per cent but French law extends collective bargaining agreements to non-unionized workers. Consequently, personnel departments devote considerable resources to detailed wage bargaining and to ensuring regulatory compliance.

Each model has strengths and weaknesses, and different implications for HR management. Supporters of the Anglo-American model often suggest that greater management autonomy aids international competitiveness because companies can respond more flexibly to market conditions. Critics suggest this flexibility has an unacceptable social cost in job insecurity. Also, they suggest that long-term competitiveness is damaged because unconstrained markets do not lead to sufficient investment in training or capital equipment.

There is evidence that the constraints within European economies (the Rhineland model in particular) have caused companies to take a longer-term view and to invest in both skills and equipment as an alternative approach to flexibility. However, this may be at the expense of both flexibility and employment levels.

## US influence

US models of HRM have influenced practices in Europe, through US multinationals and US business schools. The US approach seeks to match management of human inputs with company strategy. Two elements of this can be identified: hard and soft.

The "hard" approach considers people as another variable factor of production. Behaviour is managed in line with strategic goals. Practices include appraisal, performance-related pay and evaluation of training for contribution to strategic goals. Such an "individualized" approach is difficult where wages and conditions are determined collectively or where there is strong regulation of HR practice.

The "soft" approach also seeks to align employee behaviour with strategic goals. However, rather than being seen as passive resources, employees are seen as active partners whose creativity and commitment are vital to success. This approach is typified by attempts to build commitment and manage culture. Practices include employee involvement and communication about vision and strategy.

Research suggests that the extent of US influence on Europe varies considerably. Academic Paul Gooderham and colleagues used data from the Cranet study of European HR to look at adoption of the hard and soft models (*see* Figure 1). They found the UK to be closest to the US model (high on both dimensions). The decline of union power and lack of legal constraint has made it easy for companies to introduce individualized performance management. Also, professionalization of the personnel function has influenced the adoption of policies designed to link employee behaviour to strategic goals.

Germany came lowest on both dimensions. Here, wages and working hours are determined by unions and employers' associations. Employee relations matters are often subject to negotiation through works councils. Personnel departments focus on works councils and rarely have a strategic role. So, personnel managers play little part in developing communication about strategic objectives.

France scored high on the hard dimension. Unions have little power to block practices but do affect the role of personnel managers. Resources are devoted to complex (often hostile) industrial relations negotiations, leaving little scope for building commitment and aligning culture to strategy.

In Denmark and Norway, there was little adoption of the hard model but considerable use of the soft. Co-operation between companies and unions at a local level and high union membership make it difficult to introduce individualized performance management. However, the Scandinavian system has tended to support practices designed to enhance partnership and commitment to common goals.

In terms of legislation, Spain could be characterized as fitting the Rhineland model. However, there is a tradition of managerial autonomy and unions are weak. So Spain tends to fall closer to the UK than to Germany.

## Sources of diversity

Several factors contribute to the diversity of HR practices in European countries. Academics Paul Sparrow and Jean-Marie Hiltrop identify industry

**FIGURE 1** | Adoption of strategic HRM models

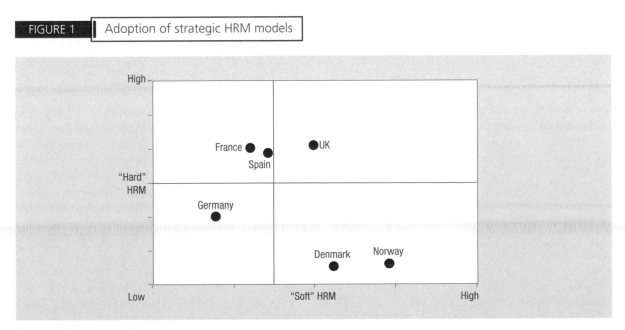

*Source*: Adaption from Gooderham *et al*.

> While a senior manager from industry might be recruited into a senior role in a bank in the UK, this would be considered bizarre in Germany.

structure, institutional structures, culture and differences in the role and development of personnel managers. First, industry structures differ. For example, the economic role played by small companies varies greatly. Small companies tend to have far fewer formalized HR policies. While small companies are less significant in the UK, in Italy about 70 per cent of workers in the industrialized private sector are employed in companies of 100 people or less. The role of the public sector also varies. In some countries (such as Spain and Italy) HR policies in the public sector have been explicitly used as instruments of social policy.

Second, economic and political institutions set an important context for HR policies. Many of these relate to different models of capitalism. Relevant institutions include employers' associations, labour unions, welfare systems and tax regimes. Third, national cultures can have significant effects. For example, there are differences in the understanding of managerial work in France, Germany and the UK. The Anglo-American notion of management as a set of skills that is separable from its context is not shared in Germany. While a senior manager from industry might be recruited into a senior role in a bank in the UK, this would be considered bizarre in Germany. In France, managers are expected to have had an intellectually rigorous training in the elite *grandes écoles*. Management is seen to require intellectual rather than interpersonal skills.

Finally, the role of personnel managers may differ. In Germany, the relationship with works councils encourages personnel managers to concentrate on operational issues. There is also an emphasis on legal skills, as there is in France. However, here, as in the UK, there has been a professionalization of the personnel function and managers have tried to link HR practice to company strategy. In contrast, in Italy and the Netherlands many personnel managers have a financial background.

## Convergence

While it is clear that there are many reasons for diversity of HR practice among European countries, there are also forces for convergence. The extent of globalization is sometimes exaggerated. However, there is no doubt that companies operating in different countries face common competitive environments. This is particularly true within the EU. In the face of common pressures there is a tendency to adopt similar HR solutions.

Research suggests that multinationals do not always seek to standardize HR practices internationally. Nonetheless, they are often important in disseminating practices among countries. Often this will be via expatriate managers or a central advisory HR function rather than a head-office diktat. However, some companies do impose a common model (more commonly US-owned companies).

Management education is also an important mechanism for the dissemination of ideas. Here US schools have been an important influence. European schools have tended to reinforce the US model rather than develop a distinctive European approach.

## EU legislation

One driver for EU action that affects HR practices is the concern to remove barriers to the movement of goods, services and people. For example, the European Commission is keen to harmonize the acceptance of national qualifications in different states. Much legislation relevant to human resource management arises out of the social agenda of the EU. The Commission is charged with pursuing a social agenda as part of economic and political union. The underlying assumptions of the social agenda are closer to those of the Rhineland model than to those of the Anglo-American approach.

There is a strong assumption in EU policy making that markets need to be tempered with adequate social protection and that the interests of owners need to be balanced with those of other stakeholders. The Commission promotes social justice, especially where there is evidence that countries may seek competitive advantage by adopting lower levels of social protection (known as social dumping). EU legislation has affected HR practices in areas such as:

- parental leave;
- working periods and paid leave;
- part-time workers;
- collective redundancy;
- transfer of an undertaking or business from one employer to another;
- informing and consulting with employees in multinationals;
- fixed-term contracts.

To take effect, EU directives must be adopted by national legislation. The principle of subsidiarity requires that the detail of implementation be left to the lowest appropriate level. In practice this means that legislation may be treated very differently under different national systems. A good example is the Working Time Directive, adopted by the Social Affairs Council of the EU in November 1993. The main provisions of this directive are to limit maximum hours of working (48 hours per week) and to provide minimum entitlements for rest periods and paid leave. It could be argued that this EU legislation is a force for convergence. In practice implementation has been diverse and is interesting for what it reveals about different national systems.

Under German law, the 1994 Working Time Statute establishes an eight-hour working day, although, subject to an average of eight hours per day over a six-month period, employers may extend the day up to 10 hours. Variations to this can be negotiated between employers and unions for a company or sector. In the Netherlands and Belgium there is a national framework, but agreements are negotiated between employers' associations and unions in each sector. In France the so-called "Aubry" law enacted in 1998 limits the working week to 35 hours, sets an annual limit on overtime of 130 hours, and sets a maximum of 10 hours per day and six days per week.

In the UK, the Working Time Regulations were ratified in 1998. The government took advantage of provisions in the directive that allow the exclusion of some groups of workers and adopted the minimum provisions. In particular, the UK was the only member state to allow individuals to opt out of the limits on working time. There is evidence that a high proportion of UK companies have made use of these individual opt-out agreements. This is partially accounted for by some organizations putting illegitimate pressure on employees to opt out, but much pressure for opt-outs has come from employees not wishing to give up overtime earnings.

So, the basic models of capitalism are reflected in implementations of the Working Time Directive. In the UK there is a continuation of the liberal voluntarist tradition with minimal legislation; in France strong government action; in Germany, the Netherlands and Belgium, emphasis on sectoral dialogue and a high standard of social protection.

## Conclusions

In any country, HR practices are embedded in complex social, economic and political structures. These structures have arisen out of particular sets of historical circumstances and lead to diversity within the EU.

There are forces for convergence, not least the ever closer economic and political union, but convergence is not automatic. Because they are embedded in wider institutions, HR practices do not always work when transferred to a new environment. Legislation and agreements at an EU level are bringing about some convergence. However, it is clear that different national implementations reflect the diversity of socio-economic systems within the EU. It seems unlikely that any Europe-wide enterprise will, in the near future, be able to implement a single set of HR practices across its European operations.

## Further reading

Adnett, N. and Hardy, S. (2001) "Reviewing the working time directive: rationale implementation and case law", *Industrial Relations Journal*, 32, 2.

Flood, P., Heraty, N., Morley, M. and McCurtin, S. (eds) (1997) *The European Union and the Employment Relationship*, Dublin: Oak Tree Press.

Gooderham, P., Nordag, O. and Ringdal, K. (1999) "Institutional and rational determinants of organizational practices: Human resource management in European companies", *Administrative Science Quarterly*, 44, 3.

Sparrow, P. and Hiltrop, J.M. (1994) *European Human Resource Management in Transition*, London: Prentice-Hall.

# Myths and
## methods of downsizing

Larry W. Hunter is an assistant professor of management at the Wharton School of the University of Pennsylvania.

There is little evidence that job cuts improve financial performance, yet in a recession they may be the only way for companies to survive. **Larry Hunter** examines the difficulties of downsizing.

Perhaps surprisingly, evidence suggests that companies which down-size achieve no financial gains and, in many cases, the aftermath of job cuts leads to poor performance and pressure to cut even more jobs.

Many academic studies have looked for evidence that downsizing leads to improvements in financial performance. The results are mixed, due in part to the difficulty of separating out several distinct phenomena. For example, in the case of a company confronting falling demand for its products, downsizing looks like the only way to survive. Asking whether this sort of lay-off might lead to positive results puts the question backwards. Lay-offs result from financial difficulties; it is unsurprising, then, that researchers have had difficulty attributing financial recovery to the lay-offs rather than changes in market conditions.

As academic Peter Cappelli notes, however, "downsizing" in its contemporary form reverses the traditional, demand-driven formulation, as companies, beginning in the 1980s, sought to improve operating efficiency by cutting jobs, even with serial execution of such programmes, even in good times. These efforts were very different from demand-based lay-offs. Executives and consultants described them using euphemisms, such as "rightsizing", "re-engineering", "restructuring" and "corporate renewal".

Studies assessing the effects of these kinds of initiatives offer little to suggest, on the whole, that they improved financial performance. Cappelli himself, in a study conducted with David Neumark, found that gains from these kinds of initiatives were scarce. Stock markets may react positively to downsizing announcements in the very short run, particularly when such announcements are coupled with a credible plan for improving performance. However, there is scant evidence to suggest that on average, long-run financial performance or stock prices are improved by job cuts.

> There is scant evidence to suggest that on average, long-run financial performance or stock prices are improved by job cuts.

Of course, looking for average effects reminds one of the statistician who had his head in an oven and his feet in a bucket of ice and on average felt just fine. These studies do not distinguish between companies that do downsizing well and those that do it poorly. Neither do most of them consider whether the companies that downsize might have problems that were more deeply entrenched and difficult to attack. In addition, these two phenomena are probably related: deeply rooted problems may be largely the result of poor management and there is surely no reason to expect companies with weak management to carry out downsizing effectively.

## Qualified losses

It is important to note that much of the downsizing, job cuts and the like that we read about do not require any lay-offs. Hiring freezes or slowdowns, when combined with natural attrition, may cut the workforce and associated labour costs. For example, nursing homes rarely lay off nurses because turnover of nursing assistants is so high that they don't need to. And when was the last time you heard of a lay-off at a local McDonald's? These are extreme examples, but when your competitors appear to be slashing jobs, it is important to understand just what they are slashing. Sometimes, it turns out, job "cuts" may even refer to the elimination of planned new positions – this gives the impression that jobs are being cut, even though total employment stays the same or grows.

Over the past decade, articles have often told of the demize of lifetime employment in Japan. The job security that large Japanese companies gave their core workforces supported practices that helped them compete effectively: good union relations; flexibility in deployment of employees; loyalty; extensive training investments; and joint approaches to solving problems. However, the Japanese model has fallen into disrepute: some of its rigidities have been revealed and its vaunted employment guarantees have begun to look more like a Ponzi scheme requiring continued growth in market share to be sustained.

Yet consider other ways in which these companies managed their employees. They typically protected their core workforce from economic shocks with layers of other workers. Older workers, those in smaller companies and women had little job security. When demand contracted, employers shed contractors and part-timers. Although these companies have been struggling for a decade, they have been able to cling to their core workforces and practices.

While the wisdom of this approach can be questioned, it is clear that Japanese companies have protected their "lifetime" employees tenaciously. More often than not, a story about a large Japanese company downsizing is not about core employees losing jobs. Rather, it refers to a hiring freeze, to reassignment from one division to another, or to a group of workers who had formally retired already and were genuinely being asked to leave for good.

Companies that aim to downsize successfully might think through the lessons from this approach. Tasks that can be pulled in from contractors and reassigned to core employees, for example, prevent companies from having to make lay-offs. Similarly, where core employees can be shifted around to parts of the business that are growing, or likely to grow, the need for lay-offs can be minimized.

Buy-outs and voluntary departures can also make things easier. However, as Japanese companies have found, this can be a very slow way to restructure in a rapidly changing world. Hiring freezes and reliance on attrition come with their own costs: it is difficult to infuse new skills and abilities into an organization when you're not hiring. Relying on attrition alone is particularly risky: in this mode, organizations are purely reactive. And asking for volunteers to leave the organization runs the risk that the most able employees leave. Intel Ireland, for example, found that its voluntary redundancy programme was oversubscribed.

## Why downsize?

Nevertheless, some companies do manage to downsize effectively and some themes can be identified among them. Effective downsizing requires clarity of purpose, credibility and clear communication of that purpose. Companies seeking to cut jobs in response to market-driven downturns, for example, can make this clear and credible by setting out straightforward criteria for re-employment should the company see its market recover. Failure to do so leads employees to suspect, often with good reason, that the market is being used as a scapegoat for other kinds of changes and in turn leads to a scepticism that makes it difficult to implement those changes.

On the other hand, companies may also seek to downsize as a way of changing the mix of skills and attributes of their workforces. In this view, downsizing can be a small part of a strategy of continuous improvement and renewal. Again, clear communication of this strategy and its underlying rationale is critical – employees, with good reason, will want to know how they fit into the plan, and if not, what they might do about it.

A third rationale is one taken by companies that begin with far-flung, unfocused empires and wish to concentrate on core competencies: adopting a "core-plus-contractor" model. Companies that have not previously given this model much thought are quite likely to discover that not all employees belong in the core. One version of this approach can be seen in many of the decisions taken by Jack Welch during his time at General Electric. Early in his tenure, Welch was known as "Neutron Jack" – he got rid of employees and left only the buildings intact. But over time, employees came to understand the logic of Welch's plans and the kinds of efforts it would take to save their jobs.

Managers might find any or all of these approaches necessary given their understanding of markets and the competitive challenges they face. None of the approaches, however, is likely to be successful if its execution is muddled. One might imagine good reasons to mask a market-based lay-off under the guise of restructuring, or vice versa. However, when employees sniff out these ruses, the consequences can be devastating.

## Facing employees

Nevertheless, many managers are faced with making lay-offs. Most employers find this process difficult and distasteful: the fall from grace of "Chainsaw Al" Dunlap, former chief executive of Sunbeam in the US, has certainly discouraged executives from crowing about making such cuts.

Many, though not all, of the problems of downsizing can be associated with low levels of trust between those making the decisions and those on the receiving end. Generally, a convincing rationale for initiating downsizing is immensely helpful. It should give objective reasons for choosing the specific positions eliminated and people dismissed, and clearly communicate these reasons and criteria.

There is a prerequisite here, however: such a rationale must exist. If, in the process of developing it, managers conclude that downsizing is a poor way forward, so much the better for all concerned. Workers keep their jobs and managers avoid the headaches. Yet that may not always be the case. Some organizations do face significant market downturns; others find themselves with a mix of human resources that leaves them unable to compete effectively. What should they do?

Interestingly, there is little persuasive evidence that downsizing requires detailed, up-front planning. In fact, a study I conducted with academics Clint Chadwick and Steve Walston suggests the opposite. Of more than 100 hospitals that went through restructuring, the study found that careful, pre-designed downsizing was associated with poorer subsequent performance. Hospital executives suggested that this was plausible. Those with detailed redundancy plans locked themselves into procedures that did not address deeper problems. In contrast, those that focused on strategic challenges were able to let details emerge in talks with employees.

More generally, such plans may be flawed because they rely on organizational charts and fail to take into account the importance of informal employee networks. When downsizing pulls individuals out of important places in such networks, whether voluntarily or involuntarily, the results can be devastating. As academics Debra Dougherty and the late Ned Bowman showed,

> No kind words can entirely overcome the fact that people do not like to lose their jobs. Even when monetary losses are not pronounced, there are psychological blows.

downsizing can disrupt networks that are crucial for sustained performance, such as those that permit innovation. In fact, the human side of downsizing is more important than detailed planning. No kind words can entirely overcome the fact that people do not like to lose their jobs. Even when monetary losses are not pronounced, there are psychological blows.

It might seem easy for employees to rationalize lay-offs caused by economic slumps: the fact that they have lost their jobs does not reflect on their individual worth. Such processes may be more debilitating than straightforward dismissals for performance failures: lay-offs can induce a sense of helplessness or loss of control that can be stressful and de-motivating. Understanding this is an important first step in approaching downsizing.

Managers themselves occupy a peculiar position with respect to downsizing. Specific people, not disembodied forces, design and carry out lay-offs. Yet managers are also on the receiving end. Their jobs and responsibilities change, and they and their colleagues are often targets of job cutting. Indeed, shrinking the supposedly bloated ranks of "middle management" is frequently central to job-cutting. Understanding that managers play these twin roles is also central to any sensible approach to downsizing.

While support for dismissed employees may be important, problems with remaining employees are more likely to be at the heart of difficulties in achieving performance goals after downsizing. Downsizing greatly affects the remaining employees and the methods managers choose to carry out lay-offs carry powerful messages to the survivors about their relationships with their employer.

The degree of dignity and compassion afforded to colleagues during termination affects the way survivors expect they will be treated. Practical guides to redundancy often advise hustling employees off the premises, keeping them away from their remaining colleagues, and generally ensuring that they are not able to damage the company. Managers applying such guidelines will find that such violations of employees' dignity arouse feelings of compassion and indignation among those remaining. Similarly, organizations sometimes avoid giving much advance notice. But this allows rumours to fester and is disrespectful. Advance notice allows dismissed employees time to explore options, gives time for both survivors and terminated employees to adjust to the changes, and sends a message of concern to survivors.

Procedural fairness is also important. Survivors will react negatively to downsizing that appears to be imposed arbitrarily, especially when employees were strongly committed to the company. A number of studies – in particular those of academic Joel Brockner and colleagues – have shown that remaining employees' perceptions of fairness during lay-offs have a number of effects on subsequent effort and performance.

However, what is unfair in one company may be reasonable in another. For example, demands to reduce "headcount" (rather than cost) may result in dismissed employees returning to work, with more pay, as contractors. This seems bizarre. Yet if the goal is not to retrench but to transform the mix of core and contract workers, and this is understood, such policies may make more sense.

## Survivors

Regardless of how clear and credible the lines of communication, downsizing is likely to increase stress and lead to feelings of insecurity among survivors. Further stress is likely to result from demands to increase productivity, from the struggle to adapt to job changes and from changes in structure. It is folly to think the sources of this stress can be made to disappear: better productivity, employee re-assignments and organizational changes are exactly what are needed to make downsizing effective.

Here, too, research by Brockner and others is helpful: not all insecurity caused by downsizing is a bad thing. Survivors do not want to be targeted for the next round, so they can be motivated. Moderate levels of insecurity, in fact, can help – but not high levels. When people remain insecure in spite of their best efforts, motivation suffers. Such employees will redirect their attention from the good of the company to protecting themselves.

After more than a decade of downsizing, US employees now understand that they cannot count on guarantees of continued employment. Europeans are coming to the same conclusion. As Peter Cappelli points out, their employers have been insistent on this point and employees have taken the lesson to heart, reciprocating with job-hopping and lower commitment of their own, particularly in the tight labour markets of the 1990s. Few sensible employees expect better treatment when unemployment rises; rather, with diminished opportunity, they are likely to become even more concerned with protecting themselves. Cappelli suggests that even if employers want to look to longer-term promises of employment, employees will not find such promises credible.

So, employers should consider ways to provide more global security even as they generate local insecurity, by assessing employees' interest in skill development. Employees who believe that their organizations are committed to keeping them employable will reciprocate with greater commitment. Such organizations may also be more likely to retain valued workers who have good labour market options.

The circumstances that lead to cost-cutting may make it difficult for companies to focus on staff development: short-term exigencies make taking a broader perspective difficult. Such challenges are intensified by the difficulty employers have in listening to employees to make sure they understand what kinds of skills are desired and few structures exist for these kinds of informed exchanges. To take an example, in a recent study of employees in call centres, my colleagues Steffanie Wilk, Rosemary Batt and I found that people had a clear idea of the skills they needed to advance both inside and outside their organizations. In particular, they knew that general

technical skills and experience with a range of computer applications would help. Yet their organizations provided them only with training to do their current jobs. These employers, should they take the decision to downsize, will find a workforce that is frightened and resistant.

## Conclusions

There is an irony here. Managers may in fact realize that approaches other than job cuts may be better solutions for the problems that they face. Yet markets and analysts make demands and job cuts are a quick way to hit financial targets. Overall, however, evidence suggests that this approach is unlikely to bear dividends even in the medium term and investors seem to understand that downsizing is not a panacea for poor performance.

Clarity of purpose, credible, two-way communication and attention to the psychological and economic well-being of employees are hallmarks of effective downsizing. This should not be a surprise: these characteristics reflect good strategic and human resource management. Organizations that downsize skilfully are likely to be well managed and it would be surprising if those that are badly managed could master such a process.

## Further reading

Brockner, J., Grover, S., Reed, T.F. and Dewitt, R.L. (1992) "Lay-offs, job insecurity, and survivors' work effort: evidence of an inverted-U relationship", *Academy of Management Journal*, June.

Cappelli, P. (1999) *The New Deal at Work: Managing the market-driven work force*, Boston: Harvard Business School Press.

Cascio, W.F. (1993) "Downsizing: What do we know? What have we learned?", *The Academy of Management Executive*, February.

Dougherty, D. and Bowman, E.H. (1995) "The effects of organisational downsizing on product innovation", *California Management Review*, 37, 4.

Pfeffer, J. (1998) *The Human Equation*, Boston: Harvard Business School Press.

# Upholding standards
## for ethical practice

Without a base of norms and values companies can end up with commercial and legal problems. **Peter Dean** sets out a way to establish a practical set of principles.

Dr Peter J. Dean is a lecturer at the Wharton School of the University of Pennsylvania and the Fels Center of Government at the University of Pennsylvania.

How can managers choose the right course of action when planning and making decisions? One way is to set ethical standards in their work practices. Such guidelines, governing areas as diverse as integrity, production and accounting, can be used by all managers, in particular those whose responsibilities include the health, welfare and protection of company stakeholders.

A few examples demonstrate how such standards might help. In 1985 Martin Marietta Corporation, now Lockheed Martin, the US aerospace and defence contractor, was under investigation for improper travel expenses. The investigation prompted managers to create an internal programme of standards governing integrity in working practices. After they had implemented the programme, employees at Martin Marietta reported better morale among the workforce and improved, sustainable relationships with many suppliers and other stakeholders.

In 1988, managers at NovaCare, then called InSpeech, one of the largest providers of rehabilitation services to hospitals and nursing homes in the US, found an annual 57 per cent turnover rate among staff. One of the explanations they gave for this was that the company lacked a common and explicit set of values. In response, managers created guidelines describing the company's purpose, fundamental beliefs and principles. Over the next decade, employee turnover reduced to 27 per cent, with executives reporting that the statement of values had made a significant difference.

Ethics are important for individuals as well as for organizations. If ethical practice is not responsibly acknowledged and housed somewhere in the organization with a plan to create an ethical culture, executives run the risk of liability. If an organization lacks a sense of responsible behaviour, personal choices and decisions on the job will begin to slide. Put a good person in an unethical environment and the environment will usually triumph over the individual. By requiring an active ethical effort, not just legal compliance, standards can lead to more than just the reduction of business misconduct. They contribute to a more successful organization.

Also, potential recruits with a long-term view of employment seek out the company that has established standards and a reputation for upholding those standards.

## Standards

Standards for ethical practice proposed here comprise norms of behaviour and decision principles within each norm (*see* Box 1). The number of decision principles may vary between companies. The standards are not comprehensive but provide a good place from which managers can consider their personal, company and cultural values before interpreting and applying them. The guidelines were drawn from the ethical standards of seven different organizations, business ethics research and experience of HR departments in large corporations.

### Integrity

Businesspeople must be honest, play fair and act in good faith to others in all dealings for the company. They should reflect on their own belief systems, values, needs and limitations to know how these might differ from those of others, and be conscious of the potential effect of these differences on their work. They must refrain from making false, misleading or deceptive statements and must provide accurate information. They avoid relationships that create conflicts of interest, as well as expensive gifts, bribery, nepotism and abuse of government relationships. They

---

### Box 1 Decision principles and norms

**Integrity**

Uphold honesty, fair play and good faith actions.

Refrain from false, misleading and deceptive statements.

Avoid conflict of interest relationships.

Disclose and clarify intentions of policies, procedures and processes.

**Productivity**

Know your area of responsibility.

Exercise careful judgement in the use of your expertise.

Know the mechanics to create a productive environment.

Master communication, management and leadership skills.

Work towards advancement of a bias-free, ethical environment.

Strive for continuous learning of skills and knowledge.

**Responsibility**

Uphold these standards in application to free enterprise.

Comply with your assigned duties and proper business conduct.

Honour all promises, commitments and contracts made.

Cause no harm.

Be aware of responsibility to the community and society.

**Respectfulness in relationships**

Honour the intrinsic worth and dignity of all individuals.

Honour the liberty, human rights and freedom of all individuals.

Be sensitive to power differences that threaten freedom.

Be aware of potential conflict between rights and duties.

Resolve all conflicts with honesty and patience, not coercion.

Create a good reputation for dependability and responsiveness.

Avoid fear of speaking about these standards with others.

Practise courage in upholding the standards.

> ## Businesspeople must be honest, play fair and act in good faith to others in all dealings for the company.

must clarify to all parties the nature of their performance and function. They must act with an expectation that each exchange in business is in effect one of many more to come. They must act with the intent of a long-term relationship

## Productivity

Professionals are expected to know about all aspects of their work and to perform in an exemplary way. They should exercise judgement to protect those for whom they are responsible. They use appropriate information, resources, incentives, research and applications to secure the best service for each stakeholder. They are aware of cultural, individual and role differences involving age, gender, race, ethnicity, national origin, religion, sexual orientation, disability, language and socio-economic status. They work continuously to eliminate the effect of bias based on the above differences.

They do not condone or participate in unfair discriminatory practices. They strive to advance individual and organizational learning, performance and development while mitigating the causes preventing stakeholder welfare. They comply with laws and social policies that serve the interests of stakeholders, the public, society and the environment. Moreover, they should possess skills such as:

- managing client relationships;
- conducting analyses;
- identifying root causes of conflicts;
- forming partnerships within a company;
- negotiating;
- conflict resolution;
- technical;
- building consensus and commitment;
- project management;
- speaking;
- facilitating change.

## Responsibility

Professionals uphold the law and these ethical standards, and prevent harm to any stakeholder. They should consult with colleagues and clients regarding ethical compliance. They should engage in proper business conduct to prevent unethical dilemmas. They should share credit for work accomplishments when appropriate and be worthy of trust as a professional. They serve the company by honouring contracts, promises and any agreed commitment.

Moreover, they should be aware of their responsibility to the community in which they work and live, to the society to which they belong and to the planet. They understand that there is a necessary confluence of a healthy ecosystem, stable governments, a healthy economy and healthy organizations. Professionals have an obvious responsibility not to bring harm to another individual, department, division, company, community or any other element in society.

## Respectfulness in relationships

Professionals recognize, respect and are concerned about the worth of individuals, their interactions with each other, as well as their rights to privacy and confidentiality within the context of fundamental dignity, financial information and worth of all people. They should advocate that restricting the rights of individuals at work should be limited and used only with clear business justification. They will be alert to the fact that legal obligations manifested as compliance policies and procedures may lead to inconsistency and conflict with the exercise of the rights of individuals.

When conflict does occur among stakeholders' obligations, concerns and rights, they attempt to resolve these conflicts in a responsible and ethical manner, avoiding or minimizing harm to others. They are sensitive to power differences among all stakeholders and do not mislead or exploit other people before, during or after professional work exchanges. Respectfulness in relationships creates confidence among stakeholders.

## Business needs and the standards

How are the standards reflected more generally in companies? The modern business environment, as well as demanding such attributes as competitiveness and technological innovation, creates a basic need for fair play, competence, keeping promises and democratic values.

In *An Inquiry into the Nature and Causes of the Wealth of Nations* (1776), the Scottish economist and philosopher Adam Smith wrote that everyone, as long as he does not violate the laws of justice, is free to pursue his own interest and to bring that interest into competition with anyone else. Many hang on to this advice and use it as the only true standard of conduct. In 1759, though, Adam Smith wrote the *Theory of Moral Sentiment*, in which he indicated that however selfish a person may be, there are principles in his nature which give him an interest in the happiness of other people. Smith remarks that this interest in others involves "fair play" and that without some ethical foundation the fabric of human society would fall apart.

Fair play is a core need of business. Without it there is no connection between the effort made to succeed and access to opportunity within which people can develop their talents and be productive for the betterment of society.

The second norm of productivity is inextricably linked with competence. Productivity results from competence unless obstacles intervene. High productivity relies on exemplary performance by workers. Individual performance can become exemplary if the organizational culture has the backdrop of the standards cited above. Understanding the mechanics to improve performance and productivity within an ethical culture is critical for mutual reinforcement within an organization.

Too often average ethical performance in a group is taken to be the standard, leading to a complacent culture. Once employee performance has become complacent, it begins to deteriorate because of the lack of an ethical backdrop. When that degeneration begins, people are increasingly resistant to efforts to bring about improvement of ethics in the culture. Performance and productivity can be improved if there is the same message of standards cited above in the organizational culture.

Keeping promises is critical for the stability of transactions. Many traders at stock exchanges promote and practise the maxim that "my word is my bond". There are other promises in the realm of business that may be more invisible. Professionals have a tacit responsibility not to bring harm to other people.

Finally, the value of respect towards individuals and relationships and values such as accountability, equality, patience, freedom, human rights and liberty should directly benefit economic life. Human rights cannot exist without people accepting their responsibilities and duties to each other in society. The purpose and importance of rights and duty always arise in relationships. Freedom is a right to one's dignity. Duty is measured in our contributions to others, the company, the community and society.

Fear of the truth itself decreases our hopes and aspirations to be free in respectful relationships. Honesty helps overcome fear and is the first step to business wisdom. Courage is doing that which you fear. Honesty helps us practise courage. For professionals, speaking the truth is often one of the most difficult things to do, yet one of the most important for growth and success.

## Companies in crisis

At the beginning of this article I outlined how standards had improved company performance in two examples. It may also be instructive to reflect on what happens when a company lacks norms and decision principles in its culture.

### Beech-Nut Nutrition

In 1987 the US Food and Drug Administration investigation of Beech-Nut Nutrition Corporation regarding the misbranding of its apple juice led to 10 counts of mislabelling by the courts at an estimated cost of $25m. The company had misled the public in claiming that one of its products contained real apple juice. The deception showed

> Freedom is a right to one's dignity. Duty is measured in our contributions to others, the company, the community and society.

that the company culture lacked integrity as well as good judgement, because it caused harm to the company and its stakeholders.

### Sears, Roebuck

In 1992, Sears, Roebuck and Company received complaints from 40 states in the US about misleading customers by selling unnecessary parts in its vehicle services departments. Although the company did not intend to defraud customers, its incentive system had gone awry with undue pressure for quotas on sales. After a long investigation, the cost of settlement was estimated at $60m. Here, we see a clear case of culture causing unethical behaviour.

With proper standards as a backdrop in the organizational culture, the loss of confidence in Sears might have been prevented.

### Salomon Brothers

In 1991, four Salomon Brothers executives failed to take appropriate action when learning of unlawful activity on the government trading desk. This failure to take action in respecting the standards of trading, stakeholders and customers led to a crisis in the perception of Salomon Brothers as a leader in the investment industry. Salomon Brothers lost nearly $1bn and the confidence of the public.

### Conclusion

Managers must go beyond complying with regulations – they should also promote standards of fair play, productivity, promise-keeping and humanistic values.

These four norms, aligned with the core business needs (integrity, competence, productivity and respectfulness in relationships) in a global economy, give direction for the rethinking of organizational culture within which ethical practice can emerge.

While they can be adopted by any part of the company, such standards offer an expanded role to human resource departments to include the responsibility for encouraging stakeholders to aspire to excellence in ethical conduct. As the chief advocates for ethical practices, HR could act as the standard bearer for ethics in the company – not just as a force for legal compliance.

## Further reading

Dean, P.J. (1997) "Examining the profession and the practice of business ethics", *Journal of Business Ethics*, 16, 15.

Dean, P.J. (1994) "Customising codes of ethics to set professional standards", *Performance Improvement Journal*, 33, 1.

Dean, P.J. (1992) "Making codes of ethics 'real'", *Journal of Business Ethics*, 11.

Donaldson, T. (1996) "Values in tension away from home", *Harvard Business Review*, September.

Paine, L.S. (1994) "Managing for organizational integrity", *Harvard Business Review*, March.

# Skills

8

# Contents

# Introduction to Part 8

**As managers rise** steadily through the organization, they acquire the technical or market-based skills in different areas of the business through training and experience. At the same time, they are expected to pick up the general skills of managing people in organizations, such as leadership, team building, negotiation and motivating employees. In this part, writers ask what people skills are required of senior managers and how they can best execute them.

# Seeking success
## by involving workers

Mark Fenton-O'Creevy is a senior lecturer in organizational behaviour at the Open University Business School.

How do managers balance tight supervision against staff self-management? **Mark Fenton-O'Creevy** outlines the pros and cons of employee involvement.

**M**anagers have long wrestled with the problem of how to co-ordinate and control the organization to achieve their objectives. A guide to farm management from the Mesopotamian civilization (written about 5,000 years ago) illustrates one approach. It suggests farm supervisors should: "Brook no idleness. Stand over [the field workers] during their work and brook no interruptions."

Many organizations have, like the Mesopotamians, exercised management via tight supervisory control, through an autocratic hierarchy. Often this has been highly successful. The Mesopotamian temple organization that produced the above guide lasted for 3,000 years. However, if the idea of tight command and control is not new, neither is the contrasting notion that involved employees are more committed and more productive. In AD 100, Columella, a Roman estate owner, wrote a treatise on estate management (*De Re Rustica*) in which he remarked: "Nowadays I make it a practice to call [estate workers] into consultation on any new work … I observe they are more willing to set about a piece of work on which their opinions have been asked and their advice followed."

## Changing patterns

In the past century, labour unions have been an important channel for employee involvement. More recently, however, union membership and consultative committees have declined, prompting growth in more direct forms of involvement such as team briefings or problem-solving groups.

Perhaps the best evidence of this comes from the UK's Workplace Employee Relations Survey (WERS). Figure 1 shows a steady decline in representative involvement and a rise in the use of direct involvement. Evidence suggests similar changes elsewhere in Europe and the US.

FIGURE 1 | Changes in the pattern of involvement*

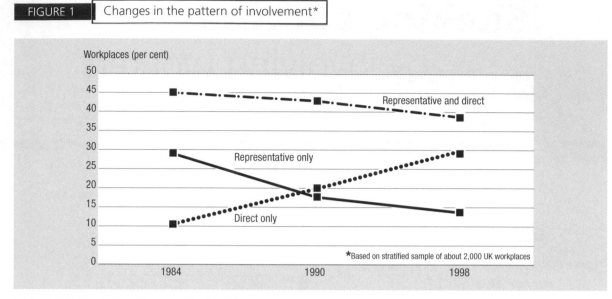

Source: Adapted from Millward, Bryson and Forth (2000)

Words such as participation, involvement and empowerment have become common parlance among managers. Is this just a matter of fashion? Will we see throughout history a swing from tight control to employee involvement and back again? Some, such as the late Harvie Ramsay, Professor of International Human Resource Management at the University of Strathclyde, have argued the latter. Ramsay suggested that when labour markets are tight and managers are under threat from organized labour, employee involvement practices are introduced to appease workers and then allowed to wither after the threat has passed. Others, such as Harvard academic Rosabeth Moss Kanter, have argued that to contrast employee involvement and control is a false dichotomy. They suggest that everyone can gain greater control through employee involvement. To understand this, we need to distinguish between control over what is achieved and how it is achieved.

By giving workers greater control over how objectives are achieved, it is said, managers can reach those objectives more easily. Greater control for workers over how they carry out tasks allows them to exploit their capabilities and understanding of the task. Genuine involvement in decisions about tasks also often leads to greater commitment. However, there is a caveat: this works only if workers understand and subscribe to managers' objectives and have the necessary skills to achieve them.

## Benefits

Employee involvement is concerned with either how best to achieve organizational goals or what the nature of those goals should be and how the benefits should be distributed. Direct involvement is typically concerned with the former and representative involvement with the latter. So, for example, improving quality is often a goal of direct involvement. Issues such as pay, working hours and the consequences of strategy for job security and the nature of work are frequently dealt with through representative involvement.

## Representative involvement

The objectives of representative involvement are generally not to improve productivity, so it would be unreasonable to judge it on that basis. Where representative involvement is mandated by law (as in much of Europe), objectives tend to be concerned with ensuring that the interests of employees are given weight compared with those of managers and owners. There is a case that this has been successful at the country level in ensuring a good climate of industrial relations and investment in both physical and human

> If workers feel that their interests are adequately addressed through a representative process, they are more likely to avail the organization of their full skills, knowledge and effort through direct involvement.

capital. Equally, some argue, the associated lack of managerial autonomy has resulted in a lack of flexibility, to the detriment of some European economies.

At the company and workplace level, research suggests, consultative committees and works councils do not in themselves affect productivity (in either direction). However, research in the motor industry by Mari Sako of Oxford University suggests that the productivity effects of direct involvement are strongest where there is also some form of representative involvement. If workers feel that their interests are adequately addressed through a representative process, they are more likely to avail the organization of their full skills, knowledge and effort through direct involvement.

## Direct employee involvement

Direct involvement processes tend to be initiated by managers and fall into two broad categories: communication-focused and task-focused involvement. Communication-focused involvement concerns systems for directly informing and listening to employees, such as "town hall" meetings, team briefings, employee attitude surveys, suggestion schemes and formal grievance systems.

These methods are in many ways weak forms of involvement. However, there is evidence of benefits where employees have a channel through which they can voice concerns. In particular, employees who feel able to raise concerns (and be listened to) are much more likely to believe that managerial processes and decisions are fair. In turn, employees who believe that fair process is followed are more likely to be committed to their organization and to remain in it, and less likely to engage in actions harmful to the organization.

Task-focused involvement concerns involvement in decisions about the work itself. Studies show that, overall, such practices have a significant positive effect on employee attitudes such as job satisfaction, commitment and organizational citizenship; they have a positive, although weaker, effect on task performance. However, it is clear that in many companies such initiatives either fail to become established or do not produce positive effects.

## Quality circles

Quality circles are small groups of employees who meet regularly to discuss quality and related issues. Their role may be to identify problems and devise solutions. Where they are part of a wider programme, quality circles are often also known as continuous improvement groups. There is little evidence that participation in quality circles (or continuous improvement groups) improves employees' motivation. However, in a review of research into quality circles, John Cotton found about half show performance improvements and about half show little or no effect on performance.

What determines their success or failure? Importantly, there seems to be a life cycle. Quality circles typically take some months before they start to deliver benefits, with the greatest success at between 6 and 18 months. Thereafter the benefits often fade away. My own research suggests that quality circles have been most successful as part of a more radical transformation of organization systems and working practices – and often as a short-term measure, rather than as an institutionalized work practice.

## Self-managing teams

Self-managing teams represent the most successful approach to performance improvement through employee involvement in recent decades. Terms such as self-managing teams, self-directed teams and semi-autonomous groups have all been used to describe team-working practices. Names and methods vary from organization to organization.

Self-managing teams complete a whole or a distinctive part of a product or service. They make a wide range of decisions, often including traditional management prerogatives. These may include selecting leaders, assigning jobs, training, redesigning processes, assessing internal performance, judging and managing quality, managing budgets and liaising with other teams.

The most comprehensive estimates of the prevalence of self-managing teams relate to UK organizations only. However, my own research with a Europe-wide sample suggests there are similar levels in other western European countries. In the UK, research on the 1998 WERS suggests about 35 per cent of workplaces use self-managing teams. However, their incidence varies considerably with the type of core occupational group in the workplace. Just over half of workplaces with professional workers as the largest occupational group use self-managing teams as opposed to only 13 per cent of workplaces with plant and machine operatives as the largest occupational group.

Research on self-managing teams is more optimistic about their benefits than that for quality circles. Most studies have found self-managing teams to improve work outcomes, work attitudes and absenteeism.

## Reasons for failure?

Economists have typically explained company behaviour in terms of the search for economic advantage. Many sociologists (while not denying the role of economic forces) have looked at the importance to company survival when establishing legitimacy in terms of relevant social institutions. For example, researchers Barry Staw and Lisa Epstein made a study of the adoption of popular management techniques in top US companies. They found that adoption was not associated (on average) with increased economic performance. However, such techniques were associated with a more positive company reputation among top executives in other companies and higher remuneration for the company's chief executive.

They concluded that chief executives are motivated to adopt such practices not because they are always economically optimal for the company but because they are seen as highly legitimate management practices, which reassure company stakeholders and send signals about the chief executive's competence to compensation decision makers.

Other evidence suggests that while new techniques may benefit early adopters, later adopters mostly do not achieve performance improvements. Why? Because late adopters are following the trend and window-dressing, while early adopters are interested in the process itself.

Adoption as window-dressing certainly explains the contrast between the mediocre outcomes of quality circles and the success of self-managing teams. The former can be "bolted on", whereas the latter require big changes to the way work is organized.

Another reason advanced for the failure of employee involvement is resistance from middle managers, who do not wish to surrender power. I am sceptical of this argument. While such resistance undoubtedly exists, it is often merely a symptom of deeper problems: for example, divisions among senior managers about the value of the initiative, or poorly conceived and designed processes for involving employees. All too often, senior managers announce they intend to empower employees and send middle managers on a brief "sheep dip" training course. These managers are then exhorted to involve and empower employees, while reward systems and promotions continue to show that what really matters is short-term performance. Core systems, structures and control over resources do not change. Consequently, behaviour does not change and middle managers become the scapegoats for another failure of vision at the top (*see* Box 1, point 1).

## How to succeed

Like anything that can deliver significant advantage, employee involvement is not an easy option. Many organizations that claim to involve employees do nothing of the sort. Many programmes are nothing but rhetoric and window dressing. So the first rule of success is: "Don't just talk about it, do it."

If employees are really to be involved and managers are to change their behaviour in ways that make this possible, then organizational systems need to change. Reward systems, training and development, modes of communication, career paths and processes for allocating resources and support all need to reinforce and support the involvement programme. So the second rule of success is: "Real employee involvement requires you to transform the organization."

As noted, direct involvement will succeed only if workers understand and subscribe to managers' objectives. This has two implications. First, objectives need to be communicated in ways that make sense to employees. Second, employees may not automatically accept those objectives as sensible or worthwhile. Objectives need to be "sold" to employees. So the third rule of success is: "Communicate and sell a

clear and engaging set of objectives" (*see* Box 1, point 2).

The reality of involvement can be tested by asking whether employees have the resources and authority to manage the work. Do they, for example, have access to meeting space, tools, computing services and other resources that mean they can implement decisions about how to organize their work? Do they have the authority to make decisions about how work is carried out, and how tasks and customers are prioritized?

This is not to say that employees can immediately be given authority and left to get on with it. Most successful instances of high employee involvement involve a gradual and negotiated handover of authority to individuals or teams, with managers and employees clear at each stage about the extent and limit of authority. So the fourth rule of success is: "Give employees adequate control over resources and real authority to manage their work."

Finally, many successful involvement initiatives have been dropped or damaged beyond repair as soon as the organization hits hard times. In the drive to reduce costs, a hidden cost can be the loss of trust and capabilities that have taken a long time to build. This is not inevitable. As some companies have found, employee involvement can be valuable in difficult times (*see* Box 1, point 3).

So the fifth and final rule of success is: "Protect and build employee involvement in the hard times as well as the good."

## Further reading

Cotton, J.L. (1993) *Employee Involvement*, London: Sage.

Cully, M., Woodland, S., O'Reilly, A. and Dix, G. (1999) *Britain at Work: as depicted by the 1998 Workplace Employee Relations Survey*, London: Routledge.

Fenton-O'Creevy, M. (2001) "Employee involvement and the middle manager: antecedents of resistance and support", *Human Resource Management Journal*, 11 (1).

Fenton-O'Creevy, M. (1998) "Employee involvement and the middle manager: evidence from a survey of organizations", *Journal of Organizational Behaviour*, 19 (1).

> If employees are really to be involved and managers are to change their behaviour in ways that make this possible, then organizational systems need to change.

Kanter, R.M. (1989) "The new managerial work", *Harvard Business Review*, November.

Millward, N., Bryson, A. and Forth, J. (2000) *All Change at Work?: British Employee Relations, 1980–1998: Portrayed by the Workplace Employee Relations Survey*, London: Routledge.

Ramsay, H. (1991) "Reinventing the wheel? A review of the development and performance of employee involvement", *Human Resource Management Journal*, 1 (4).

# Unlocking the secrets
## of business innovation

Thomas Mannarelli is an assistant professor of organizational behaviour at Insead's Asia campus.

Good managers make quick, sound and efficient decisions. However, they must be willing to accept ambiguity and uncertainty when dealing with creative product ideas, says **Thomas Mannarelli**.

**M**anaging creative talent has always been a challenge. In business, however, creativity has only recently been given the attention it merits. The rise of information technology and globalization has focused attention on product and service differentiation. While much has been said about the value of knowledge, managers are discovering that what you know is only a piece of the puzzle. It is the way knowledge is used that determines a company's performance. Easier access to constantly changing information hasn't made life easier; in fact, it has put most organizations on a more level playing field. To remain competitive companies must continue to find and hone innovative solutions to market problems.

When executives think of managing creativity they often think only in terms of how to manage the creative person. Certainly managing creativity at the individual level is a vital component, but managers must think beyond the person to maximize the creative potential of their organizations. Social psychologists have discussed the importance of various facets of creativity, which include not only the person but also the product, the process and the situation. As these facets are described in detail, it will be clear that they are not distinct but closely related. So, when motivating creative people, managers must think about more than just individual employees.

## When experience counts for little

In one sense, the creative product (defined broadly as a product, idea or service that is both novel and useful) is the essence of creativity. Regardless of the inventiveness of the people involved or the processes of production, it is only from the product or service that an organization can derive the benefits creativity provides.

> Traditional analytical models of decision making, while appropriate for evaluating choices for which there are ample historical data, can often kill off creative ideas that might be extremely valuable.

Yet managing the product may be the most important (and probably the most difficult) part of managing creative people. While employees give their blood, sweat and tears to a new product, it is the executive who must make the painful decision of whether or not to back it, alter it or reject it. Such judgements about whether to invest the company's resources can also be interpreted as a referendum on the creator's competence.

The problem is that managers typically make decisions about product ideas in the same way they decide about conventional issues such as financing and resource allocation. Yet creativity poses a fundamentally different problem for decision makers. Traditional analytical models of decision making, while appropriate for evaluating choices for which there are ample historical data, can often kill off creative ideas that might be extremely valuable.

An executive from a US record company bemoaned the fact that the new album from one of his label's most successful acts, while very good, did not contain any "hits". The disappointed band members were sent back to the studio to keep working on it. When asked how he knew that the album had no hits, the executive said that his judgement was not based on any mystical talent but on an ability developed over the years to spot hit songs, and a realization that a hit is one of those things that everyone recognizes when they hear it.

Perhaps he is right most of the time and that may be sufficient. But, then again, maybe it's not. In an infamous example, Decca Records turned down an opportunity to sign The Beatles in 1964 because it believed guitar music was no longer marketable. Decca was not the only one; virtually every major label rejected the band except George Martin, an inexperienced producer and head of the small EMI subsidiary Parlophone Records. Even Martin conceded that his decision had more to do with the enthusiasm of the band members and of their manager, Brian Epstein, than it did with his belief in the quality and marketability of The Beatles' music.

This phenomenon is not unique to music. History is replete with similarly faulty conclusions drawn by astute executives and other experts. Western Union declared in 1876 that the telephone, with all of its shortcomings, was of no value. In 1977 Ken Olsen, founder of Digital Equipment Corporation, concluded that there was no reason why people would want to have computers in their homes. And Fred Smith's economics professor at Yale University gave him a "C" grade on a paper outlining his idea for what would later become Federal Express, claiming that his plan for overnight package delivery, while interesting, was not commercially feasible.

## Key decisions

The point is that creative product ideas cannot be judged using the same informational shortcuts that managers habitually employ to make other decisions. Good managers are quick, certain and decisive. This type of behaviour is continually rewarded and reinforced. Subordinates, board members and shareholders alike look to managers for their wisdom and experienced leadership to make sound and efficient decisions. Therefore, it is difficult for managers and stakeholders to accept uncertainty about decisions involving creative products.

That is not to say managers cannot use their knowledge and expertise to analyze creative propositions. On the contrary, it would be foolish to suggest otherwise. But good managers of creativity have learned to be cognizant of what they know and what they think they might know. Compared to a typical product evaluation, creative products call for an agnostic approach. Product ideas must be assessed realistically, assuming a high degree of uncertainty about their ultimate usefulness. Managers must be more willing to tolerate the ambiguity that accompanies such uncertainty and must not fall into the trap of assuming that just because something did not occur in the past, it cannot occur in the future.

The idea of product agnosticism could also be seen as a form of self-management. Executives typically reach their positions after establishing a track record of making good decisions. After some time such confidence in decision making becomes habitual. And that is when the danger sets in.

An agnostic approach asks only that managers reserve judgement, at least temporarily. Allocating time and effort to fully appreciate the possibilities of a counterintuitive idea can mean the difference between signing The Beatles and letting them go. One would be hard-pressed to find many examples of creative entrepreneurs, inventors, scientists and the like who were not told at least initially that their ideas were crazy or unworkable. Only after much tenacity and perseverance do these mavericks prove their critics wrong.

Albert Einstein once said, "If at first the idea is not absurd, then there is no hope for it." Perhaps when it comes to creativity, managers should learn how to think more like physicists and less like traditional managers.

## Motivation

Early research on the creative personality suggested that perhaps creative individuals were neurotic or suffered from social or psychological impairment. Systematic tests of this hypothesis proved it unfounded; creative individuals were actually found to be normal or above average in terms of mental health and stability. The original hypothesis may have stemmed from the fact that creative people face a lot of opposition to their ideas in professional environments. In response to the barriers they face, they often lash out with frustration.

However, the misunderstanding of creative people may also have something to do with the way in which most managers understand motivation. Early behaviourist theories of motivation proposed that people respond positively to reward and negatively to punishment. While there is obviously some truth in this, subsequent research has demonstrated that motivation is much more complex. Creativity is inextricably linked to motivation. It blossoms when people engage in tasks without expectation of reward or a vote of approval. Instead, they do it for the pleasure and feeling of accomplishment that accompanies the activity. Further, creativity (and intrinsic motivation) on a given task is reduced when external factors are emphasized.

That is to say, when creative people are performing a task, if the extrinsic reasons for engaging in the task are more important than the intrinsic reasons, they will tend to perform less creatively. Outside factors encourage people to focus purely on the accuracy and consistency of the outcome; while the task may be accomplished, creativity is blocked and interest in the activity stifled. This is not to say that creativity can be promoted by eliminating compensation for performance – the most salient extrinsic factor. Managers of creative individuals do have the means to influence employee motivation.

## A full-time culture

One approach is to move away from traditional tools of motivation, such as salary and promotion, to remove perceptions of organizational control over work and to allow creative employees to focus on the intrinsic attributes of the task. Managers must be willing to relinquish some control over subordinates and allow a higher degree of freedom to perform not only in terms of the product outcomes but also the means they employ to reach their objectives.

Probably the most effective way of increasing the intrinsic motivation of creative people is to establish a culture of creativity. This is easier said than done. First, there are no foolproof methods for creating a culture; an organization's culture evolves organically, influenced by many factors, some within and others outside the control of managers (*see* 'A cultural evolution in business thinking' in Part 4). So while organizations frequently try to change their cultures, the outcome is never certain. Furthermore, if such a transformation involves a radical departure from the existing culture, the process can be lengthy, typically requiring years of effort.

However, if managers are committed to a creative cultural transformation, success can best be achieved by acting on many fronts. The first

> If managers are committed to a creative cultural transformation, success can best be achieved by acting on many fronts.

and probably the most straightforward is a physical transformation, which borrows from the theory of "scientific management" advocated by Frederick Taylor in the early 1900s. Taylor's theory suggested, among other things, that work should be designed in a methodical and scientific fashion so that performance was optimized. Scientists should be able to determine the conditions (such as light levels, room temperature, ergonomic desk design and so on) for optimal productivity through rigorous research.

Although many of Taylor's ideas have been rejected for their robotic treatment of human beings, his impact was undeniable. Interestingly, many of his principles are being applied in creative industries to foster the ideal working environment. Advertising agencies, consultants and research and development laboratories are increasingly turning to architects and interior designers for help construct physical workspaces that enhance communication, interaction and openness. Companies in Silicon Valley have been praised for their informal work environments, ranging from casual dress codes to flexible work schedules and elaborately decorated workspaces.

Policy changes and office design cannot be expected to improve creativity directly but they do contribute to a more relaxed, informal and less bureaucratic environment – all qualities that encourage organizational commitment and intrinsic motivation.

Managers can also foster a creative culture by procedural improvements. When advertising executive Alex Osborn came up with the famous brainstorming process in 1941, his idea addressed the creative needs of his particular industry. The fact that brainstorming is now used (although frequently incorrectly) in all types of organizations is a testament to both the broad desire of managers for creative solutions to problems and the need for tools to help stimulate creative thought.

Brainstorming is not the only technique available. Lateral thinking, mind-mapping and many others are also used. Creative consultancies provide such tools, and even the more general consulting companies are adding a wide array of creativity techniques to their repertoire of resources.

Often organizations identify one technique as their primary tool. However, there may be great value in using several techniques. Some take longer than others and the choice of technique may depend on time constraints. Some methods suit groups while others are designed for people working alone. Furthermore, different techniques provide different benefits. For example, some are more effective at stimulating radical divergent thinking, others incorporate more systematic and logical thought processes.

Finally, the use of several techniques can augment efforts to develop a more creative culture. Many techniques incorporate a high degree of playfulness and fun into their procedures. Working in organizations and teams that use these techniques can be more exciting and more emotionally rewarding. By changing techniques, the process never becomes dull or routine.

Managers can also establish a creative culture through an "authentic transformation". Here the question is simple: do managers really believe in and value creativity from employees? An organization can adopt the most effective creative processes, craft the most creative physical environment and implement more informal company policies, but if there is no belief in the value of creativity from senior managers, the transformation is doomed. Certainly, this commitment must be communicated in words, but such words must also be backed up by enthusiastic support and visible actions that demonstrate the company's commitment to innovation.

Perhaps the most important point about establishing a culture of creativity is that it cannot be a part-time effort. Often managers argue that creativity is desirable only when it is needed and that it can hinder operations when not needed. In fact, the flow of creativity cannot be turned on and off at will. If creativity is encouraged only at those rare times when managers demand it, an organization will never become creative by habit.

## Conclusion

The past decade has witnessed an astonishing period of innovation. While creativity contributed greatly to the economic growth of the late 20th century, it can also be argued that economic growth also contributed greatly to creativity. Although managers routinely stress the importance of creativity for prosperity, in practice the resources devoted to creative endeavours are often treated as expendable.

When times are good, managers are more willing to invest time and money in unconventional ventures and take risks with novel ideas. But when the climate changes, creativity is seen as a luxury that can no longer be afforded. In these challenging economic times, the importance of creativity should be given added emphasis. It may be precisely what is needed to lift struggling economies out of the doldrums.

## Further reading

Adams, J.L. (1986) *Conceptual Blockbusting: A Guide to Better Ideas*, Reading, MA: Addison-Wesley.

Amabile, T.M. (1996) *Creativity in Context*, Boulder, CO: Westview Press.

Csikszentmihalyi, M. (1996) *Creativity*, New York: HarperCollins.

Kao, J. (1996) *Jamming: The Art and Discipline of Business Creativity*, New York: HarperBusiness.

Michalko, M. (1991) *Thinkertoys: A Handbook of Business Creativity*, Berkeley, CA: Ten-Speed Press.

# In search of
## strategic meaning

HR can make a difference in a strategic role – for better or for worse, says **Theresa Welbourne.** The important factor is to build positive relationships.

Theresa M. Welbourne is an associate professor of organization behaviour and human resource management at University of Michigan Business School and president and chief executive of eePulse.

**H**uman resource management has been changing for some time. Its early focus on labour and industrial relations shifted to personnel administration and has moved on to strategic human resource management. However, senior HR executives are by no means consistent about what they are doing differently now that they are "strategic".

One group of executives might say: "We now report to the board and are involved in strategy; we help with mergers and acquisitions, for example." Another, by contrast, complains: "We continue to report through the accounting or finance department, we are busy dealing with paperwork and much of our job is being outsourced." Even when pushed, neither group can say how their work has changed. It seems that the work of the HRM department has changed little. If so, what contribution can the department make?

Before trying to answer this question, managers should ask why saying that HRM has taken on a strategic role should change anything. Is it any more "strategic" than any other function such as marketing, sales, accounting, finance, technology or public relations? At the same time, there has been growth in executive coaching, consulting and HR outsourcing. What does this say about the future?

## The executive effect

With academic Linda Cyr, I conducted a study on people management issues within high-growth and high-change organizations. We explored the effect on performance of having a senior HR executive reporting directly to the chief executive. (In practitioner and academic journals, this is one agreed definition of "strategic HRM".)

The research was done on a sample of companies we called the "fruit flies" of management. These are companies going through initial public offerings – they live and die quickly, allowing a researcher to study cause and effect in conditions that may be closer to those found in a laboratory. Generally, they start up operations, obtain a product, hire a management team, decide how to organize themselves and are given a sizeable amount of money at IPO with which to grow their operations. The study included approximately 200 variables that described the companies at the time of their IPOs, revealing information about strategy and structures, and investigated more than 500 organizations.

Having a senior HR executive reporting to the chief executive did affect company performance. However, the relationship was complex. Sometimes the HR executive had a positive effect on longer-term company performance (growth in stock price and earnings over three years) and sometimes the effect was negative. Under conditions of change, the HR executive effect was positive; when the company was experiencing little change, the effect was negative.

It seems unsurprising that the HR executive effect may not be significant in some cases but odd that there is a condition under which it is markedly negative. Following this research, I conducted a series of case studies with large and small companies to investigate these mixed aspects of HRM. An examination of initiatives in these companies seems to explain how HRM can help or hurt an organization. This article reviews the experiences of two such organizations: Northwestern Memorial Hospital and eGM, a division of General Motors.

## Relationships

Northwestern Memorial Hospital inhabits a new $580m building in central Chicago and serves about 40,000 inpatients and 800,000 outpatients a year. Its strategic plan calls for it to develop and maintain the "best patient experience".

The aim of eGM is to create products and services for General Motors that will help the company to get closer to its customers; its strategic plan demands that it "revolutionize the customer experience". Here, customers are defined as car dealers, consumers, employees and other stakeholders of the company. In both cases, senior managers tried to build strong relationships with employees. They went about this by carefully listening to employees in the same way that they listened to their customers, then responding in simple ways that built loyalty. Such relationships require constant communication and both companies used innovative technology to help managers build their relationship management skills. Primarily, they used weekly electronic communications with workers to provide senior managers (and HR executives) with data on the state of the workforce.

## Hospital taskforce

The technological approach was particularly challenging for Northwestern Memorial Hospital because many employees did not have access to computers. Nurses, technicians, janitors and housekeeping staff – employees on the operations side – spend little time in front of a computer terminal. However, the hospital's strategic plan called for improving communication, obtaining good results on its best people strategy and bringing technology to employees.

The hospital launched a weekly programme in spring 2001 that encouraged workers to discuss their views on the hospital's performance or working practices. A third of employees on e-mail replied at least once to the communication (the hospital employs about 7,000 people). However, while 64 per cent of managers responded, only 23 per cent of people in an operations role replied (in these jobs e-mail and computer use has not yet been integrated into employees' day-to-day work).

The problems of obtaining information and helping employees use computer technology were eclipsed by the challenge of responding to what employees actually wrote. Four themes emerged:

> The problems of obtaining information and helping employees use computer technology were eclipsed by the challenge of responding to what employees actually wrote.

- inadequate staffing: at a time of low resources, there were numerous comments about some staff not doing their share;
- unsatisfactory computers, fax machines and copiers;
- management issues – a lack of communication, support and coaching from managers;
- excessive workload and a lack of fulfilment.

The hospital created a taskforce of managers and HRM representatives to address each issue and formulate responses. The approach bears similarities with customer relationship management: the hospital used focus groups to help it understand, improve and monitor its relationships with employees.

## High energy culture

Mark Hogan, eGM's president, took a similar approach but faced a problem. If the response to the survey showed that employees wanted assurances of job security, higher pay or a nicer building (with a shorter commuting time), he could not satisfy them – no car company could. Instead, he asked employees what questions they had for him. Some of the most common questions were:

- What are the strategic goals of eGM?
- What is the company's short-term outlook?
- Are there plans to relocate within the next year?
- How much of a stake does the company have in OnStar [a GM product]?
- Will Mark Hogan continue to share news by voice-mail updates?

Simply by answering these questions, Hogan was able to encourage employees and keep them informed of the company's plans. In the same way that most companies respond to customers, eGM used weekly employee communications to create a high-energy, communicative culture.

The company runs a string of more traditional programmes, covering topics such as performance management systems, succession planning and leadership. These initiatives may be symbols of performance but they do not get at the culture of the company. The HR team at eGM concluded that only by a continuing dialogue with employees could managers hope to influence the ingrained habits of corporate culture.

## Customers and staff

What lessons can be learned from these cases? The key to building positive relationships is not just in obtaining frequent data but in interpreting and responding to the data. If a company asks customers what they think about its product but fails to change the product (or fails to explain why it will not be changed), customer relations will suffer. When customer relations suffer, so do sales.

The same happens with employees. When managers ask about the workplace, employees respond; if managers are unwilling to react, productivity suffers; when productivity suffers, customer service and sales suffer.

If relationships are accepted as being crucial for long-term success, then managers have to talk to customers and employees to remain in business. In reality, however, many employers are so afraid of what employees will say that they do not ask. Yet managers must ask; they need to collect systematic, representative data and respond to it. Often, that response is simpler than expected.

The future of HRM lies in managing relationships. HR executives can improve their own performance and the financial performance of their organizations by learning to be relationship management coaches. Using marketing and sales methods normally associated with customer relationships is one way of gaining momentum quickly among employees.

Companies should consider other alterations in the role of HRM. First, administrative HR work such as payroll administration can be outsourced or placed in the accounting department. Second, HR executives with the relevant skills can create a new department called "relationship management". Senior managers should hire someone to lead this function, with the title of chief relationship

## Companies should consider other alterations in the role of HRM.

officer. The HRM department should go beyond relationships with employees and ensure that the organization takes a strategic approach to relationships with all stakeholders.

What organization has both a strategic approach to its relationships with employees, investors, customers and suppliers, and a senior executive who influences business decisions, branding and strategy because that person has real-time information about the people in all of these groups? Management consultants are starting to understand that employee and customer branding, and identity are important for long-term success, but few people are helping individual managers think about the people who are important to their own success.

Not many organizations take on this task as an internal responsibility, but managers are hiring executive coaches to help them improve relationship management. At the same time, a $75bn market in customer relationship management is growing fast and a $30bn market in managing employee relationships is gaining momentum. It is clear that companies are interested in this area and a strategic approach to relationships can help a company succeed. What is the role of HRM in this movement?

In our IPO research, HRM in fast-growth companies was concerned with relationship management. Executives help their leaders deal with the amount of change in the companies – under conditions of fast growth, relationships are tested constantly and need to be managed. When little change occurs, however, HRM often stays within its traditional domain. The department's members develop programmes that often do affect relationship management but, unfortunately, they often do so in a negative manner. When was the last time that performance appraisal or job analysis made anyone feel good about the company? Companies may continue to change the way they do HR tasks, often making them more quantitative, complex and bringing in principles of scientific research, but these large-scale programmes do not necessarily build relationships.

Northwestern Memorial Hospital and eGM used customer relationship models with their employees. The simplicity of the programmes helped managers in two ways. First, weekly employee metrics helped them lead their business better. Second, frequent communication with employees allowed managers to improve productivity by responding to short-term tactical problems that came up during the process, by monitoring the progress of strategic initiatives and making changes as needed and by acting on employees' ideas, suggestions and complaints.

Problematic issues cannot always be resolved or result in action, but acknowledging staff concerns and trying to solve a problem is greatly appreciated by employees.

## Conclusion

Trust comes only with time. Most organizational growth is stifled because employees will not go the "extra mile". Why should they? They have learned not to trust – their actions are not appreciated and many are scared in a climate of redundancies, downturn and political uncertainty.

Northwestern Memorial Hospital and eGM have gained competitive advantage by telling employees that they are as important as customers. They, and other companies, can focus on relationships as a strategic asset and reap the benefits.

## Further reading

Ghoshal, S. and Bartlett, C.A. (1997) *The Individualised Corporation*, New York: HarperBusiness.

Pfeffer, J. (1998) *The Human Equation*, Boston, MA: Harvard Business School Press.

Schmitt, B. and Simonson, A. (1987) *Marketing Aesthetics*, New York: Free Press.

Welbourne, T.M. and Cyr, L.A. (1999) "The human resource executive effect in initial public offerings", *Academy of Management Journal*, 42, 6.

Some relevant articles are available at: http://www.eepulse.com/research.html.

# The ups and downs
## of leading people

Michael Useem is a professor at the Wharton School of the University of Pennsylvania and director of its Center for Leadership and Change.

Managers have to be ready to take up the reins of leadership, says **Michael Useem**, and that includes calculating risks, voicing concerns and guiding uncertain superiors.

An unexplored yet critical side of leadership is upward leadership, or getting results by helping to guide your boss. Rather than undermining authority or seizing power from superiors, upward leadership means stepping in when senior managers need help and support in a way that benefits everyone.

Leading up is a matter of offering a superior your strategic insights or persuading a boss to change directions before it is too late. It requires an ability to work in two directions at once, of stepping into the breach when nobody above you is doing so – and of listening to those below you before you step off a cliff yourself.

Upward leadership is not always welcomed. Many managers have worked for a supervisor who ran the office with a fine level of detail or misjudged the future. To come forward when a superior does not encourage it can be risky, but if the upward leadership works – whether welcomed or not – it can help transform decline into growth and, occasionally, turn disaster into triumph.

Upward leadership is not a natural skill but it can be mastered and there are few better ways to appreciate its exercise than to study those who have had to apply it. Watching their efforts can provide lessons for leading up when it really counts.

## Bold subordinates

In 2000, the then US vice-president Al Gore defeated Bill Bradley in the campaign for the Democratic presidential nomination. Many factors contributed to the defeat but among them was Bradley's reluctance to reply to stinging attacks by his opponent. His instinct had been to run his campaign above the fray – less as "a 21st-century politician," said *The New York Times*, "than as an Old Testament prophet."

Although his campaign suffered defeat after defeat in the early stages, Bradley might have recovered his momentum had he hit back hard. To do that, though, the candidate needed to be led into the fray, a form of leading up that no one working for him proved willing to risk. Bradley tended to take his own counsel more than that of campaign advisers. For their part, they did not always say what he needed to hear. An aide summed up the problem just after Bradley withdrew from the campaign in March following defeats in two states: "These people were always concerned about what their relationship with Bill should be, as opposed to just doing what it takes to win."

The apparent inability of Bradley's staff to distinguish between leading up and currying favour may have contributed to the aspirant's decline. However, the cause goes back to the man who had created such a mindset in the first place. Had Bradley pressed those who worked for him to do their best by him, even if it meant voicing criticism, they might have bolstered his run for the party's nomination.

Leading up can require fortitude and perseverance. Managers might fear how superiors will respond and doubt their right to lead up, but all carry a responsibility to do what they can when it will make a difference and to tell a superior what he or she ought to hear. Many strategies and more than a few organizations have failed when the middle ranks could see the problems but hesitated to challenge their command.

From the other point of view, there is also an obligation on managers to encourage people below to speak up and tell them what they need to know, to fill in for their shortcomings when future success is threatened.

A culture of upward leadership is built, not born. For that, managers should regularly insist that more junior staff examine proposals and challenge errors. Asking those of lesser rank to say what they candidly think and complimenting them for doing so are among the small measures that can make for a big improvement in attitude.

## A culture of upward leadership is built, not born.

## Risk and reward

Some individuals begin with a head start but everybody can improve their ability for upward service. In 1997, David Pottruck, chief operating officer of broker Charles Schwab, faced a critical decision in his career, in which the outcome depended greatly on his upward leadership skills. Could he convince his chief executive and company directors to make a radical move into internet-based client trading? It would be expensive and risky but it could also be highly advantageous.

Founded in 1974, Schwab's annual revenue exceeded $2bn by 1997. Through its thousands of customer service representatives, the company bought and sold shares for a million clients and in the astounding bull market of the 1990s everyone seemed to benefit. The rise of the internet, however, threatened to undo all that, undermining a rich network of relationships painstakingly assembled over many years. The web furnished free and fast access to company information that had long been the brokers' province and it opened a way to trade stock at a fraction of the time and cost required to call a broker.

For those willing to forgo personal contact, Schwab had built an electronic trading service, charging just $29 a trade. Many customers, however, still wanted real dialogue with real people and it was from these people that the serious money came – as much as $80 a transaction. For how long, though, would these clients continue to pay $80 when they knew other clients were trading for just $29?

One solution would be to bundle full-service and online trading into one offering and so give all customers the combination that many increasingly wanted. In the spring of 1997, Pottruck decided that the two-tier system had to go, even though he was personally responsible for building much of it. In its place, he would create a single full-service offering with internet trading and he reasoned that it could cost no more than $29 a trade.

Pottruck turned to his boss, Charles Schwab, for approval. Charles Schwab had already embraced the internet. He had appreciated the power of the web early and had pushed the company to move online in 1995. The founder was known to have a feel for market trends and as Pottruck explained his thinking, Charles Schwab immediately affirmed his interest in the proposed move. However, he also posed hard questions: how much would it cost, how would it affect the organization and how soon could benefits be expected? Charles Schwab was willing to take large risks and place big bets when the odds were known, and he pressed Pottruck to nail them down.

Pottruck instructed his staff to assess the effect of slashing the full-service commission of $80 and providing full service to everybody at $29 a trade, including 1.2m customers using the limited-service internet option. The strategists came back with a shocking conclusion. If the company allowed account holders to migrate, it would depress the company's revenue in 1998 by $125m and its earnings by $100m, more than a fifth of its projected pre-tax profits. Stock markets would be likely to drive down Schwab's share price with a vengeance.

Although he was sure of the long-term chances of the new offering, Pottruck was less sure whether returns would arrive quickly enough to avert financial disaster. The plan would require vigorous support from the chief executive and board members if it were to succeed. Pottruck himself was in the best position to make the case.

He gave Charles Schwab the financial implications of the low-price full service and warned of the effect on profits in the short term. Following weeks of discussion, Schwab endorsed the plan. The founder always insisted on putting customer service first and Pottruck had made that his guiding principle; Schwab had consistently stressed careful analysis, which Pottruck had done; Schwab had delegated much to those he trusted and Pottruck had already earned his confidence.

The next step for Pottruck was the company directors, without whose wholehearted approval it would be foolish to proceed. Pottruck brought his plan to the board in September 1997. Some directors wondered why any change was needed since the year was already proving to be the best in company history. After-tax profits were approaching $270m, and what Pottruck was now proposing would slash them by a third or more. Others wondered whether the options had been studied thoroughly. Still others asked whether the downside could be weathered. Pottruck's confident response was: "It will be fine but it will take some time" – possibly a year and a half or more. The directors duly agreed on what would be the company's most fateful decision of the era.

On January 15, 1998, Schwab announced it was offering web trading for $29 a time and was extending all services to all customers – consultations at branches and by telephone, and personal advice. The first quarter's results – as Pottruck had forecast – were devastated. Schwab was indeed cannibalizing its full-service, high-priced accounts. Quarterly revenues had been growing at 6.5 per cent per quarter in 1997; now they declined by 3 per cent. Pre-tax income had been rising by 8 per cent per quarter in 1997; now it dropped by 16 per cent. Yet the expectation that the world was moving to the web proved prescient. By the end of 1998, the number of Schwab customers with online accounts had nearly doubled and Schwab finished the year with 20 per cent growth in revenue and 29 per cent rise in profit.

Meeting the internet challenge at Schwab required keen insight and a reasoned capacity to risk much when others doubted the proposed path. It also depended on a boss ready to be persuaded and a board ready to be moved. However, that readiness was not automatic. Rather, it was the product of steps that Pottruck had earlier taken to establish a relationship of confidence with those above him.

Learning to lead up is a lifelong endeavour and it is greatly helped by a willingness to learn from past mistakes and superiors who are willing to suggest how it is done. Taking risks is a defining element of any leadership and calculated management of risk is essential. To succeed as a risk-taker on behalf of superiors, decisions need to be taken quickly and accurately. In spite of the uncertainties and large stakes that may be involved, if decisions are for managers to take, it is essential for them to do so rather than kick the responsibility upstairs.

The first step in winning the support of superiors and the board is to ensure accuracy. The second is to communicate carefully why the proposed course of action is necessary and how it can be accomplished with the minimum upheaval.

## The cost of failure

When organizations foster upward leadership, the benefits can be great. Conversely, the costs of ignoring or discouraging it can be enormous. Consider this example.

In February 2001, the nuclear submarine USS Greenville suddenly surfaced and collided with a Japanese fishing boat, the Ehime Maru. The boat overturned and nine passengers were killed. A navy investigator reported that a visiting officer on the Greenville had sensed that Commander Scott D. Waddle was rushing preparations and cutting corners to give a demonstration to 16 civilians on board – but the visiting officer had said nothing to the commander about his concerns.

Similarly, Waddle's second-ranking officer, who carried the most explicit obligation to challenge questionable procedures, had failed to voice his doubts about his commander's pace, including an abbreviated periscope inspection of the horizon just before the surfacing. The subordinate officer, the investigator found, "was thinking these things, but did not articulate them to the commanding officer". The investigator concluded that the crew members so respected their captain that they were reluctant to challenge him. Commanding officer Waddle, he found, "doesn't get a lot of corrective input from subordinates because he's very busy giving directions and the ship has experienced a lot of success when he does". Had the institution more effectively stressed its principle of upward challenge, had the visiting officer and the commander's subordinates been emboldened to question their commander's actions, the fatal event may have never happened.

Even short of the loss of life, the cost of failure for upward leadership can be huge. Consider the price of such an error for the chairman of Samsung Group, Lee Kun Hee. In 1994, he decreed that Samsung should invest $13bn to become a car producer, aiming to make 1.5m vehicles by 2010. Car manufacture was already a crowded field, plagued by global over-capacity, but Lee was a powerful chieftain and a passionate car buff, and none of his subordinates questioned his strategy.

A year after the first cars rolled off the line in 1999, however, Samsung Motors sold its assets to Renault. Many of Samsung's top managers had silently opposed the investment and Lee later told them he was puzzled why none had openly expressed their reservations. By then, though, Lee had reached into his own pocket for $2bn to placate his irate creditors.

## Courage to lead up

A common element among those who successfully lead up is a driving urge to make things happen on high, an unflinching willingness to take charge when not fully in command.

The exercise of upward leadership has been made easier by contemporary expectations in many companies that managers learn not just from their superiors but from all points of the compass. The phrase "360-degree feedback" has come to mean a manager's annual task of gathering reaction from direct subordinates and immediate bosses. So it is with leading up: instead of just motivating those below, managers must also muster those above; instead of just learning from those above, managers need listen to those below.

Such leadership can be inspired when executives are willing to take the time to create the right culture. Once established, a company-wide emphasis on leading upwards serves as a kind of inertial guidance system, continually reminding everybody that they are obliged to stand up without the need for superiors to ask for them to do so.

---

The exercise of upward leadership has been made easier by contemporary expectations in many companies that managers learn not just from their superiors but from all points of the compass.

## Box 1 **Principles of leading up**

### For the company manager

- Building superiors' confidence in you requires giving them your confidence.
- The bond between manager and executive should be a relationship based on an open flow of information and respect.
- The more uncertain or irresolute your superiors are about achieving a goal, the more clear-minded and determined you must be in formulating and executing your strategy.
- If your superiors do not appreciate a grave threat, transcend the normal channels of communication to drive home the message.
- Persistence often pays but it requires determination to stay on a rocky path when you have persuaded those above and below you to follow.
- However hostile your superior, however harsh your message, the well being of those in your hands must remain foremost.

### For the chief executive

- If you want subordinates to offer their best advice, you must value and make use of it.
- Stay tuned to what your subordinates are implying or communicating through other means. Because their personal stake in you and the company is large, they may appreciate your situation better than you do yourself.
- If you expect those below to support your leadership and step into the breach when needed, they will need to understand your strategy, methods and rules. That requires repeated restatements of your principles and consistent adherence to them.
- Downward leadership and upward leadership reinforce one another. If you are effective at the former, it will encourage the latter; if you are adept at the latter, it can inspire the former.

## Further reading

Collins, J. (2001) *Good to Great: Why some companies make the leap ... and others don't*, New York: HarperCollins.

Freedman, D.H. (2000) *Corps Business: The 30 management principles of the US Marines*, New York: Harper Business.

Kennedy, J.F. (1964) *Profiles in Courage*, New York: Harper and Row.

Pottruck, D.S. and Pearce, T. (2000) *Clicks and Mortar: Passion-driven growth in an internet-driven world*, San Francisco: Jossey-Bass.

Useem, M. (2001) *Leading Up: How to lead your boss so you both win*, Crown Business.

# The failure
## factor in leadership

Manfred F.R. Kets de Vries
is Clinical Professor of
Leadership Development
and Raoul de Vitry
d'Avaucourt Chaired
Professor of Human
Resource Management at
Insead.

It is tempting to blame external forces for the failure factor in leadership. But responsibility lies much closer to home, argues **Manfred Kets de Vries**.

Organizations are like cars. They don't run themselves, except downhill. They need people to make them work. And not just *any* people, but the *right* people. The effectiveness of an organization's leadership determines how the organizational "machine" will perform. Unfortunately, not all executives are the paragon of leadership excellence. Some leaders show an irrational side – a shadow side that can negatively affect other people in the organization and even, in extreme cases, bring down the organization itself. That shadow side can cause havoc in the organization. When I ask executives what their greatest source of stress is, a full 70 per cent say dysfunctional leadership.

Where does this shadow side come from? Why do perfectly normal-looking executives turn into problem cases and wreak havoc around them? What is this failure factor in leadership all about? It's tempting to assign responsibility for the failure factor in leadership to external forces, citing the words of Euripides: "Whom the gods want to destroy they first make mad!" But we can find responsibility much closer to home, in our own inner psychological theatre. Let's look at some of the most common reasons why leaders develop the failure factor.

## Conflict avoidance

Though we tend to think of leaders as dominant and unafraid, many have a tendency towards conflict avoidance. There is a large group of executives who have a desperate need to be liked and approved of. The need to be loved echoes in every line scripted for their inner theatre. Afraid to do anything that might threaten acceptance, they're unable (or unwilling) to make difficult decisions or to exercise authority. They become mere empty suits, unwilling to accept the fact – and it *is* a fact – that boundary setting sometimes takes precedence over conciliation.

Conflict avoidance is neither a successful nor, in the end, a popular management style: the leader who always appeases is like someone who feeds crocodiles hoping that they'll eat him last. There's nothing bad about being nice, but there comes a point when every leader has to say: "My way or the highway." I don't have an exact formula for success, but I know a sure formula for failure, and that's trying to please *everyone*.

A good case example of conflict avoidance is former President Clinton. I sometimes argue that if we want to know something about a male leader, our best source is his mother. If we're lucky, she'll reveal some of the underlying dimensions of her son's personality. And so it is with Clinton. His late mother, in her autobiography, claimed that if her son went into a room with 100 people, of whom 99 liked him and one didn't, he'd spend all his time and his formidable energy trying to win over that one last holdout. He realized the dysfunctionality of this pattern, however, and eventually used a chief of staff to make unpleasant decisions for him while he was in the presidency.

Richard Branson, chairman of the Virgin group of companies, has similar characteristics. He perceives himself as the chief ombudsman of his organization and wants to be liked by his people. Like Clinton, he came to realize this weakness and generally has other people in his organization making the unpleasant decisions for him. However, on multiple occasions Branson has rehired people who've been fired by others somewhere in his organization.

## The tyrannization of subordinates

Another pattern that leads to leadership incompetence is the tyrannization of subordinates. This pattern describes the Genghis Khans of the work world – those abrasive (and sometimes sadistically oriented) executives who obviously graduated with honours from the Joseph Stalin School of Management. Robert Maxwell, with his tendency to engage in abusive behaviour, was clearly at the head of his class. Former Prime Minister Margaret Thatcher also possessed some tyrannical characteristics. She would make statements such as, "I don't mind how much my ministers talk as long as

they do what I say," or "I'm extraordinarily patient provided I get my own way in the end." The "Iron Lady" could be a bit of a bulldozer.

A more recent example of destructively abrasive behaviour can be seen in Al Dunlop, alias "Chainsaw Al", Former CEO of Scott Paper and later Sunbeam. An advocate of shareholder value ad absurdum, he believed that only short-term thinking mattered. What happened to a company because of his interventions in the long run wasn't his concern. Of the eight companies he was involved in, six no longer exist. When he started at Scott Paper he laid off one-third of the senior management and 70 per cent of the workers in one fell swoop. He once said: "You're not in the business of being liked … If you want a friend, get a dog. I'm not taking any chances; I've got two dogs!" Finally, his leadership style caught up with him, however: his own board members fired him after he engaged in "creative accounting" to make his sales figures seem rosier than they actually were.

The tyrannization of subordinates sometimes triggers a response that Anna Freud called "identification-with-the-aggressor syndrome". Through unconscious impersonation of the "aggressor" (that is, the abusive boss), subordinates assume the leader's attributes and thus transform themselves from threatened to threatening, from helpless victims to powerful actors. This is a defensive manoeuvre, a way of controlling the severe anxiety caused by the aggressor. The people in the one-down position hope to acquire some of the power that aggressor possesses. Unfortunately, all they accomplish is to become aggressors themselves, thus increasing the total organizational aggression.

## Micromanagement

Another cause for leadership derailment in micromanagement. This is seen in executives who are so detail-oriented that they can't let go of control. Not trusting anyone else to do a job as well as they themselves, micromanagers are unwilling to delegate. I once consulted for an entrepreneur who'd been quite successful at building up his company. He was a control freak, however. Given his developmental history – where things had

> Not trusting anyone else to do a job as well as they themselves, micromanagers are unwilling to delegate.

been running out of control – letting go of control evoked highly emotional imagery. For example, he was in the habit of opening all the mail that came to the company, and he wanted all e-mail forwarded to him. This level of involvement was manageable as long as the company was in the start-up phase, but once it had become a $20m operation, the entrepreneur's lack of trust in the capabilities of others had a stifling effect on all organizational processes.

To illustrate this dysfunctional pattern from another perspective, I offer a cartoon I once saw. It showed an executive coming home to his wife and saying: "I did it. I just fired all 324 of them. I'm going to run the plant by myself!" Funny as this cartoon may be, micromanagement clearly isn't the way to get the best out of people. In fact, all it's good for is ruining morale and destroying organizations.

## Manic behaviour

Manic executives, possessed of apparently boundless energy, push themselves and others to the limit. But they're so hyperactive that they don't always notice what it is they're doing (even when what they're doing is dead wrong). From a clinical perspective, "manic" behaviour can be seen as a defence against depression. Executives engaged in such a manic behaviour pattern need to realize that there's a vast difference between working hard and working smart. Another cartoon comes to mind to illustrate manic behaviour. Two executives are talking to one another about a third person. The first executive says: "He hit the ground running, but he was going the wrong way!"

A look at the history of Xerox reveals the effects of disconnected, manic behaviour. In 1976, the market share held by Xerox was around 88 per cent. Six years later is was only 15 per cent. Yet Xerox executives kept going their merry

way. The firm became increasingly good at repairing machines and selling copying paper, but no one gave much thought to technological innovation. No one noticed that customers weren't as taken with broken-down machines as management was. On the contrary, customers liked problem-free machines. Canon, a Japanese competitor adept at reading customers, identified Xerox's weaknesses and was determined to gain market supremacy. In just a short time it had succeeded.

Manic behaviour forces companies to lose sight of their main mandate. These manic leaders became so inward-looking that they forget their main constituency: their customers. Leaders shouldn't look in the mirror; they should look out the window! Only if they're externally directed can they remain close to their customer base.

## Inaccessibility

Inaccessibility of leadership is another common problem. Some executives are so full of self-importance that they have no time for others. It wouldn't occur to them to manage by example or to walk around the workplace and marketplace listening to their primary constituencies. Lofty and unapproachable, they shield themselves behind a battery of secretaries and assistants and closed-door policies. One executive in a company I was visiting said: "Our president is like the yeti, occasionally seen in high places." Is it that such executives are looking for more grandiose people to interact with, or are they afraid that if people come to close they'll discover a fraud with very little to say?

## Game-playing

Every organization has its "operators" – political animals who are master power calculators. Like inaccessible leaders, these game-players can talk and think only about themselves and their attention falters when others talk (unless they themselves are the subject of discussion). Furthermore, their personal goals sway the organizational goals.

Game-players follow their own golden rule: credit goes up while garbage goes down. They refuse to let their subordinates shine, using and abusing them rather than helping them grow and develop, and they do everything possible to steal the attention from their superiors. They try to hog the limelight, whether it's aimed below or above them. Not surprisingly, game-players experience high turnover among their people. They would do well to heed Ann Landers's advice: "Don't accept your dog's admiration as conclusive evidence that you are wonderful."

## Generational envy

Many senior executives have a hard time dealing with their successor, even if they themselves have named the "crown prince". A major reason is that CEOs are, almost by definition, masters at power calculation; power is an important property to them, and they know how to acquire and manipulate it. Appointing a successor changes that power equation. Power starts to flow away to the new candidate as soon as that person has been named, and CEOs experience subtle changes in power relationship patterns almost immediately. Loyalties shift quickly, relationships realign; new power structures begin to emerge. I've often said, tongue in cheek, that the major task of a CEO is to find his likely successor and kill the bastard. Unfortunately, clinging to power through the derailment of that successor usually has disastrous effects on the organization.

The acid test of excellent leadership is what happens when the leader is no longer there. How seamless is the succession? Does the process occur without too much drama? Is the company still performing successfully after the old CEO has gone? Has the leadership in the company done sufficient planning for leadership succession? If not, give some thought to Charles de Gaulle's comment that the graveyards of the world are full of indispensable men. If after reflection you really believe that you're indispensable, put your finger into a glass of water, withdraw it, and note the hole that you've left.

Executives incapable of leadership development may suffer from generational envy. One indication is being resentful of the young "upstarts". They're like Cronos eating his children. They sent promising subordinates to the organizational equivalent of Siberia or fire them

for supposed incompetence – a "murder" if ever there was one – and then rationalize that fate so effectively that they think they're doing both organization and subordinates a favour.

A *New Yorker* cartoon shows an obviously powerful executive sitting behind his desk smoking a big cigar. In front of the desk stands a young executive, listening deferentially. The text reads: "You remind me of myself at your age, Collins. You're fired." Clearly, this narcissistically inclined executive is possessed by generational envy. Putting their interests far above the interests of others, such leaders spurn good corporate citizenship and use young people only as extensions of themselves. As long as the young people are willing to accept that role, all is well. when they want to go their own way, however, envy strikes, as in the cartoon. This "desertion" is not taken lightly by executives who (having themselves had fantasies of overthrow – and more – when they were young) fear that the young people may try to depose them.

## Escaping psychic prison

All of the above behaviour patterns contribute to the two Ms of failed leadership: *mistrust* and *malaise*. The acid test of effective leadership is the extent to which people in the organization trust their leader. If the trust level is low, some kind of malaise will occur; it's inevitable. Though the details will vary from firm to firm, some symptoms are universal: creative thinking will be suppressed, the "not-invented-here" syndrome will prevail, a "kill-the-messenger" culture will hold sway, infighting will take place, a cover-your-back mentality will predominate, and "bureaupathology" (that is, an excess of paperwork and supportive documentation) will emerge. When these two Ms sneak in, the consequences can be detrimental for an organization, particularly when the executive who opened the door to them occupies a senior position.

Many executives don't pay much attention to their inner world. In fact, they keep themselves busy just to make sure they don't have time to reflect. It's not necessarily a *conscious* avoidance, but it's an avoidance nonetheless. They run faster and faster, giving very little thought

> Many executives don't pay much attention to their inner world. In fact, they keep themselves busy just to make sure they don't have time to reflect.

to what they're running for or where they're running to. They're like the proverbial rats on a treadmill.

Some of them are stuck in what amounts to a psychic prison. And yet they rarely try to escape from their self-imposed house of detention. They're mired in their old ways of interacting, engaged in what psychoanalysts describe as repetition compulsion, an (unconscious) urge to re-enact troubling scenarios in the hope that repetition will eventually lead to liberation from this need. Many otherwise very bright people engage in a from of magical thinking: they believe that by doing the same thing over and over again, they will produce a different outcome. They fail to realize the common sense behind the old Native American saying: "When you discover that you're riding a dead horse, the best strategy is to dismount!"

The challenge for many leaders is to find a way out of that prison – to find other, better ways of doing things. Although at the age of 30, two-thirds to three-fifths of one's personality is formed (according to estimates of developmental psychologists), there's always ample room for change. Mental health is all about having a choice. And we *do* have a choice, always. It's true that our inner theatre stays largely the same – a certain amount of "hardwiring" is inescapable – but we can choose to react differently to our core wishes.

Leaders need to be the architects of their own fate, the authors of their own script. If we turn that scripting over to others, we're not really living, we're just playing a part. How much better it would be to *own our own lives*. And we can – if we're willing to open ourselves to the possibilities of change. If we are unwilling to do so, we will be the architects of our own decay!

Copyright Manfred Kets de Vries 2002

This article is adapted from *The Leadership Mystique* (London: Financial Times Prentice Hall, 2001).

# Rewards

**9**

# Contents

# Introduction to Part 9

**H**R managers report that they spend the highest proportion of their time on issues relating to salary, bonuses and benefits to employees. In recent years, companies have begun to recognize the need to design and manage reward systems for all employees, incorporating any sophisticated stock options benefits, pensions and other provisions. Here, authors describe the main features of such a system and ask whether all-employee share incentive schemes actually improve corporate performance.

# Rewards
## that work

Thomas B. Wilson is president of the Wilson Group, a compensation consulting company (www.wilsongroup.com).

Compensation systems should provide more than just a way of paying people. **Tom Wilson** sets out the options and shows how a portfolio of programmes can be assessed.

Is a compensation system simply a way of paying people? Or is it a channel by which managers can communicate important messages about strategy and values? In comparing their compensation levels with those of other companies, are managers more interested in being consistent with industry practices or in doing things differently to create a competitive advantage? Do they think of compensation as a cost of doing business or as an investment from which they expect to see desirable returns?

Compensation programmes have a more substantial impact than managers realize. This article explores how organizations can use rewards to drive strategy and reinforce values.

## Reward systems

There are four main types of reward programmes. First, salaries or wages are the regular payments people receive for their services while employed by a company. Second is bonus or incentive pay, based on the performance of the individual, business unit or company – commonly known as variable compensation. The amount depends on results and is not guaranteed. The difference between a stable salary and variable compensation varies widely. Third, most organizations provide financial security or services for which people would normally have to pay themselves – known as benefits. Such services include health insurance, pensions and retirement benefits, and transport. They are not considered tools needed to do the job. Finally, companies are increasingly using formal recognition programmes to award individuals for achievements and special contributions. These awards usually take the form of certificates, public recognition, commendation letters or promotions. The value of these awards is largely symbolic, though this is not to minimize their importance.

There are two contrasts to be drawn when considering these four types: cash rewards versus non-cash rewards; and all-employee rewards versus rewards for performance achievements. One set provides stability, security and entitlement; the other provides opportunity and appreciation. This framework can be used to assess a company's portfolio of programmes and allows managers to determine whether programmes are consistent with strategy and values.

Having placed the company's programmes in one of the quadrants defined by this framework (cash versus non-cash and secure versus contingent), managers should ask themselves: in which areas do I want to lead or match my competitors? What will be of most value to my people? How effective are these programmes in delivering their intended value? By answering these questions, managers can establish a strategy for compensation and benefit programmes and assess the return on investment they deliver. They can identify priorities for change, then develop a plan for implementing it.

## Competitive position

To answer the first question, one needs to know what other companies are doing. Certain trends in compensation can be identified. Salaries remain an important component, but as they meet the basic security needs of individuals, other aspects become more important. The trend for salary increases has not changed much over the past few years. Increases reflect what companies feel they need to pay to stay competitive. In the past decade, for example, salaries in the US have been increasing by between 3.5 per cent and 5 per cent a year.

While most executives have always received bonuses, over the past five years surveys show the percentage of companies offering them to professional and managerial positions has grown from 59 per cent to 79 per cent and for hourly and administrative positions from 27 per cent to 45 per cent. Further, stock option plans have increased from 66 per cent to 74 per cent for professionals or managers and from 20 per cent to 29 per cent for hourly/administrative workers. The use of other awards is also increasing (*see* Table 1).

| TABLE 1 | Other types of award |
|---|---|

| | % of companies offering awards |
|---|---|
| Flexible time schedules | 73 |
| Non-monetary recognition awards | 72 |
| Hiring bonuses | 70 |
| Employee referral bonuses | 68 |
| Spot cash recognition awards | 50 |
| Formal career planning | 21 |
| Retention bonuses | 26 |
| Broad-based stock options | 34 |
| Pay based on skill or competency | 19 |
| Cash profit sharing | 19 |

*Source: US Compensation Planning Survey* (2001) William M. Mercer

Understanding what prevails in the marketplace allows managers to assess the company's ability to attract and retain staff. However, the value lies in creating programmes that are suited to the organization and enhance its ability to optimize the talent it employs. An integrated reward strategy encourages innovation, not imitation.

While there is an abundance of data on the prevalence of programmes, there is little reliable data on the philosophy or practices of reward systems. In my research, about 70 companies were questioned on how they used rewards to drive performance and reinforce their culture. The following examples describe two approaches to reward strategies.

A major US airline sets its hiring rates of pay low in the marketplace. When recruits pass through the highly involved selection process and are hired, they receive rapid pay increases during the first two years if they demonstrate that they can learn quickly, perform well and fit with the company. The company's variable pay programmes

Understanding what prevails in the marketplace allows managers to assess the company's ability to attract and retain staff.

are linked to team results and each individual also has a stake in the success of the company through profit sharing and stock options.

Benefit plans conform to industry standards and the company tries to provide workers with high value at minimum cost. It makes much use of recognition programmes: it is reported that an individual or a team is recognized for a business-related contribution every hour of the day. One of the criteria for hiring or promotion to the position of manager is the ability to recognize and reward performance. Because of these factors (as stated by the chief executive) the company is a leader in terms of growth, profitability and shareholder value.

In a second example, consider a large financial services company. Since it is difficult to retain margins while competing on fees and interest rates, the company distinguishes itself by service. This is highly dependent on its people. So it uses different forms of individual variable pay, commission plans and special bonus awards for those interacting with customers and team incentives for those in sales and service functions.

It has adopted many performance awards for both individuals and teams, believing recognition provides the highest return on investment. It has several core benefit programmes, but distinguishes such programmes with features that are considered "fringe" in the industry, such as competency-based career development and access to online benefit programmes. Because of these factors, the company excels in terms of return on assets, growth and customer retention.

In these cases, the companies know what competitors do but find their own path. Consequently, their reward systems have given them a unique culture and a competitive advantage.

## What people value

The traditional method for assessing reward programmes is to compare them against two factors: what others are doing in the marketplace and whether the programme met the budget allocated to it. What is wrong with this perspective?

When a company conducts market studies for its products or services, it often examines potential customers' needs and determines what will influence their behaviour. To apply this framework to reward systems, the most important affinity groups or segments must be defined. Most companies do this when they develop programmes for executives, sales, production and service employees. Other factors may also intervene such as age, gender or education.

In a preliminary research study we asked participants to rate more than 75 items. The data was examined by age, gender and educational levels. The two items that all groups rated as the most important were high-quality leadership and healthcare benefits. Most differences emerged when examining data by age. Employees aged between 20 and 29 valued career advancement, training and involvement in major decisions (in addition to items noted above). Mid-career individuals (aged 30 to 49) valued paid time off, challenging work and regular performance feedback, while established employees (aged 50+) wanted involvement in important decisions.

There were also differences by education. Those with high school diploma or associates degree valued paid personal time off and career advancement opportunities. Those with a bachelor's degree valued challenging work assignments and involvement in work redesign. Those with masters' degrees or higher valued challenging work assignments and involvement in key decisions.

It is important to use such findings as a guide to understanding what people value. Some programmes can be highly valued by all employees and can make an organization distinctive. Other programmes can be used to enable people to "earn the rights" to specific things they personally value through performance programmes. The company will need to assess the cost of these programmes compared with their effect.

## Programmes

The value of a reward programme is determined by its recipients and the results they produce. While there is no single approach that works, it does not mean any programme will be effective. As in most strategies and programmes, it must be properly designed and implemented to work well. A few features tend to emerge consistently as the most important.

For programmes focused on providing security and stability, it is crucial for the employee to understand the programme fully. Second, managers must find the right balance between consistency and responsiveness to the individual's needs. Many companies have developed flexible benefit systems to enable employees to tailor programmes according to their needs. Companies might offer annual gatherings or parties, sometimes including families, as a mechanism to reinforce the community spirit of the company. Those who travel a great deal may have cars or special arrangements to support their responsibilities and personal expectations.

Programmes also need to make the organization distinctive. Some companies have put details of schemes on the web to help people to understand how they are structured. Employees can plan for retirement or sign up for training. A company can always find ways to make its programmes worth more to employees.

When rewards are focused on opportunity and performance, managers should devote a good deal of attention to the measures that determine when an award pays out. Programmes linked to performance require a clear understanding of the measures, goals or standards and the actions people need to take. Second, feedback on progress is critical. Whether a company uses a scoreboard or regular discussions of progress, people need to know how well they are doing and see how their efforts are making an impact. Without feedback, programmes can rapidly become entitlements and people lose the connection to performance. A useful guideline is to have three to five checkpoints between the beginning and the end of the period. In addition, goals should be both challenging and achievable. If the effort is too simple, it will not inspire the performance one seeks; if it is seen as impossible, people are likely to make an effort but remain sceptical.

> Whether a company uses a scoreboard or regular discussions of progress, people need to know how well they are doing and see how their efforts are making an impact.

Performance-based programmes include cash, such as commissions, incentives, bonuses and recognition awards. Managers should think beyond the basic question of how much people receive from such awards. Consider this example. Two medium-sized service companies each had an annual goal-sharing programme for managers and employees. Payouts were based on the annual results of the entire organization. Both achieved about the same results for the initial year of the programme.

In the first company, senior managers conducted a series of employee meetings. They discussed the company's annual results and the impact of these results on their customers and market position. They held open discussions of the challenges faced and what people did to overcome them. When it came time to make the awards, executives randomly passed out the envelopes containing each individual's cheque. They asked them to find the person who was named on the envelope and, as they handed over the envelope, tell them something they appreciated about what they had done during the year. For without the combined efforts of all individuals, managers said, there would be no cheques to distribute.

In the other company, better managers sent e-mails or held brief discussions with the employees about their bonus payments; most did nothing. Otherwise, bonuses were deposited directly into the individual's bank account. Little else was said.

What is the difference in the impact of these two approaches? What do you believe would be the value given to the bonus cheques in each case? Which approach provided the highest return on investment?

## Conclusion

Managers can transform compensation, benefits and recognition programmes into a reward system that drives an organization's strategy and core values. For the organization such a system is an opportunity to encourage and reinforce those things that make it successful. For the individual it is an opportunity to be paid fairly, to share in the success of the company and to be rewarded for commitment and performance. Reward systems can be viewed as a cost of doing business or a source of competitive advantage. If you share the strategic view, this is the best time to assess what is working and what is not.

## Box 1 Equity and bonuses in tough times

The principles outlined in this article can be applied in different economic circumstances. When a company and its markets are growing rapidly, variable pay programmes – through cash or stock options or equity – are highly attractive. People will often see an immediate gain. However, if a company comes to rely on these tools, it exposes itself to substantial risk. The technology industry is witnessing the result of such reliance since equity values have plummeted.

Managers have addressed their over-reliance on equity plans in two ways: some have balanced it out with increases in variable pay, leaving stock option awards in place; others have increased or replaced existing options with new ones set at a lower price. The aim is to accommodate both individual interests and shareholder interests, but this is never an easy objective to achieve.

In a downturn, managers may come under intense pressure to award bonuses or variable pay-outs regardless of performance, mainly to retain important contributors. However, when the link between these payouts and performance is broken, employees quickly come to perceive such bonuses as entitlements. To avoid this, managers must instead focus on setting clear goals, discussing performance frequently and finding ways to celebrate successes without bonus payouts.

When performance is strong and cash is plentiful, managing rewards is easy. When performance suffers and payouts are minimal or non-existent, the task of management is to reinforce support for people's efforts without undermining the principles of their contingent reward programmes. This is the real leadership challenge.

## Further reading

Risher, H. (ed.) (1999) *Aligning Pay and Results*, New York: Amacom.

Tulgan, B. (2001) *Winning the Talent Wars*, New York: Norton.

Wilson, T. (1999) *Rewards That Drive High Performance: Success stories from leading organisations*, New York: Amacom.

Wilson, T. (1995) *Innovative Reward Systems for the Changing Workplace*, New York: McGraw-Hill.

World at Work (2001) *Annual Total Salary Increase Budget Survey for 1997–2001*, Scottsdale, AZ.

# Firm benefits from
## share-owning workers

Martin J. Conyon is an assistant professor of management at the Wharton School at the University of Pennsylvania.

Richard B. Freeman is a professor of economics at Harvard University and co-director of the Centre for Economic Performance, London School of Economics.

Employee ownership plans are on the rise. **Martin Conyon** and **Richard Freeman** present the evidence to justify their popularity.

There has been a resurgence of interest in employee ownership plans. In the UK, chancellor Gordon Brown committed the government to a policy of encouraging ownership in the belief that it has beneficial social and economic effects. The 2001 US tax law improved the tax advantages of Employee Stock Ownership Plans (ESOP) – the major form for employee ownership in the US – while limiting the potential for employees to abuse the system. Korea passed a law that gave greater tax advantages to a similar plan. Ireland lowered tax rates for broadly based employee stock options and France reduced taxation on qualified stock options.

In spite of recent increased volatility in equities (which have complex implications for stock option granting policies), the trend in capitalist countries is clearly towards increasing financial participation by staff in their companies. The forms of participation and ownership that receive tax-favoured treatment vary across countries, depending on governmental policy stances. The US favours stock options and collective ownership of shares through ESOPs. The UK has schemes that increase individual ownership of shares through options. France prefers profit-sharing. The Belgian government has enacted a law that allows companies to choose between cash-based profit-sharing and share-based profit-sharing.

Do companies that adopt employee share schemes perform better than others? Second, do companies that use shared compensation systems provide employees with information so that they can perform their jobs better? Namely, is shared compensation associated with greater employee involvement and democracy of enterprise?

This article examines whether promoting all-employee share ownership has been good for company performance. Arguments for the use of shared compensation schemes are reviewed and evidence to evaluate the effectiveness of schemes is considered.

# The case for

Why is it important to encourage employees to own shares? The answer is that it can benefit employees and companies alike, increasing the size of the economic pie and improving the well being of company and worker. The chief benefits, and some limitations, include the following.

## Incentives

Probably the most important reason for pushing stock options down the organizational hierarchy to all employees is the perceived beneficial effects on incentives and employee behaviour. In turn, employee motivation increases, as, hopefully, does organizational success.

Owning shares or stock options can be a powerful motivation. Fixed salaries simply reward individuals for turning up at work – they focus on the input side of work rather than the output side. Straight salary systems do not encourage employees to focus on value-enhancing opportunities. Piece-rate pay does not allow for the co-operative nature of production methods and is hard to administer when technology changes the nature of production and goods.

Ownership of an asset, such as a share option, on the other hand, directly encourages employees to increase the price of that asset, namely the share price. In effect, employees are persuaded to think and behave like owners.

## Recruitment and retention

By offering competitive pay packages, which include share-based remuneration, companies can attract and retain employees in competitive labour markets. This is especially the case if staff turnover rates are high. In addition, recruitment and retention effects may be particularly important for start-ups, companies with high growth opportunities or smaller companies. At the same time, share-based plans reduce the danger that an employee will leave to work for a competitor that does provide such compensation.

Owning shares or stock options can be a powerful motivation.

## Tax incentives

There are important tax and other institutional incentives for companies to offer wide employee ownership. The UK government, for example, is committed to encouraging employee ownership and nurturing an enterprise culture. It gives tax advantages to both employees and companies under the employee share plan introduced in July 2000. Employees who meet the scheme requirements and hold shares for five years or more do not pay income tax on their shares. Employers, too, can benefit from corporation tax relief. The tax relief may induce individual companies and employees to choose the various schemes, but the social test of their value is that they increase economic well being beyond the tax breaks themselves.

## Institutional context

Benefits from increased incentives and subsequent performance do not come automatically. Changes in management style and context, notably greater employee communication and devolved decision making, should accompany increased share ownership. For companies to be successful, the management process and corporate culture is central to implementing equity-based compensation.

In the US, Cisco makes extensive use of an all-employee stock option plan. Kate DCamp, global compensation leader at Cisco, stresses that stock option programmes alone do not create an ownership culture: they are simply one manifestation of it. Cisco believes in open management, working through teams whose employees are empowered to make significant decisions. Moreover, employees won't be motivated by options if they don't understand them, so the company runs an education programme.

The key is to use financial rewards to create an ownership culture.

# Any downside?

The benefits of all-employee share ownership should be set against potential problems. The first is the "line-of-sight" argument. Companies should only give equity incentives to employees who can influence outcomes. For this reason, share options are often given to senior managers and directors. These people clearly have the power to affect the strategic direction of the enterprise, earnings potential and the stock price. However, employees further down the hierarchy might find the link between their work and how it shapes performance more difficult to identify. The benefits of wide ownership simply might not materialize.

Then there is the "free-rider" problem. In most work settings, individuals will be rewarded after meeting a group or aggregate measure of performance rather than an individual one. Any extra effort by an individual that improves performance is shared among all participants. When reward is divided among very many employees, it may contribute only a small amount to an individual's compensation. So, any given employee might be tempted to avoid his or her share of the effort, hope that co-workers put in the effort to generate performance increases, and then pick up his or her share of the pie. If everyone acts in this way there will be no gains to be shared.

These arguments have led some economists to doubt that all-employee share plans can improve company performance. At the minimum, these arguments make it clear why the simple introduction of pay that varies with company performance may fail to induce workers to do a better job, and why economists are forced to talk about corporate culture instead of pure pecuniary incentives.

## Empirical evidence

However, what of the evidence that relates employee share schemes and company performance? A growing body of research, based on data from the US and UK, shows a positive link between company performance and employee share ownership. In the US, the National Center for Employee Ownership (NCEO) provides online information on the benefits (www.nceo.org).

A study by academics Joseph Blasi and Douglas Kruse covering more than 300 companies between 1988 and 1994 found that sales, employment and labour productivity growth was about 2.4 per cent higher than in non-ESOP companies. Another

**Companies offering stock options have greater sales, more employees, greater capital intensity, higher shareholder returns and higher labour productivity.**

study discussed on the NCEO website found that the performance of 229 new-economy companies offering broad-based stock options was significantly better compared with their counterparts without such plans. Companies offering stock options have greater sales, more employees, greater capital intensity, higher shareholder returns and higher labour productivity. It may not be possible to extrapolate these studies but they do suggest employee stake-holding can improve performance.

UK-based researchers, too, have examined the issue. John Cable and Nick Wilson used a sample of 52 British engineering companies from 1979 to 1982. They had detailed information on profit-sharing schemes. Their analysis showed that companies with profit-sharing arrangements performed 3 per cent to 8 per cent better than those without. In addition, quality circles, briefing groups and job rotation also had a positive effect on productivity. Having both profit-sharing and employee involvement added most to productivity.

Sandeep Bhargava considered the effects of profit-sharing in a sample of 114 UK companies between 1979 and 1989 and found that profit-sharing had a significant effect on profitability. Other UK researchers have found similar patterns of results. UK academic analyses have added to the picture of a modest positive effect. Saul Estrin and colleagues reported a productivity improvement of about 6 per cent in cases where profit-sharing bonuses were 5–10 per cent of wages. Other studies, too, reported in their 2001 paper, suggest that shared compensation arrangements tend to enhance performance.

In short, evidence reveals a positive, albeit small, effect of profit-sharing on company performance. As noted above, though, introducing a shared compensation system is a complex task that needs to be accompanied by changes in the management system. For example, information sharing, communication and decision-making processes may need to be adjusted.

## Further evidence

Our recent work presents new UK evidence on the effects of shared compensation on enterprise performance. We used several data sets and examined the effect of share schemes approved by the Inland Revenue on company productivity. Information was based on a survey of all UK listed companies carried out in 1999.

The objectives of the research were twofold: first, to see whether companies that used Inland Revenue approved systems had superior levels of performance; second, to evaluate whether companies that did use such arrangements also had greater levels of employee involvement in decision making or information sharing.

Various findings emerged. First, companies had an appetite for using share-based compensation with all employees and this had been growing in the mid-1990s. For example, the approved profit-sharing scheme allows companies to provide free shares to employees without tax liabilities. Figure 1 shows that about 19 per cent of companies responding to the 1999 survey had an approved profit-sharing scheme in 1995 and this rose to about 25 per cent in 1998.

The research also established that companies with certain schemes had greater productivity compared with companies that did not (*see* Table 1). The results indicate that only in two cases (approved profit-sharing and the company share option plan) can a positive productivity effect be established. The effect of the different shared compensation systems seems to square with previous observations. Approved company share option schemes cover selected employees, typically senior managers and executives, who can affect company performance in response to stock options. Profit-sharing also rewards employees with shares and appears to be associated with higher productivity.

We also examined the effect of such plans on share prices of the sample companies that used approved profit-sharing or all-employee share schemes. An index of their share prices from 1991

| TABLE 1 | Compensation schemes and productivity |
| --- | --- |

| Compensation system/ Inland Revenue scheme | Productivity effect |
| --- | --- |
| Approved profit-sharing | 17% higher |
| Approved profit-related pay | 4% higher |
| Approved SAYE | 3% lower |
| Company share option plan | 12% higher |

*Source*: Conyon and Freeman (2001)

| FIGURE 1 | Companies with approved profit-sharing scheme |
| --- | --- |

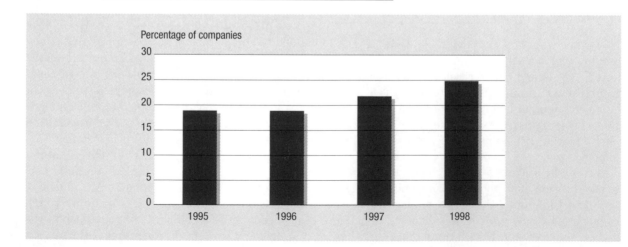

FIGURE 2

**FIGURE 2** | Share-based compensation schemes and company performance

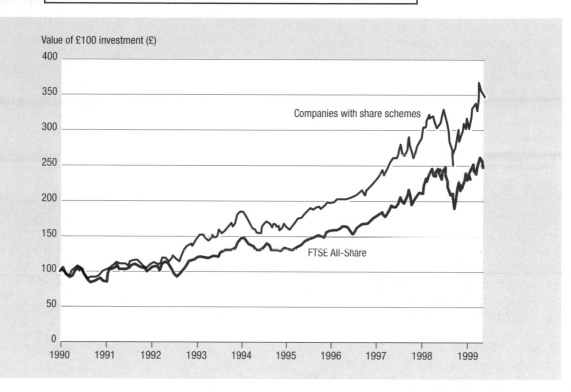

Value of £100 investment (£)

Companies with share schemes

FTSE All-Share

to 1999 was formed. It was found that a £100 investment in the portfolio of companies that used share-based compensation plans grew to £350, while the same £100 invested in the FTSE All Share Index in 1990 was worth about £250 in 1999 (*see* Figure 2). Again, the evidence is that companies using broad-based share plans seem to perform better than those without such plans.

To see whether companies with shared compensation systems tended to consult and communicate more with employees, we used survey data on consultation, communication and information sharing. In particular, we know whether a company has "a joint committee of managers and employees primarily concerned with consultation rather than negotiation"; "a formal structure for information sharing with employees" (such as provision of data on financial status, production and labour market position, market strategy); and finally "a formal structure for communication between all levels of employees and management" (such as quality circles, newsletters and suggestion schemes). We aggregated these results to define a situation

**TABLE 2** | Compensation schemes and communication

| Compensation system/ Inland Revenue scheme | Communication and information sharing |
|---|---|
| Approved profit-sharing | 18% more |
| Approved profit-related pay | 11% more |
| Approved SAYE | 14% more |
| Company share option plan | 4% less |

*Source*: Conyon and Freeman (2001)

where the company has at least one of these systems (*see* Table 2).

Generally, the results indicate a positive correlation between information sharing/decision rights and the use by companies of shared compensation structures. Shared compensation increases the likelihood of companies using consultation, information sharing and communications systems. It makes the use of shared compensation more effective.

## Conclusion

The use of shared compensation can increase company performance by providing direct financial incentives to employees. The type of incentive scheme may matter, but there are on average benefits to companies from using shared compensation practices. With renewed policy interest and with companies facing a new set of all-employee share incentive schemes, such evidence is encouraging in terms of the benefits to productivity.

## Further reading

Bhargava, S. (1994) "Profit-sharing and the financial performance of companies: evidence from UK panel data", *Economic Journal*, 104.

Cable, J.R. and Wilson, N. (1989) "Profit-sharing and productivity: an analysis of UK engineering companies", *Economic Journal*, 99.

Conyon, M.J. and Freeman, R.B. (2001) "Shared modes of compensation and company performance: UK evidence", National Bureau of Economic Research working paper W8448 (http://papers.nber.org/papers/W8448).

Estrin, S., Perotin, V., Robinson, A. and Wilson, N. (1997) "Profit-sharing in OECD countries: a review of some evidence", *Business Strategy Review*, 8, 4.

NCEO (2001) "Performance effects of options in 'new economy' and unionized companies" (http://www.nceo.org/library/option_corpperf_new economy.html).

# Recruitment, testing and **training**

# Contents

# Introduction to Part 10

**J**ob candidates can be sifted and selected in a number of ways, but for most companies the interview is still the crucial determinant of the recruitment process. Here authors describe and debate several means of linking assessment of a recruit with his or her likely future performance, including the increasingly popular psychometric test. Other authors in this part discuss the role of training in corporations. It is clear that training improves performance, yet managers should be open-minded about the kind of training employees demand – generic training may paradoxically achieve the best results.

# Beyond
## the interview

Rob Yeung is a senior consultant at Kiddy and Partners, organization and business psychology consultants.

Simon Brittain is a partner and head of assessment at Kiddy and Partners.

The search continues for an inexpensive process that can deliver a perfect correlation between assessment and future performance. **Rob Yeung** and **Simon Brittain** examine the options.

The world of business is fickle. Only a short while ago, companies were talking about the "war for talent", with leading blue chips, investment banks and consulting companies fighting with dotcoms and other start-ups over the best individuals. Today's climate is very different – with waves of redundancies and many people thankful to have a job at all. However, boom or bust, good recruitment and selection practices are essential.

During a boom, organizations may recruit managers who have a talent for launching services and products and thinking about new markets. However, the skills needed in a downturn are very different. The emphasis switches to recruiting managers who can cut costs aggressively, retrench and manage in the aftermath of mass redundancies. Research shows that while recruiting the wrong individual can have a huge impact on a healthy business in terms of opportunity costs, it can be fatal for an ailing one.

Unfortunately, the frightening reality is that many organizations – particularly companies without HR representation at board level – do not have selection practices that allow them consistently to distinguish outstanding candidates from those who are merely competent, or to select managers who are different from those cast in the current mould. As such, these organizations handicap their ability to compete effectively.

The history of recruitment and selection techniques is littered with practices that range from astrology to assessment centres. This article considers past methods and current thinking in behavioural, or competency-based, methods of recruitment and selection.

# A compelling body of evidence indicates that the traditional, unstructured interview has very poor predictive validity.

## The interview

The interview still forms the basis for most selection procedures. Typically, a manager will look at a candidate's curriculum vitae and ask questions that he or she believes will help to predict whether a particular candidate will perform successfully. A critical concept in selection is that of predictive validity – or the extent to which measurement of some characteristics of a candidate will predict on-the-job performance. There are many characteristics that could be measured as well as an enormous diversity of performance criteria, which could include anything from salary growth to manual labour productivity, sales earnings or ratings of success by peers. However, a compelling body of evidence indicates that the traditional, unstructured interview has very poor predictive validity.

Interviewers are prone to unconscious bias that they can only dimly perceive. Many recruit in their own image, choosing people with similar backgrounds or personal interests rather than possibly better, but dissimilar, candidates. They may also be deceived by the "halo effect", wrongly believing that a candidate who has charm and good interpersonal skills will also be good at everything else. Different interviewers can have different standards – resulting in excellent candidates being turned away by overly harsh interviewers or poor candidates being offered jobs by benevolent interviewers. As such, the interview is only marginally more successful at predicting job performance than astrology (*see* Figure 1).

## Other methods

Surprisingly, graphology (the analysis of handwriting samples) is used by many companies in continental Europe, where is it common practice for candidates to submit a handwritten covering letter with their application, whereas it is rarely used in the UK or the US. However, research has consistently failed to find a significant correlation between graphology and job performance.

Neither are references very good predictors of job success. For a start, candidates tend to choose referees who provide a flattering reference. Referees can also be reluctant to give poor references, for example when an employer feels guilty for having made employees redundant. On the other hand, references can occasionally eliminate candidates who have exaggerated their experience or lied about their qualifications, thereby boosting the predictive validity of an overall selection process.

As Figure 1 indicates, work sample tests are among the best methods of predicting whether a candidate will perform successfully on the job or not. Such tests ask candidates to do the tasks that will be required of them in the job for which they are applying, so this might be a typing test for secretaries or taking apart and repairing a gearbox in the case of a motor mechanic.

In-tray exercises have become popular for simulating the demands of many office-based jobs.

| FIGURE 1 | Selection method and performance |
|---|---|

| | |
|---|---|
| **1.0** | Perfect prediction |
| **0.9** | |
| **0.8** | |
| **0.7** | |
| **0.6** | Assessment centres (for promotion) |
| **0.5** | Work sample tests |
| **0.4** | Assessment centres (potential performance) |
| **0.3** | Structured interviews |
| **0.2** | Typical interviews References |
| **0.1** | Chance prediction Graphology Astrology |

They require that candidates sort through a pack of documents and respond in writing to the most important – usually against the clock. However, they have been criticized for asking candidates to write what they might normally say to others – it is difficult, for instance, to see how an in-tray exercise alone could identify a person with good negotiation or presentation skills. Second, employers simply do not like relying too heavily on in-tray exercises as they are loath to recruit without face-to-face contact. As a result, organizations have been turning to competency-based approaches to recruitment and selection.

## Competencies

Competencies are statements about the characteristics that result in effective, superior performance in a job. Typical management competencies, for example, focus on skills such as innovation, leadership and change management. Companies such as Royal Bank of Scotland, Consignia, Amazon and Goldman Sachs use competency frameworks.

Adopting competencies helps a business to identify criteria that can be used to assess employees not just for recruitment but also to appraise performance, develop people and identify successors. In the context of recruitment this method allows managers to identify the skills that they are seeking in employees. A business could also highlight competencies that it needs. For example, if an organization is trying to switch from a short-term sales focus to a longer-term consulting relationship with customers, it might include a competency to do with "partnering with customers".

Competencies must be unique to each organization. A company that takes a set of competencies off-the-shelf will adopt a generic model that has limited relevance to its particular competitive market, the style of its managers and its culture. The rise of competencies has redeemed the interview. In spite of having low predictive validity, the interview continues to be integral to selection. Candidates expect a chance to put their case and potential employers like to meet prospective colleagues. Once competencies have been identified, it becomes straightforward

to train managers to interview using them so that decisions become more consistent and more able to predict job performance.

## Assessment centres

Structured, competency-based interviews have greater predictive validity than traditional interviews but assessment centres are even better. Candidates can be confused by the term, believing it describes the location, or perhaps a dedicated building. However, it merely refers to an approach that uses several methods to give a thorough picture of the strengths and weaknesses of a candidate.

As with the structured interview, an assessment centre tests candidates against a set of competencies. However, the centre differs in that it is likely to comprise not only an interview but also written exercises, psychometric tests, cases studies, group discussions and simulations (see Box 1). There are likely to be several assessors. Assessment centres rarely run for less than a day and can last for a week. A centre may even be designed to assess a single candidate.

Simulations are particularly important because they have led to a great increase in the predictive validity of selection methods, allowing assessors to observe behaviour against a set of competencies rather than just self-reports of behaviour. As an example, rather than asking prospective sales executives how good they think they are at dealing with customers, why not actually watch them trying to handle an irate customer?

The major disadvantage of assessment centres is their expense. There is a development cost, perhaps to create fictitious company materials and write role-play scenarios. There is also the cost of training assessors and having them present throughout the duration of the assessment. Accordingly, assessment centres tend to be used for senior managers, internal promotion or for important roles in the business – such as high-flier graduate recruitment programmes (see Box 1). Even though assessment centres are regarded as the best method for selecting candidates, their cost may go some way to explaining why they have been taken up by relatively few organizations. In particular, UK companies lag their

Box 1 **Sample assessment centre timetable**

**08:45** Introduction: candidate (for director post) welcomed and briefed on the schedule.

**09:00** Personality inventory: 150 self-report paper and pencil questions completed by candidate; results used to help interviewer probe management style.

**09:45** Interview: assessor interviews candidate in detail against the role's competencies.

**11:00** Business case analysis: candidate introduced to a fictitious company and given in-tray exercise to analyze and complete. This may include detailed financial statements and forecasts to scrutinize, perhaps a budget to prepare, along with memos, letters and faxes to respond to in writing.

**13:00** Presentation: candidate asked to present summary recommendations on the fictitious company to an assessor, role-playing the company's chief executive.

**13:30** Working lunch: while finishing the in-tray exercise.

**14:00** Direct report meeting: candidate given 30 minutes to prepare for a meeting with an underperforming employee. The employee is played by a second assessor.

**15:00** Board meeting: candidate given 20 minutes to prepare for a meeting with two peers to discuss a difficult issue. Both peers are played by assessors.

**16:00** Aptitude test: timed test to measure the candidate's critical thinking ability.

**16:45** Debrief: candidate's opportunity to ask final questions.

**17:00** End of day: candidate leaves. Assessors discuss candidate's performance and recommend whether to hire or not.

German and North American competitors in their use.

However, organizations that balk at investing in assessment centres may be guilty of short termism in that the costs are outweighed by the financial benefits, especially at senior levels. For example, academic Craig Russell examined the value of competency-based selection in 98 candidates for executive roles in a Fortune 50 company. Monitoring their performance over three years, he calculated that general managers selected using a competency-based process each generated an additional $3m in annual profit as compared with recruits who were selected using a previous process that was not based on competencies.

On the other hand, organizations that have already adopted assessment centres must not rest on their laurels. While some leading organizations quickly embraced the concept, many early centres were designed without sufficient consideration of how and why performance during the assessment is supposed to link with future job performance. For example, it is difficult to see how asking a group of candidates to build a structure from toy bricks could be said to predict managerial competence. Such organizations could be opening themselves up to legal challenge from talented candidates who may be rejected for seemingly irrelevant reasons.

## Assessing selection

Research has tended to focus on the effectiveness or predictive validity of selection methods. However, organizations must also consider other criteria in devising selection methods.

- *Practicality*: the ease of use of a selection method. For example, line managers can be trained relatively easily to conduct competency-based interviews, whereas they would need extensive training to work in an assessment centre.

- *Generalizability*: the extent to which results can be used across levels and job roles. A verbal reasoning test may have high predictive validity for administrative staff, but may be worthless for selecting managers who need to coach and develop others. Similarly, an assessment centre for senior managers is likely to be too demanding for graduate entrants.

- *Cost-effectiveness*: what will be the payback of investing in better recruitment and selection methods?

- *Acceptability*: not only to candidates, but also to the line managers taking part in the selection process.
- *Legality*: to ensure selection does not infringe candidates' human rights or discriminate unfairly against minority groups.

## The future

The holy grail of selection would be an inexpensive selection process that could deliver a perfect correlation between candidate assessment and future performance. Given the diversity and unpredictability of human behaviour, this is unlikely to happen; however, assessment specialists do continue to seek ways of improving selection methods.

### Technology

The purpose of an assessment centre is to mimic work situations. However, most centres are run as paper and pencil exercises – candidates are presented with printed materials and asked to write down their responses.

Organizations will increasingly incorporate technology in assessment centres to add to their realism, which should also enhance their validity. The application of technology would, for example, allow managers access to computers, voicemail and other tools they would have in their own offices. However, HR managers will need to convince line managers that such technologies deliver better recruits for the additional cost.

### Retaining candidates

While organizations are getting better at recruiting the best candidates, they could pay greater

---

The holy grail of selection would be an inexpensive selection process that could deliver a perfect correlation between candidate assessment and future performance.

---

attention to retention during the selection process. It is often the case that the way an organization treats candidates during the assessment process is indicative of how it treats employees. Many organizations are guilty of expecting candidates to jump through hoops without explaining the purpose of each stage and then failing to give feedback to unsuccessful candidates. Good candidates often have several job offers, so recruiters must make the process as much about helping candidates to choose the organization as vice versa.

### Change

Currently, when a vacancy arises, the role is first defined and then candidates are sifted and assessed to find the best person. However, organizations are increasingly changing at such a pace that roles can soon be redefined or made redundant. It is no longer enough to find the best candidate for today's needs. Recruiters must be able to identify candidates who will meet not only the company's current needs but also its uncertain future needs.

## Further reading

Arthur, D. (2001) *The Employee Recruitment and Retention Handbook*, New York: Amacom.

Cook, M. (1998) *Personnel Selection: Adding value through people*, Chichester: Wiley.

Russell, C.J. (2001) "A longitudinal study of top-level executive performance", *Journal of Applied Psychology*, 86.

Ryan, A.M., McFarland, L., Baron, H. and Page, R. (1999) "An international look at selection practices: Nation and culture as explanations for variability in practice", *Personnel Psychology*, 52.

Schmidt, F.L. (1998) "The validity and utility of selection methods in personnel psychology: Practical and theoretical implications of 85 years of research findings", *Psychological Bulletin*, 124.

# A missing link
## in the strategic plan

Gary Latham is Secretary of State Professor of Organizational Effectiveness at the Rotman School of Management, University of Toronto, and a past president of the Canadian Psychological Association.

Value for money from training can come about only if companies can improve understanding of their strategy and ensure employees can carry it out, says **Gary Latham**.

Companies in Europe and North America spend $1bn a year upgrading the knowledge, skills and abilities of their employees. What do they hope to achieve? They want each division, unit and employee to understand the overall strategy and, more importantly, to make it happen. Second, they hope to bring down barriers – such as lack of knowledge and skills or ingrained bad habits – that hamper execution of company plans.

Therefore, training and development aim to create what Jack Welch, former chief executive of General Electric, called "the boundaryless organization". In such an organization, active steps are taken to eliminate an attitude of "I know nine things, so I will teach you eight" and replace it with one of "I will teach you nine things by the end of the day and a tenth thing tomorrow morning". Managers want to bring about changes in employees' ways of thinking and behaving. To accomplish this, psychologists recommend improving each person's self-awareness, knowledge and skills, and their motivation to apply newly acquired knowledge and skills on the job.

Self-awareness includes understanding one's roles and responsibilities. Training can give workers insights into any gap there might be between their behaviour and the organization's culture or values. It might also show how others see them and how these perceptions affect the way others pursue the organization's goals.

Why is there such an emphasis on knowledge and skills? First, technological innovation requires that office workers be retrained five to eight times during their careers. It is hardly surprising if people become frustrated as their jobs require more problem solving, analytical skills and teamwork than they have been trained to deliver. In addition, with mergers and acquisitions, and globalization, managers need to be sensitive to changes in the organization's culture, as well as the various cultures of the places in which the company operates. The Center for

> Just as managers develop a strategy, they must also develop the human resources capabilities to implement it.

Creative Leadership (CCL), an educational institution in the US, reported that the main causes of the derailment of a successful leader is lack of interpersonal skills and their inability to cope with change.

There may be some truth in the adage "a poorly developed plan that is brilliantly executed is better than a brilliant plan that is poorly executed". In most companies, senior managers spend time in the autumn revisiting the company's strategic plan, only to find that in January employees quietly file the plan in a drawer. Just as managers develop a strategy, they must also develop the human resources capabilities to implement it.

At Travelers Insurance, senior executives recognized that the company would have to transform itself. They set out a plan for change with an emphasis on customer service. Managers were trained to manage the transition to new technologies and all employees were trained in computer skills so they could address clients' needs with appropriate company services immediately.

Is training and development worth the cost? Only if programmes are evaluated to see whether objectives have been attained. Without this, managers cannot improve the training process and they will see no improvement in how workers carry out strategy.

## Training design

Psychologists say: understand the outcomes that people expect and you will understand why they do what they do; change their expectations and you will change their behaviour. In terms of our argument, effective training is based on analyzing people's needs. This analysis should show senior managers, and the people who will be trained, what needs to be done. In short, they must see the links between what they do and expected outcomes – between taking or not taking the training and the likely impact that will have on company strategy. If there is no difference in results after training, the programme is unlikely to be supported. Any training analysis has to be explicit about what people must start doing, stop doing and continue to do to execute strategy.

Since the second world war, organizational psychologists have emphasized active participation, feedback and practice to make the most of the skills and knowledge that a course confers. In the past two decades, four principles have also emerged that are central to increasing the efficacy of training in motivating an individual or group to acquire the skills necessary for resilience.

Efficacy refers to the belief that one can bring something about. It is critical to motivating people to master the knowledge and skills taught on a training course and to apply them. Research has shown that people with high self-efficacy commit to goals that are difficult to achieve and more valuable to the organization. Obstacles and setbacks add to the challenge and excitement of pursuing them. People with low self-efficacy look for tangible reasons to abandon the goal. They perceive the same obstacles and setbacks as proof that the goal is not attainable and are more likely to give up. The four ways of increasing efficacy are:

- Arrange tasks to enable early successes and provide some tasks that all but guarantee early successes. Success inculcates confidence; trainees can say: "I now think I can do this."

- Find people similar to the trainees who have either mastered the task or are in the process of doing so; this enables the trainee to speak to people with whom they can identify and who have achieved the course's aims. A problem with benchmarking – a common element in courses – is that the less effective person or group may be discouraged by the fact that "best practice" appears unattainable. Support from "significant others" who have achieved these goals can help.

- Ascertain who is the "significant other" for the person or group. Who whispers in their ear? Psychologists have found that people tend to behave according to the expectations of those who are significant to them. This is both good and bad: influential people can either build us up or tear us down. Trainers should make participants more aware of these effects; those who undermine confidence can then be put in perspective and those who boost it can be sought out.

- Set learning goals. Learning goals should be set when the person lacks the knowledge or skills to perform the task; outcome goals should be set when the issue is primarily motivation rather than learning. Outcome goals refer to a desired end state, such as "increase revenue by 18 per cent". Learning goals emphasize the discovery of ways of solving a problem or mastering a task, such as "find five specific ways of increasing revenue". When people set outcome goals before they have mastered the task, their performance gets worse. Because they are anxious about failing, they jump from one incorrect approach to another. Instead of setting outcome goals, trainers should ask participants to seek out methods of approaching the task. Performance improves dramatically when learning goals are set.

## Evaluation

Another psychological truism is: "That which gets measured gets done." For many, the presence of a metric signals that an activity is valued in the company. If the system of measurement is not aligned with the organization's vision and values, however, most people will concentrate on the metric and ignore the vision. To ensure that the knowledge derived from training is applied on the job, managers must figure out a way of measuring the expression of that knowledge in the trainee's performance – and build this metric into performance appraisals.

Similarly, pay and promotion must to some extent depend on the transfer of training skills to the workplace. For example, when clerical workers were given training in self-management, their productivity declined relative to that of their untrained colleagues. Interviews with the clerks who had been trained revealed that after they were given autonomy, they believed that they deserved higher pay than clerks who had not been trained. They became so disgruntled at not receiving a pay increase that their output declined. The moral is this: that which gets appraised and rewarded gets performed on the job.

Randomly selecting people to be trained first and comparing their performance with those who have yet to be trained can show the value of training and development. If there is a significant difference in the performance of the two groups, the training is clearly worthwhile. If managers then train the remaining group and performance increases to the level of the first trainees, this is additional proof of the programme's effectiveness.

## Technology-based training

In an effort to reduce the costs of training, organizations are increasingly turning to courses offered on the web and on CD-Roms or DVD-Roms. The latter are particularly effective for creating realistic job simulations. Sales employees can be given practice in dealing with irate customers, nurses in dealing with patients and nuclear power plant operators with emergencies.

Microsoft offers a host of computer-related courses from independent training producers over the internet. The company contends that a classroom course that normally costs $2,800 can be taken for $395. Companies such as Booz Allen & Hamilton, JC Penney and Eli Lilly use their intranets for employees to share knowledge, skills and abilities critical for the advancement of their strategy.

Most technology-based courses automatically assess what the worker has learned. Trainees are not able to move to the next exercise until they have mastered the current one. As well as the courses being cheaper, trainees taking computer-based courses are not forced to travel outside the workplace. Further, these courses allow for differences in learning rates among people. Unlike human trainers, the internet does not get impatient with a slow learner, nor does it hold back the quick learner because of colleagues having difficulty with the subject matter.

## Senior management

The training of senior managers has become a major source of profit for business schools in Europe and North America. Organizations such as the London Business School and the University of Toronto customize programmes to suit the strategy of client organizations. These programmes are mini-MBA courses that last between 5 and 20 days.

Although the content is tailored to the needs of the client, the themes are usually the same: leadership skills for senior managers; building teams; and the development and implementation of a customer-driven strategy. In short, these programmes focus on organizational behaviour, strategy, marketing and finance. Companies are also forming alliances with institutions to offer MBA degrees to a student body that consists solely of their employees, supervisors and customers.

## Development and succession

In the 1990s, Jack Welch said: "Choosing my successor is the most important decision I'll make. It occupies a considerable amount of thought almost every day." Welch recognized how important leadership was in the pursuit of strategy.

A survey by CCL suggests that career development and succession planning encourage the organization to scan its business environment. This also shows the company intends to change and, ultimately, planning ensures survival. The downside is that the process disrupts work. Employees learn about and begin to apply new priorities and procedures. The study found a 33 per cent failure rate for executive succession. Further, there is often a drop in performance as staff turnover rises.

As well as being fair, leaders must be seen to be fair. It is less important who gets what (such as an assignment or promotion) than that there are procedures to determine what gets distributed to whom (for example, how profit is shared). If systems exist, employees tend to ask:

- Is the system representative of the thinking of the organization at large or that of a select few?
- Are systems followed consistently?
- Are procedures ethical? If they were published in the business press, would the organization beam with pride or blush with embarrassment?
- Do I have a champion who makes my strengths and development needs known to others?
- Is there an appeals process? If important data is misinterpreted, will I be seen as a team player or a malcontent if I try to correct things?
- Do I have a voice? Will people listen to me before making decisions?

If managers take these questions into account, employees are likely to accept the process.

---

## As well as being fair, leaders must be seen to be fair.

---

Career development and succession plans should then be linked to business strategy.

### Self-management and coaching

The skills of coaching and managing oneself have become more important as cost cutting has removed layers of management. Such skills also increase involvement in the workplace.

Drawing upon principles from clinical psychology, academic Colette Frayne and I developed a training programme to reduce absenteeism among unionized government employees. In brief, the training taught people to set high goals in relation to their job attendance, to monitor ways in which the environment helped or hindered them from reaching that goal, to identify and administer rewards for working towards it, and punishments for failing to work towards it. Such self-regulatory skills taught employees how to manage personal and social obstacles to attendance, and raised their perceived self-efficacy that they could exercise influence over their behaviour. Attendance was much higher in the training group.

### Conclusion

To ensure strategy is carried out, employees must have the skills to do what is asked of them. They must see the relationship between what they do and the outcome they can expect for themselves. Learning rather than outcome goals should be set when the way to achieve a goal is not readily apparent. Training programmes must focus on the employee's self-efficacy, the belief that "Yes, I can".

Finally, managers should evaluate programmes rigorously. If people are not implementing strategy more effectively after training, or more effectively than those who were not trained, kill the programme.

This article is drawn from *Developing and Training Human Resources in Organisations* by Gary Latham and K. Wexley (Prentice Hall, 2001).

# Investments that
## build on human nature

Charles Galunic is an associate professor of organizational behaviour at Insead.

John Weeks is an assistant professor of organizational behaviour at Insead.

With the demise of job security, companies need other strategies to encourage commitment. **Charles Galunic** and **John Weeks** propose generic training, which, ironically, makes people more mobile.

O nce, managing people was simple – or so we are told. Jobs were standardized and just needed filling, skills were learned in school, and workers were happily married to companies by efficient formal contracts. And they all lived happily ever after, soothed into docility (and perhaps mediocrity) by the benevolent assurance of lifetime job security.

Even allowing for a generous dollop of myth, things have changed. Job definitions now evolve, advanced skills take time to define, and unstated and shifting mutual obligations – not formal contracts – inform the employment relationship. Developing people, not just managing them, has become a necessary yet tricky task. Investing in human capital is complicated by the fact that the skills companies need keep changing and it is risky because money is spent on training people who may soon leave.

No wonder managers struggle with how to invest in developing and motivating their people at a time when investment in people, not just technology, is returning to centre stage. So how should managers invest in their human capital?

Fortunately, some things have not changed. Human nature remains remarkably stable. People want to feel competent and secure, they are consistent in reciprocating good or bad deeds; and they are influenced by, and often imitate, behaviours that surround them. Nothing changes from the sandpit to the boardroom, so managers should revisit these truths as they think about investing in people.

In the rush to transform employees into independent agents, managers believe that if they call them "talent" they can handle them at arm's length. Use formal contracts to stipulate the task, the thinking goes, and career development falls on employees. If employees fail to develop into value creators, it's their own fault. However, in managers' eagerness to create self-standing agents it may have been forgotten that investments in human development have to keep pace. Moreover, these investments must be

# If employees fail to develop into value creators, it's their own fault.

mindful of employee needs and motivations, and here is where human nature can help. People like to feel secure, especially about their livelihoods – few have jobs with pay-offs so large that they can ignore safety nets. Companies need to bear in mind human reciprocity when investing in employees. Reciprocity is an attribute that should embolden managers to make what may, at first, appear as unorthodox and risky investments. And remember that people are natural imitators. Employees will treat each other – and their customers – as they are treated by the organization.

## Job security

It is difficult to speak of job security without first outlining what is meant by the employment relationship. Most employees start with a written contract. This documents the basics: title, salary, responsibilities and so on. However, written contracts are poor at dealing with the minutiae of tasks and behaviour that may be asked of employees over time, which are unforeseen and impossible to codify.

In other words, much of what organizations expect from employees is not stated and develops as the relationship progresses. Certain exchanges are repeated – such as flexible working hours for weekend business travel – and shared assumptions plant themselves in members' minds, forming part of the organization's culture.

These perceptions of the mutual obligations between employers and employees form what is called the psychological or social contract. This contract is more balanced than the formal one, obligating the employer, not just employees, to behaviour in certain ways. Although seldom codified, it is reproduced constantly and so always on the minds of employees. Break this and employees will know. Nevertheless, breaking or modifying this social contract is exactly what companies have been doing. Former understandings were simple: employees gave employers loyalty and commitment in return for job secu-

rity. As job security lost its status, eroded by waves of downsizing, employees lost their corporate religion.

Many books lament the loss of organizational commitment and wonder how companies can halt the slide. Many remedies have been proposed and some tried. A prime example is to pay more attention to compensation (if not necessarily to pay more), particularly pay-for-performance, which aims to obtain high-commitment behaviour by paying for it. Other examples include flexible working hours, generous spending to support telecommuting and lifestyle-friendly perks, from gyms and nurseries to coffee and confectionery.

Although such initiatives may encourage employees to work hard, they are no substitute for job security. There is something precious in knowing that one's ability to earn a living is secure, a sense of freedom and independence that things like modest increases in pay, nurseries and other perks have a hard time matching.

The difference between job, or more broadly occupational, security and these perks is also the difference between the material and psychological benefits of an occupation. People derive not only material benefits and independence from jobs but also a sense of identity – a feeling of competence, a place that supports social links and family relations. Threaten this, and companies threaten something near a person's core.

This creates a dilemma. How do companies halt the erosion of employee commitment and loyalty, an unquestionable strategic advantage, if demands for competitive flexibility destroy job security? Is there a way to cultivate dedication and align behaviours to organizational ends without lavish perks or, on the other hand, simply imposing more controls? The answer is that there is no flawless way. The idea of "employability" has forced people to see themselves and their companies in a different light. The company no longer serves as a clan but as a much looser association, something approaching a talent agency, replete with fashionable but depersonalized practices such as sharing desks. Ironically, managers were dumbfounded when these agents had the nerve to start job-hopping. Many became frenzied, forcing an arms race in perks and pay that has made some of them vulnerable to recession.

## General skills

There are ways to restore commitment without again offering job security. Part of the answer lies in how companies develop employees. Company-specific investments are made all the time, of course, and these are vital, perpetuating the skills and capabilities of the company and possibly a source of competitive advantage.

Other investments can play a significant role in generating employee commitment and loyalty. These "generalized investments" focus on general skills and education to raise the professional level of employees. Topics include leadership and personal development, technology, finance and teamwork. Whereas run-of-the-mill training focuses on things the company knows how to do – but employees do not – generalized investments are about expanding horizons. In a sense, these investments are the difference between training and education. Crucially, compared with company-specific training, generalized investments make employees more employable and, potentially, mobile. Certainly from the employee's perspective, increasing employability is what these investments are all about.

It doesn't take a suspicious finance director to recognize this advice as heretical and risky. Strategic thought has advocated that all resources should be as company-specific as possible and so help distinguish the company from competitors. Indeed, not long ago, *The Economist* distrustfully asked why companies should spend money on improved skills when those employees could be "poached at a moment's notice". It may seem extravagant to develop employees in ways that make them more mobile.

However, that is the point. From the perspective of employee security – in a broader, occupational sense – these investments go a long way to restoring confidence. In turn, employees are likely to respond with greater commitment. The value proposition of generalized investments is that, in their response to them, employees will distinguish the company through greater commitment, dedication and individual performance.

## Evidence

There is corroborating evidence. Generalized investments in a sample of insurance agents have been found to raise their commitment substantially. In this case, investments included general managerial development and technology investments, both of which could be easily used by other companies. Further, the raised commitment translated into greater satisfaction with agents, profitability and expectations of continued benefits.

Why should companies expect such an effect? Why wouldn't employees stay around just long enough – and do just enough – to grab these investments and then leave? Clearly, some will. After all, young consultants and investment bankers commonly justify their insane hours and short careers with the knowledge that in a few years they can take their accumulated wisdom – company-specific and general – and go off into industry. Like most investments with interesting returns, there is risk. Nonetheless, the insurance agent study strongly suggests that people tend to respond well to such investments. Human nature, once again, explains why. People are exceptionally consistent reciprocators. In the words of anthropologist Marcel Mauss, generosity creates obligation. Successful salespeople learn this early in their careers; managers need to also. Give employees something of value and they tend to respond in kind. Company-specific investments, or those that bound employees more tightly to their companies, also tended to generate some, albeit more modest, levels of commitment. What makes generalized investments different, and perhaps more powerful, is their altruistic quality. It is easier to dismiss organizational investments in human development that are purely focused on productivity and profits.

On the other hand, it is more difficult to dismiss these investments when they show concern for employees' continued viability as professionals – and at apparent cost and risk to the company. These investments should provide returns, but employees will notice that they are more attractive in the employment market and have more control over their future. This can weigh heavily on the mind.

## Generalized investments offer a way to interpret the employment relationship in emotionally engaging terms.

Indeed, because such investments signal concern for the individual per se, rather than as an agent of the company, they can generate a particularly strong need for reciprocity, manifested in greater commitment. Just ask British Airways, whose popular Managing People First programme in the 1980s focused on self-development and leadership – not on skills – and was important in raising employee dedication and the company's transformation under Colin Marshall.

In short, generalized investments offer a way to interpret the employment relationship in emotionally engaging terms. A steady supply of sweets in a competitor's canteen will be less likely to lure employees away.

There are other advantages to generalized investments. For one thing, because they are not tied to things the company already knows, they are likely to generate innovation. In this sense, development involves not just the individual but, in the longer run, the organization, whose pool of ideas and routines should expand.

## Imitation

Human nature suggests a further and neglected advantage. People are especially adept at imitation. This is not just triggered mimicking of something that is already known, such as yawning. Rather, as psychologist Susan Blackmore describes in *The Meme Machine*, imitation involves acquiring understanding and appreciation about the behaviour being observed, something that separates humans from other species and is an important source of individual development.

Of course, anthropologists such as Dan Sperber and Ulf Hannerz caution that imitation is seldom as simple as copying. It involves mutations and is influenced by the status and power of the source. Nonetheless, much of what employees know how to do – what amounts to organiza-

tional culture – was acquired through selecting and imitating ideas and behaviours that compete for attention and circulate around companies.

It is because people are natural imitators that generalized investments may have multiplying effects, helping to mould an organizational culture that is less selfish and provincial, and more co-operative and loyal. This is partly because commitment can be contagious. It is also because organizational policies that are backed by leaders communicate something about desirable organizational behaviour.

Further, it is because employees are likely to reciprocate altruistic organizational acts by imitating such behaviour in their dealings with colleagues. Just as imitation is the greatest form of flattery, employees may copy the spirit of generalized investments and so mimic such altruistic acts. A company's social contract says something not only about how employees should treat the company but also how they should treat each other.

## Caveats

A few caveats are in order at this point. Obviously, a good amount of employee development will be – and should be – highly company-specific. If a company doesn't provide training in its culture, methods and routines, it may mean that it does not have capabilities that are distinct. It is not an issue of company-specific or generalized investments but of balance. Indeed, generalized investments are likely to stand out more in the minds of employees than the usual corporate training. Remember that an important part of generalized investments is to elevate the professional level and well being of employees – if this message is lost, or implemented in an insincere way, a good portion of this investment may be lost.

Another consideration is that because this form of human development can become personal, its communication and implementation needs to be handled delicately. Tell an employee that you are sponsoring him for a programme on, say, taking care of his health or public speaking and he may feel insulted. As always, it is wise to link these initiatives to corporate values and strategy, and introduce them without singling out individuals.

Finally, remember that sometimes policies aimed at generating high-commitment organizations can work too well. Employees may devote more of their time to the company than is necessary or acceptable. Like many management tools, these investments will further blur the divide between work and private life. Good management is about finding balance and is genuine about its concern for employee welfare – there is nothing like hypocrisy to disengage employees.

No one knows what shape future social contracts between employees and employers will take. However, the value placed on human development will continue to increase. The best and the brightest are likely to choose companies that provide professional or occupational – not job – security. Generalized investments should not be regarded as a luxury or a perk but as a genuine investment in people and organizational culture. It is also safe to say that human nature will not change and managers may be well served by respecting the basics.

## Further reading

Blackmore, S.J. (1999) *The Meme Machine*, Oxford: Oxford University Press.

Evans, P., Pucik, V. and Barsoux, J.-L. (2002) *The Global Challenge: Frameworks for international human resource management*, Chicago: McGraw-Hill.

Galunic, D.C. and Anderson, E. (2000) "From security to mobility: Generalized investments in human capital and agent commitment", *Organization Science*, 11, 1.

Ghoshal, S. and Bartlett, C.H. (1997) *The Individualized Corporation*, New York: HarperBusiness.

Ridley, M. (1998) *The Origins of Virtue*, New York: Penguin.

Waterman, R.H.J., Waterman, J.A. and Collard, B.A. (1994) "Toward a career-resilient workforce", *Harvard Business Review*, 72, 4.

# In search of
## the best performers

Victor Dulewicz is a professor of management studies and head of the HRM and organizational behaviour faculty at Henley Management College.

The concept of emotional intelligence has expanded the potential of psychometric testing, says **Victor Dulewicz**, but online availability threatens established standards.

Surveys have shown that a high proportion (about two-thirds) of large and medium-sized companies in the UK use psychometric tests and questionnaires for recruiting staff and developing them, and for building, recruiting and assessing teams. Such large-scale usage shows that companies see real benefits in testing. However, there are limitations, which are likely to increase as testing using the web becomes more popular.

This article describes benefits, problems and trends in psychometric testing, focusing on internet testing and the assessment and development of emotional intelligence.

## Benefits

Psychometric tests (use of the term here includes questionnaires) are not a new fad and nor do they only measure IQ, as many people believe. They are designed to assess not only mental abilities and aptitudes, such as verbal, numerical and spatial reasoning, but also personality characteristics, interests and values and, very recently, emotional intelligence.

Such tests have been the most widely used scientific assessment tool for the past 100 years, for a number of good reasons. First, they are normally based on well-researched models in the study of psychology and so have a sound scientific base. Concepts or traits measured are clearly defined and so there is usually a common understanding of these among users. They are developed rigorously using trials that can take years of painstaking research.

Second, the results produced are objective. This is achieved by taking the person's "raw" score and comparing it against the range of scores previously obtained from a reference group such as the general population, managers or graduates. Thus, one can state that this person's score is higher than, say, 75 per cent of UK graduates. Third, users have to adhere to high professional standards of practice. To obtain tests in the first place, people must be trained and accredited by the publishers. Fourth, and most relevant to the bottom line, validation studies have demonstrated the value of tests for predicting performance in a wide range of jobs.

Validation is usually done by correlating scores with measures of performance on a job or training course. An article in 2002 by Ivan Robertson and Mike Smith, psychologists at Umist, shows that ability and personality questionnaires are effective predictors of performance, especially when compared with other selection methods. Furthermore, cost-benefit and utility analyses conducted over 20 years using widely accepted models have consistently shown large savings when the cost of using valid tests is compared with the actual or likely benefits of selecting higher performing staff as a direct result of using tests. Generally, the higher the level, the greater the cost savings found.

So, rigour, objectivity and validity are the main reasons these tests are widely used. Inevitably, though, they have limitations. First, while the validity of ability tests is widely accepted, doubts linger in some quarters about personality questionnaires, partly because more informal tests or quizzes have sprung up, many of which are on the web. Since personality questionnaires are based usually on self-reporting, there can be problems resulting from inaccurate self-perception or from "motivational distortion" – when someone presents a favourable self-image.

Nevertheless, adjustments can be made to take account of this and Robertson and Smith's research has shown it does not seriously affect the ability to predict performance. Moreover, these problems are not unique to testing. In selection interviews, such problems can be even more acute.

Second, ability tests do sometimes have what is called "adverse impact" – some groups may be at a disadvantage because of, say, language or cultural factors. The most common example is when someone whose first language is not English sits a test written in English. They may not fully understand every question and so their performance may suffer. However, reputable test

> Assessment centres, which often include tests as part of their programmes, are required to cover competencies not amenable to testing.

designers and publishers are aware of such problems. Users are urged to review results and to take action whenever these problems arise.

Third, tests must be administered by people who are trained and qualified, and materials are restricted to them. Unfortunately, this can add significantly to the cost and can lead to the superficial attractiveness of so-called tests that have been devised in a day and can be used by anyone.

Fourth, tests cannot assess all competencies needed for a job, so they can never be a perfect predictor of performance. As a general rule, the higher the job level, the less predictive power tests have. Assessment centres, which often include tests as part of their programmes, are required to cover competencies not amenable to testing.

Finally, test results are extremely useful for self-development, for example careers guidance or personal development, but they cannot provide the degree of detailed and comprehensive behavioural data generated by development centres. These can be valuable for personal development when drawing up action plans.

## Emotional intelligence

Two recent developments have taken place. The first relates to what is being measured; the second relates to how people are being assessed. For most of the last century, tests were designed to assess mental abilities, aptitudes, personality characteristics, interests and values. However, a concept has emerged which has captured the public's imagination. Emotional intelligence has been defined as achieving goals through the ability to manage feelings and emotions; to be sensitive to and to influence other people; and to sustain motivation and to balance motivation and drive with conscientious and ethical behaviour.

Its roots can be traced back to the 1980s and the work of Howard Gardner, an academic psychologist. However, it was Daniel Goleman's book *Emotional Intelligence* that brought the idea to the world's attention. Goleman argued that a person's success in any aspect of life is due not only to their IQ but more importantly to their EI as well. He subsequently turned his attention to employees and in 1999, on the BBC Radio 4 programme *In Business*, he claimed: "EI is twice as important as IQ and technical skills ... The higher up the organization you go, the more important EI becomes."

Studies have found that EI contributes to the performance of various groups of workers including managers, team leaders, salespeople and even board directors. Also, EI is an important component of leadership. In *On Becoming a Leader*, Warren Bennis said: "In those fields I have studied, emotional intelligence is much more powerful than IQ in determining who becomes a leader." Our own research has confirmed this, including work on directors.

As implied above, EI can be measured. There are now two or three psychometric tests that provide an accurate profile of an individual's EI. There are also courses to help people to develop aspects of their EI, in particular self-awareness, interpersonal sensitivity and influence.

## Assessment

Ability tests have recently been introduced which are aimed at assessing job-specific abilities such as fault-finding and financial appraisal. They are closer to the job simulations found in assessment centres than to conventional psychometric tests. Publishers claim that people find them more relevant and interesting and that the tests offer a taste of real work tasks.

A major innovation is "adaptive testing", whereby software tailors the test for each respondent by generating questions based on previous answers to an initial standard set. This makes testing sessions much shorter and it enables the questions to be varied when people have taken the test before. It can also be very useful in graduate recruitment, where applicants may be given the same test on several occasions.

Over the past century, few other factors have had a greater impact on the testing industry than the internet. A search on the web for personality-type questionnaires will find hundreds, most of which are not psychometric tests but simple quizzes or lists of questions.

Recently, however, publishers have begun to put their tests online and HR professionals have shown some demand for internet testing. A 2001 survey by People Management found that "more than three-quarters of the HR professionals want the [online testing] service". However, 30 per cent did have reservations – they did not want it yet, mainly because packages did not give them sufficient control over the testing environment.

Advocates of online testing point to a number of advantages. It offers access to anyone with a computer linked to the web, the results can be processed almost instantly, and a report can be generated and sent off in a few minutes. Publishers can then use the data for development work and research to improve tests and demonstrate their effectiveness. Results can be used by companies to screen applicants for jobs and to reduce large applicant pools quickly and effectively. In addition, the web could significantly increase the number of people able to take tests for self-development purposes and dramatically reduce the associated costs.

Any breakthrough raises concerns, however, and testing using the internet is no exception. Critics contend that testing should be conducted under controlled conditions – ability tests, for example, should be timed to the nearest second, and this is difficult to achieve remotely. Questions are also raised about the confidentiality of results and reports, and about who should have access to the data. Further, how can the lay person determine whether a web-based test is a reputable psychometric instrument or just a trivial quiz?

The question many people find most difficult to resolve is: how can the tester verify the identity of the person responding? If the test is being used for selection purposes, many candidates would be tempted to ask, and perhaps pay, someone to take the test for them. While sophisticated recognition systems have been invented, using fingerprints or the iris of the eye, one would still need to have the correct original against which to compare the specimen presented by the test-taker.

> ## The question many people find most difficult to resolve is: how can the tester verify the identity of the person responding?

Finally, technical issues remain, many of which relate to compatibility of different operating systems and software. If the testing system is not highly reliable, ability testing under strict time conditions becomes risky. If the test breaks down mid-way, for example, one cannot ask the candidate to start again, because of the practice he or she will have had.

SHL, one of the largest test publishers, launched its first web-based service in 2000. Its director of research and development, Dave Bartram, reported that clients were already seeing benefits in terms of time and cost of recruitment. However, he accepted many of the problems and proposed that testing on the web could take place under three sets of conditions:

- uncontrolled (no training or accreditation required) and unsupervised, the test-taker merely registers on the internet;
- controlled but unsupervised, where the user registers the candidate and checks their identity;
- controlled and supervised, where a qualified test user conducts all aspects, exactly as would happen in a face-to-face situation.

Tests used under each condition would have different classifications for use. Bartram, who is president of the International Testing Commission, also noted that the commission "is already considering a classification and accreditation scheme that all publishers could adopt and would provide an indication of the qualities of an instrument (for example, whether its psychometric properties have been evaluated) and the conditions under which it has been designed to be used".

Robert McHenry, chairman of test publisher OPP, has argued against online tests and warned against assuming that testing will be easier, cheaper and more convenient when it comes to remote candidates. At the moment, he claims, internet test sites lack convenience. In future, systems based on software sent by e-mail will allow managers to assess candidates using a combination of computer-based and telephone tests.

Test publisher ASE is taking a twin-track approach. Traditional tests will remain restricted to trained users on limited access sites and less formal instruments will be designed for unprotected environments, with appropriate "health warnings". The company has also been experimenting with "distant feedback" on tests via electronic media and this method appears to work well. However, it is important that the feedback skills of test users are enhanced so that results are returned electronically in the most sensitive and meaningful way.

## Conclusion

The internet can provide the test user with many worthwhile benefits, but unless standards of control and supervision are maintained, there is a clear danger that those benefits will be compromised. Reputable tests could become debased as they enter the public domain and professional standards may decline. They would eventually become indistinguishable from unregulated online tests, and companies and recruits would lose out. Further, ethical concerns about the use of personal test data and reports need to be resolved.

On the wider front, psychometric testing has many advantages for assessment and development purposes but, as with all goods and services, caveat emptor applies. Choosing appropriate tests requires investigation and professional advice from occupational or organizational psychologists, and users are strongly advized to order tests from publishers that adhere to national standards. In the UK, the British Psychological Society reviews tests; overseas users are advised to contact equivalent bodies such as the American Psychological Association.

People choosing to use the web for testing should think hard about the professional and technical issues before going ahead.

## Further reading

Bartram, D. (2001) "Frames of Mind", *People Management,* June 14.

Bennis, W. (1989) *On Becoming A Leader*, Reading, MA: Perseus Books.

Goleman, D. (1995) *Emotional Intelligence: Why it can matter more than IQ*, New York: Bantam Books.

Higgs, M.J. and Dulewicz, V. (1999) *Making Sense of Emotional Intelligence*, Windsor: NFER-Nelson.

McHenry, R. (2001) "Frames of mind", *People Management*, June 14.

Toplis, J., Dulewicz, V. and Fletcher, C.A. (1997) *Psychological Testing: A guide for managers*, London: Chartered Institute for Personnel and Development.

# Subject Index

# Name Index

# Organization Index